perspective for the absolute beginner

A Clear & Easy Guide to
Successful Perspective Drawing

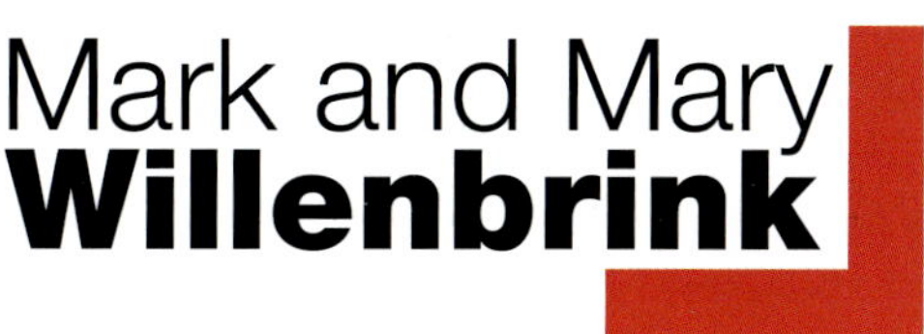

Mark and Mary
Willenbrink

NORTH LIGHT BOOKS
CINCINNATI, OHIO
www.artistsnetwork.com

Contents

What You Need

Paper
80-lb (170gsm) dark gray construction paper
medium-texture sketch paper
medium-texture drawing paper
tracing paper

Pencils
0.05 mechanical
2B
4B
6B

Other
craft knife
double-sided tape
drawing board
heavy cardboard sheet
kneaded eraser
large highly reflective spoon
lightbox or transfer paper
masking tape
pencil sharpener
ruler
straightedge
triangle
T-square

Optional
angle ruler
color wheel
pencil extender
plastic eraser
proportion wheel
value scale

Introduction

Both magicians and artists entertain with illusions. While the magician uses smoke and mirrors, the artist's platform is a flat two-dimensional surface to convince the viewer that the art appears three dimensional. This book is about visual illusion in the form of perspective, which includes linear perspective, atmospheric perspective and color use. You'll learn what tools to use and how to use them, the terms and principles related to perspective, along with tricks and techniques to create depth in your artwork through lines, values and color. Get ready to entertain and be entertained with the illusion of perspective.

Putting Perspective Into Perspective

Since Renaissance times perspective has been studied and more realistically portrayed in art. Commenting on the importance of perspective, Leonardo da Vinci stated, "Perspective is to painting what the bridle is to the horse, the rudder to a ship."

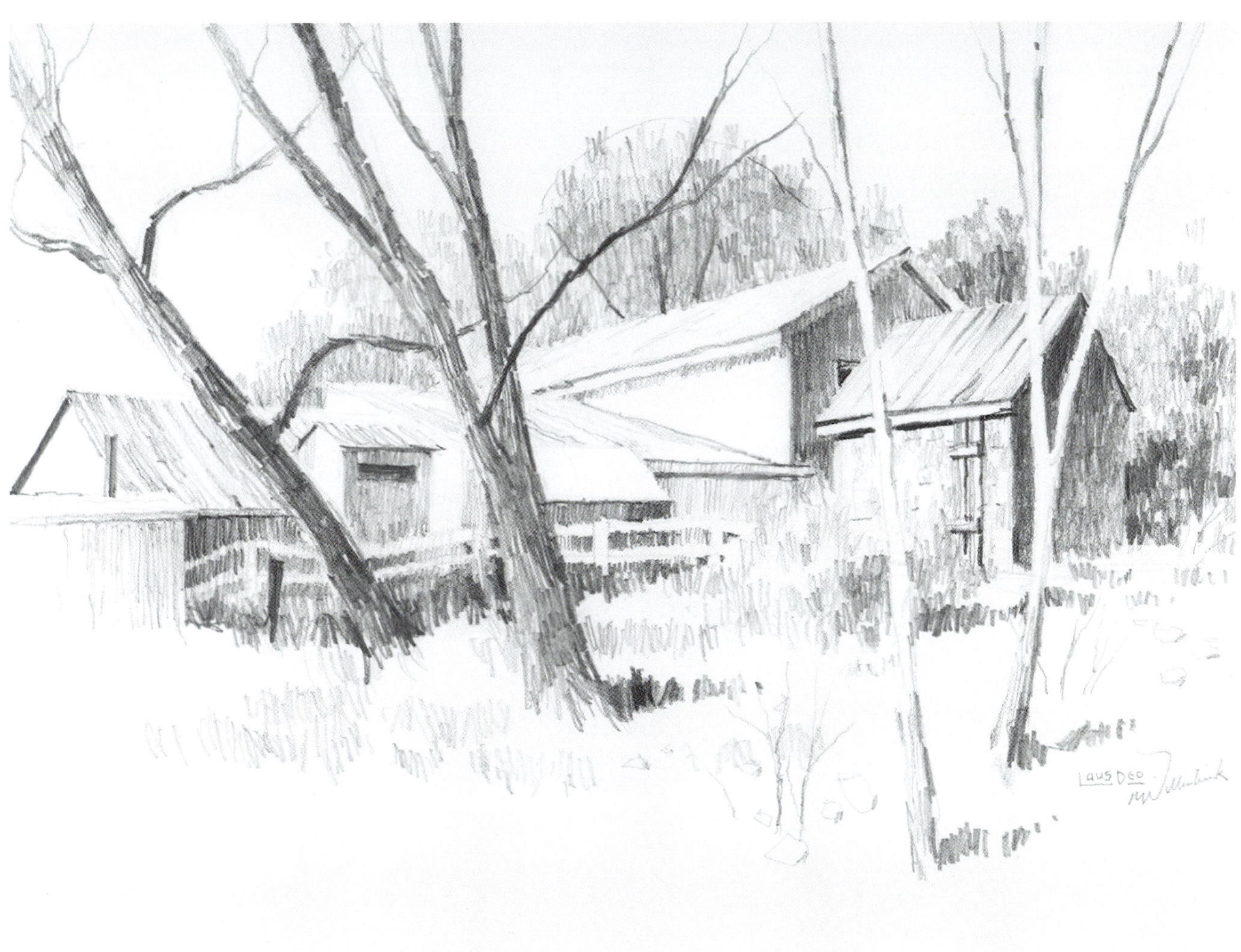

Farm Buildings
Graphite pencil on drawing paper
7½" × 9½" (19cm × 24cm)

Drawing Tools

When starting an art project, consider whether it is to be a sketch or a drawing. A sketch may be a quick study, whereas a drawing is a finished work of art. For this reason, it is necessary to have the right supplies for your intended results.

Pencils

As with other art supplies, pencils vary in quality. The cheaper pencils may have grit in the core, which can scratch the paper surface when applying pencil strokes. Pencils also have variations with their casings and cores.

Drawing pencils typically have a wood casing and a core made of graphite, charcoal or carbon. The core is also referred to as lead, although pencils don't contain actual lead. Graphite pencils produce controlled linework and dark values; however, their results are never black, but dark gray. Charcoal pencils can produce blacks, but they are soft and smear easily, making detail work difficult. Carbon pencils may include graphite or carbon in their lead. They can make blacks similar to charcoal pencils but with firmer lead, like that of graphite pencils.

Black and white colored and pastel pencils can be used in conjunction with gray paper. Black colored pencils create rich darks, and white pastel pencils make brilliant bright whites and work well on a gray paper surface. The drawbacks are that colored pencils are hard to erase and don't overlay well, and pastel pencils are chalky and smear easily.

Hardness Ratings

The hardness rating of pencil lead is usually stamped on the casing. Hard lead pencils are labelled with an H, while soft lead pencils are labelled with a B (for black). F and HB lead pencils are in between the hardness of H and B lead pencils.

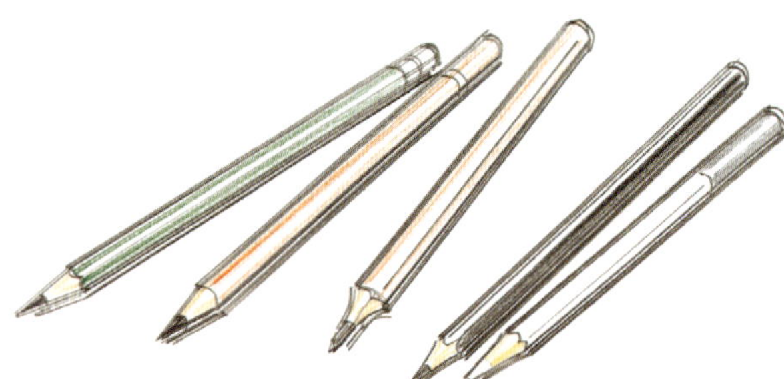

Graphite, Carbon and Charcoal
Drawing pencils typically have a core made of graphite, carbon or charcoal.

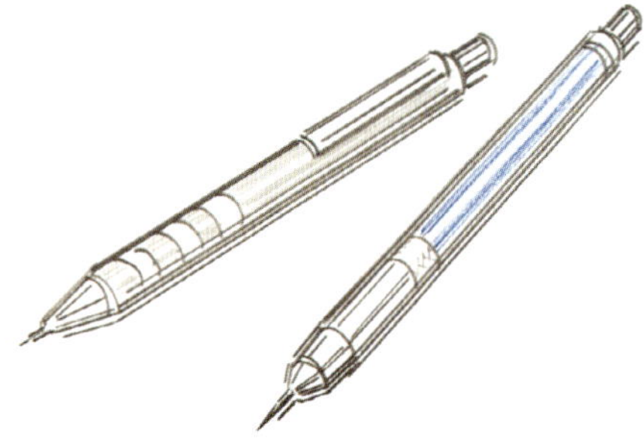

Mechanical Pencils and Lead Holders
Mechanical pencils produce fine, controlled lines that are useful for precise perspective renderings. Lead holders can make wider strokes or fine lines. Both mechanical pencils and lead holders use refillable graphite lead.

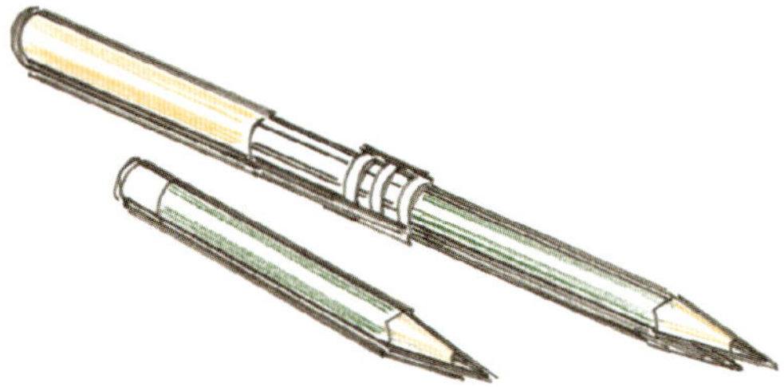

Pencil Extenders
Pencils that have been shortened by sharpening can be lengthened with a pencil extender for continued use.

The Right Tools for the Job

Though it might be tempting to skip this part about supplies, it's well worth your time and energy to learn how to use the materials suggested in this book. Using the proper tools will allow for a more enjoyable experience with more accurate results.

The numbers refer to the degree of their characteristic: the higher the number, the greater their degree (characteristic). This means the lead of a 6H pencil is harder than that of a 2H pencil, and the lead of a 6B pencil is softer than a 2B pencil. With their ability to retain a sharp point, hard lead pencils work well for detail work on smooth paper, whereas soft lead pencils are better at creating rich darks on paper with a rougher surface. Depending on the results you want, having pencils with a range of lead hardness at your disposal is useful.

Mechanical Pencils and Lead Holders

Mechanical pencils and lead holders have reusable metal or plastic casings that use refillable graphite lead. While mechanical pencils use narrow lead, which can produce only narrow lines, lead holders (also called clutch pencils) use lead that is the width of typical pencils, giving them the ability to make narrow or broad lines.

Woodless Pencils

With no outer casing other than a coating of lacquer, woodless pencils can make wider strokes than average pencils. However, they are also prone to breaking.

Pencil Extenders

A pencil extender has a wood handle with a metal sleeve at one end. By placing the sleeve over a pencil that has been shortened by use, the pencil is lengthened and made easier to handle.

Pencil Sharpeners

Pencils can be sharpened with a manual or electric sharpener, or by hand with a craft knife and sanding pad. The lead of a lead holder is sharpened using a rotary sharpener.

Erasers

Through the process of drawing, you may need to remove linework with a kneaded or plastic eraser. The puttylike consistency of kneaded erasers makes them useful for lifting light pencil lines by pressing the eraser against the paper surface or by rubbing gently back and forth over the surface area to be erased. Darker pencil lines can be erased with plastic or vinyl erasers, which produce residual strings, making cleanup easy. Other erasers may leave crumbs or possibly stain the surface of the paper. An eraser shield can be used to control where the work is being erased.

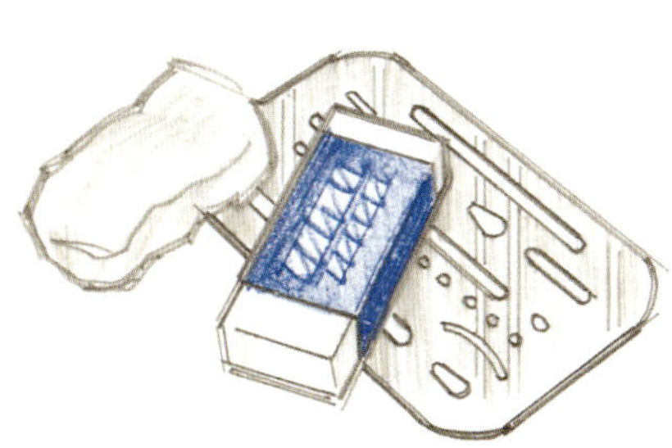

Kneaded and Plastic Erasers and Eraser Shield

Kneaded erasers are useful for erasing lighter linework, while plastic erasers work better for darker linework. An eraser shield is a handy tool for isolating an area on the drawing for erasing.

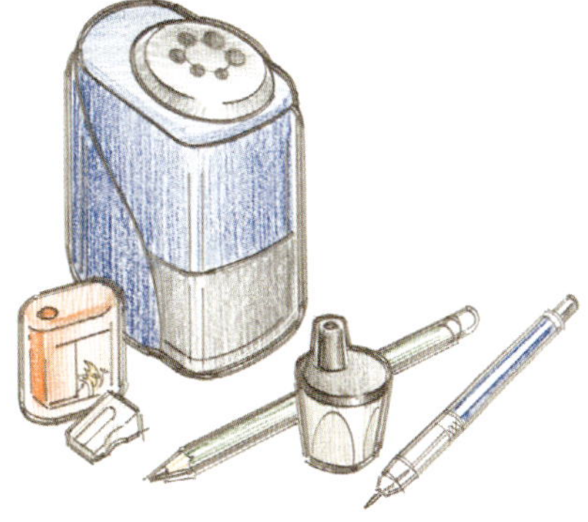

Pencil Sharpeners

Manual sharpeners can be small and portable, which is ideal for travel use. Electric sharpeners tend to be larger and are for home or studio use.

The lead of a lead holder is sharpened using a rotary sharpener. To do so, insert the lead holder in the top, then, with the lead exposed, spin the top of the sharpener.

Sharpening by Hand

Sharpening by hand is especially useful for sharpening soft lead pencils such as charcoal pencils, which tend to get chewed up in conventional manual or electric sharpeners.

To sharpen by hand, grip the pencil in one hand and a craft knife in the other, with the blade away from your thumb and toward the point of the pencil. (Always be cautious when using a craft knife!) Trim the wood by pushing the thumb holding the pencil against the thumb holding the knife. Reposition the pencil by rolling it in your hand and trim again. Continue whittling away the casing so that the lead core is evenly exposed. Sand down the lead on a sandpaper pad to make the point.

Paper & Drawing Boards

There are several factors to consider when choosing paper and drawing boards.

Paper

Sketch paper is thin, lightweight, and typically ranges between 50–70 lbs. (105–150gsm). Drawing paper is thicker and heavier, usually 90 lbs. (190gsm) or more, and can withstand erasing and heavy pencil pressure.

The paper content will determine how well the paper holds up over time. Sketch and drawing papers are commonly made from wood pulp, cotton or a combination of both. Wood pulp or cellulose contains acid, which causes deterioration and yellowing over time. Cotton is acid free, making it a better ingredient for paper because it won't age like wood pulp. The best papers made from cotton are those made from long fibers, which are better suited for heavy pencil pressure and erasing than short-fiber papers.

Paper surface texture, also referred to as tooth, may be rough, smooth or in between. Rough surface papers are compatible with soft lead pencils such as charcoal. Smooth surface papers are compatible with lead that is not as soft, such as graphite pencils.

An alternative to traditional drawing paper is Bienfang Graphics 360 marker paper. It is only 13.5 lbs. (28gsm), making it easy to trace on without the aid of a lightbox. However, because it is very thin, wrinkling can occur just by simply resting a hand on the surface. These wrinkles can be avoided by placing a sheet of copier paper under your hand when drawing.

Drawing Boards

The smooth, hard surface of a drawing board provides support for the paper and allows for better pencil pressure control than cardboard or a pad of paper. Drawing boards are made of Masonite, laminate or soft wood and are especially useful for perspective drawing. They are available in many sizes.

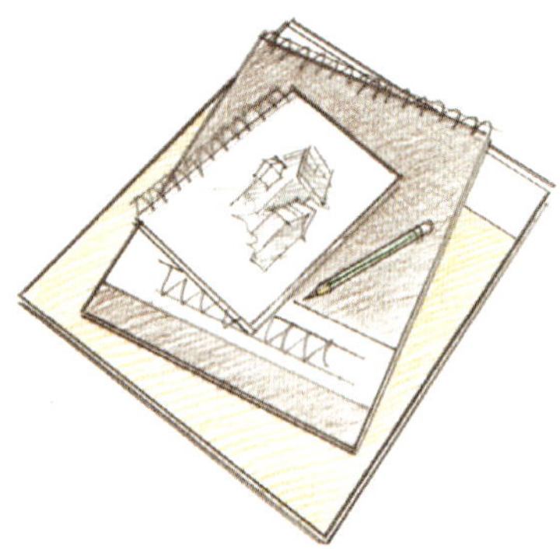

Different Papers, Different Uses
Sketching and drawing papers are available as pads in a variety of sizes. Drawing paper can also be purchased as large, individual sheets, which can be cut down to size for use. Gray papers are also an option. They provide a middle value to which lights and darks can be added with pastel white and black colored pencils.

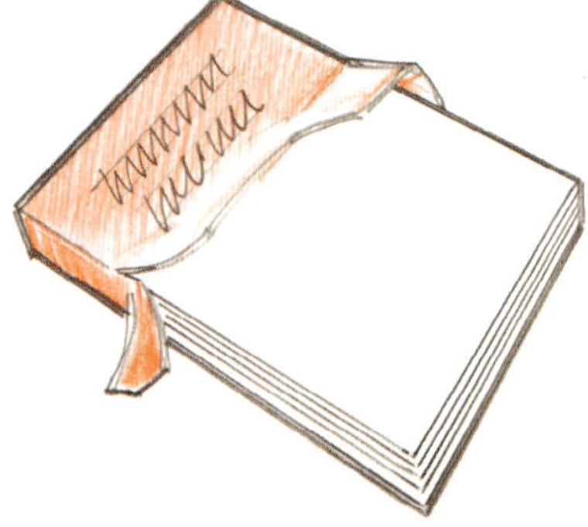

Sketching with Copier Paper
Because it is inexpensive and readily available, copier paper may seem less intimidating to practice drawing on than standard sketch paper. Its smooth surface works well with graphite and mechanical pencils.

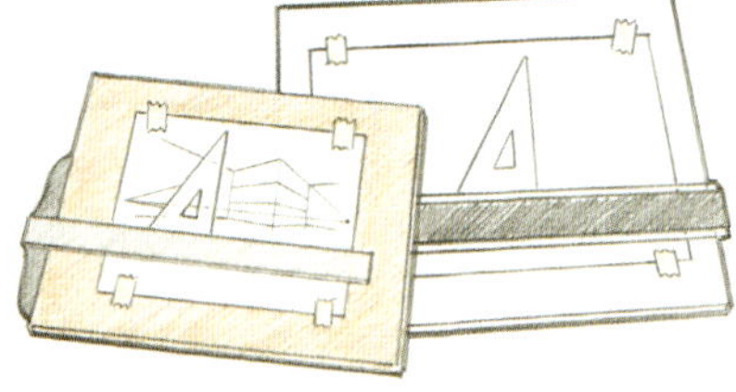

Portable Drawing Boards
A Masonite sheet can be used along with a small plastic T-square and triangle as the drawing surface and tools for making small perspective drawings. A parallel straightedge board has a laminated surface with a horizontal straightedge attached that can be moved up and down as a T-square.

Stick a Pin in It

The surface of most wood boards is soft enough to allow pushpins to be stuck into them. When making a perspective drawing, pushpins can be placed at the vanishing points. Then a straightedge can be placed up to the pushpin to draw lines to the vanishing points.

Additional Supplies

Besides the basic tools, additional supplies such as a lightbox, transfer paper and proportioning devices can be used for successful perspective drawing.

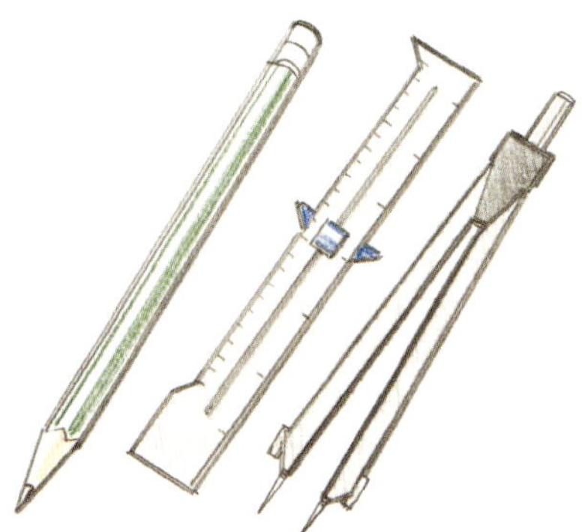

Proportioning Devices

Proportioning is a basic drawing skill that compares measurements. Though a pencil can be used as a proportioning device, for more accurate results, a sewing gauge or dividers may be used.

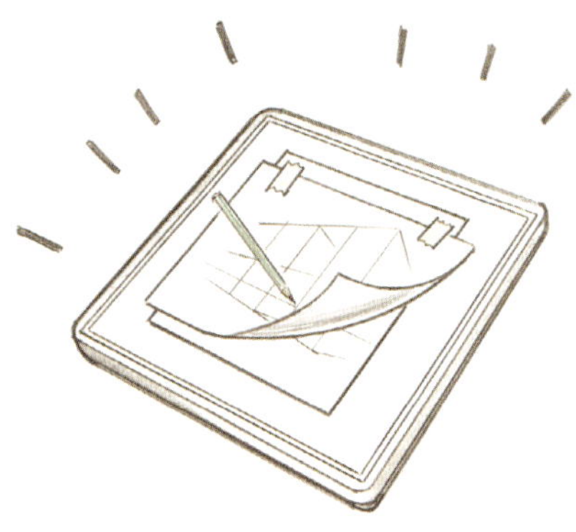

Lightbox

A lightbox illuminates an image from behind, allowing you to trace a sketch onto drawing paper. This way the unwanted lines, which would have to be erased later, are not carried over to the finished drawing.

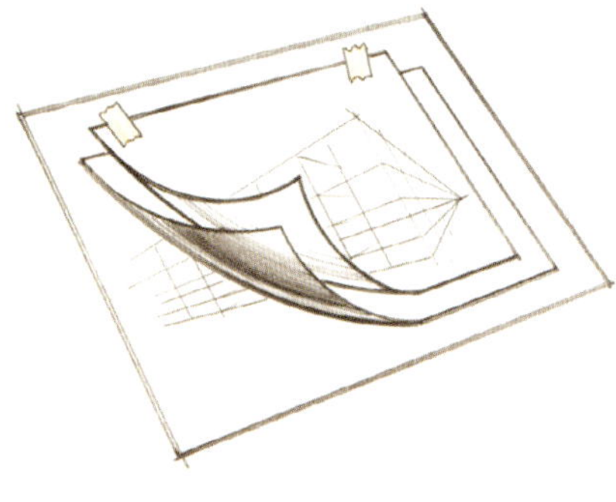

Transfer Paper

An alternative to tracing a sketch is to transfer the image using transfer paper, also called graphite paper. Tape the sketch paper to the drawing paper, then place the transfer paper (graphite side down) between the two sheets. Transfer the sketch onto the drawing paper by tracing over the image, avoiding unwanted lines.

Transfer paper can be purchased ready for use, or you can make your own. To make transfer paper, cover one side of a sheet of tracing paper evenly using a soft graphite pencil or stick. Slightly dampen a cotton ball with rubbing alcohol and gently wipe it across the tracing paper to bond the graphite. Allow the paper to thoroughly dry before use.

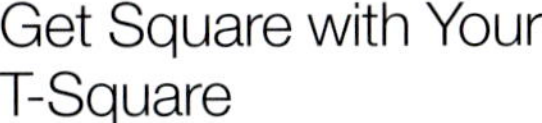

Get Square with Your T-Square

Depending on its complexity, perspective drawing can require precise vertical, horizontal and straight lines. Many artists use T-squares, triangles and straightedges throughout the course of drawing to achieve accuracy with their artwork. A T-square is used for making horizontal lines. It can also be used with a triangle for making straight vertical lines. To get accurate lines when working with a T-square and triangle, make sure the end of the T-square is snug against the edge of the drawing board and the triangle is snug against the edge of the T-square.

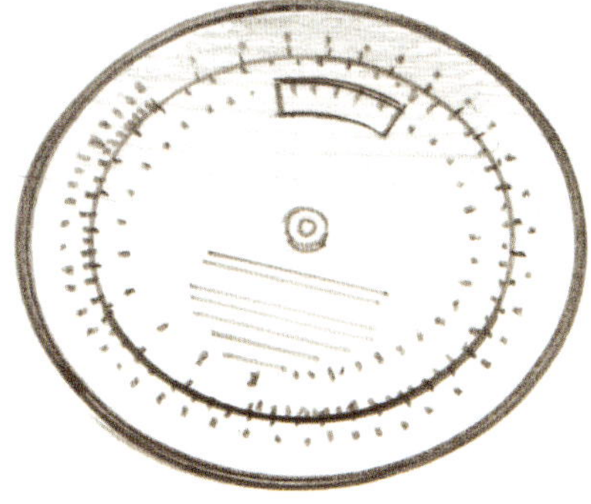

Proportion Wheel

A proportion wheel, made of two thin plastic discs, is used differently than the aforementioned tools. It provides measurements and percentages to enlarge or reduce a sketch that is to be copied on a copier. The sketch can then be traced or transferred onto drawing paper from the copy.

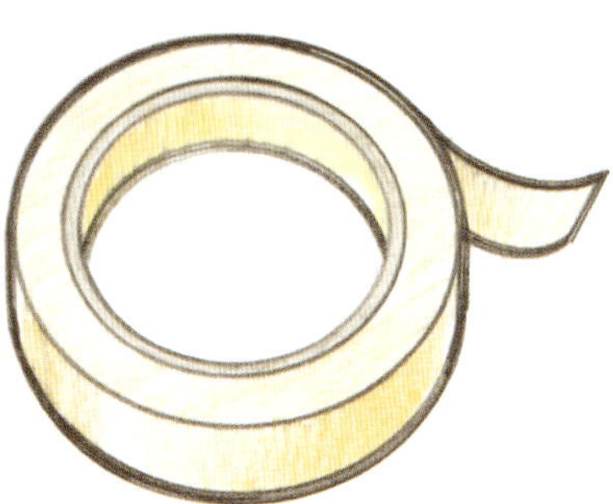

Masking Tape

Masking tape is used to adhere one sheet of paper to another or to adhere paper to the drawing board surface.

Basic Drawing Skills

The approach to completing drawings in this book has two stages. The first stage is to develop a structural sketch of the subject. The second stage is to create the finished drawing complete with values, which uses the structural sketch as its foundation.

To develop the structural sketch, the subject's perspective is blocked in by means of proportioning, transposing angles and aligning. Utilizing these skills is sure to improve the accuracy of your drawings.

Blocking In

Blocking in is the process of placing the basic shapes of the subject for the foundation of the structural sketch.

Proportioning

Proportion compares the sizes of the features of the subject against each other. A pencil, sewing gauge or dividers can be used when observing a photograph, however, a pencil or sewing gauge works best for proportioning a live subject.

Transposing Angled Lines

Angled lines may seem more difficult to place correctly than vertical or horizontal lines. Transposing angled lines of the subject to the sketch can be achieved with relative accuracy using a straightedge such as a pencil or an angle ruler.

Aligning

Aligning compares the line with the placement of the elements of the subject. Aligning can be vertical, horizontal or angled.

Start Big and Basic
Start the sketch by placing the big, basic shapes with light sketchy lines. The first lines of a sketch are used as a point of reference and aren't intended to be accurate. Rather they are used for comparison of additional lines that will develop into an accurate sketch.

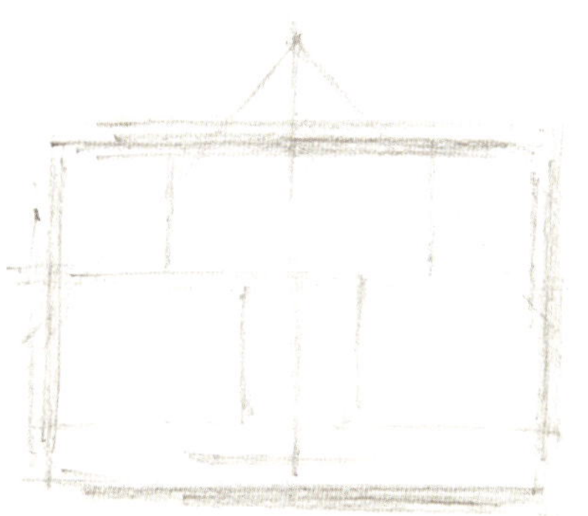

Develop the Form
Once the basic shapes are placed with relative accuracy, develop the form by adding elements that are progressively smaller and more clearly define the subject.

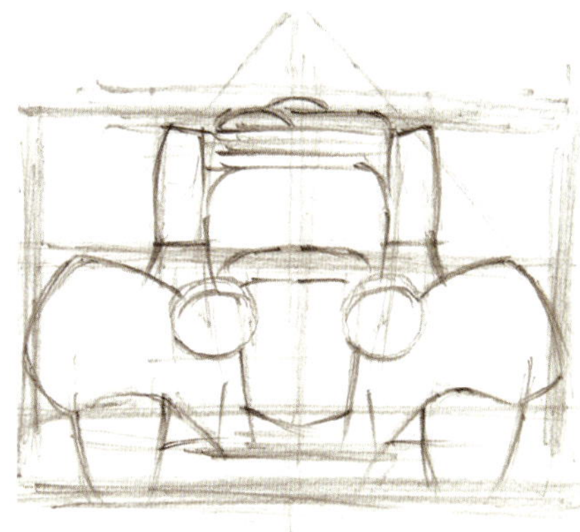

Add Smaller Forms
Add the smallest forms and refine the overall sketch.

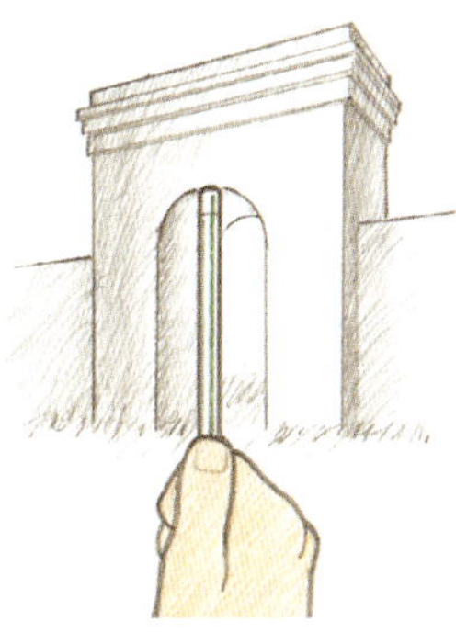

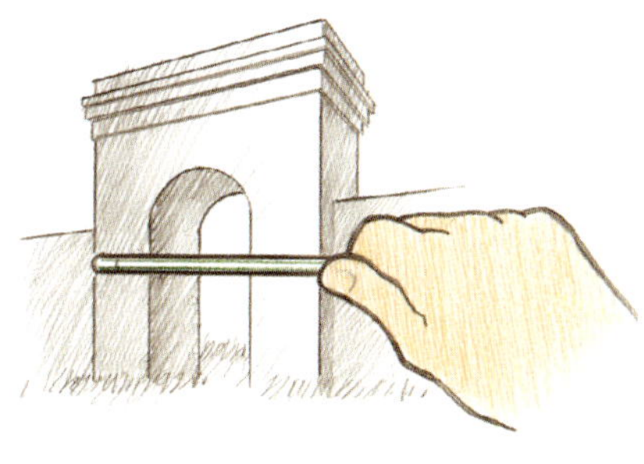

Determine a Unit of Measurement

Observe the subject and select a portion of the features that can be used as a unit to measure by. With this example, the height of the arch can be used as a unit of measurement.

Compare the Distance

Use the unit of measurement to compare the distance of other portions of the subject. Notice that the height of the arch is the same distance as the width of the entrance.

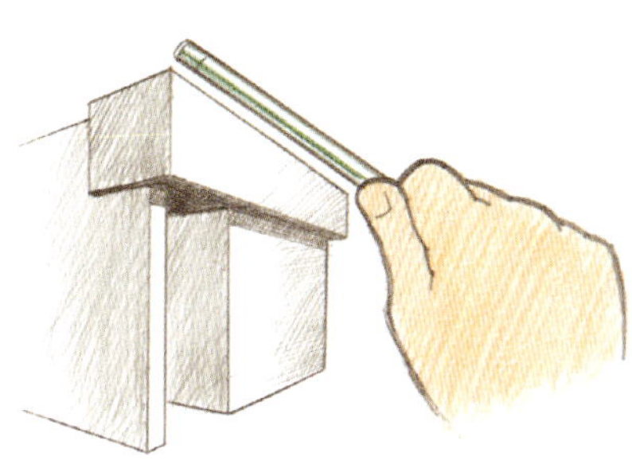

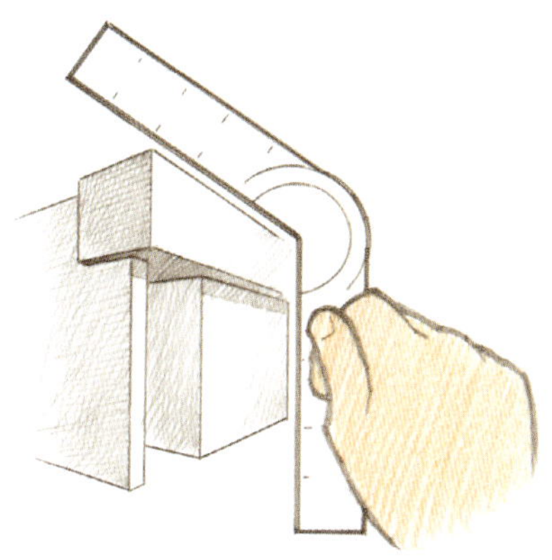

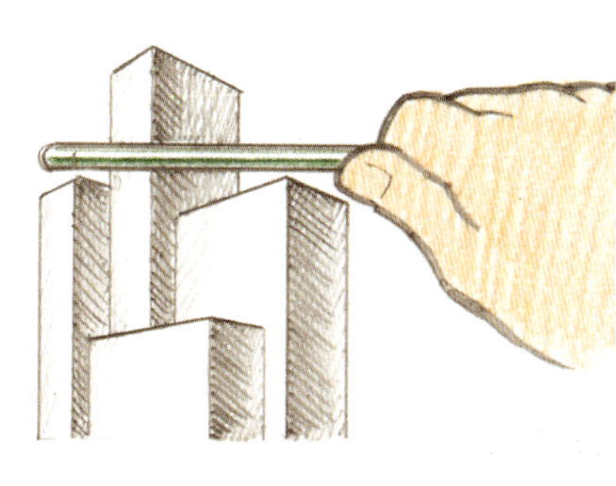

View and Sketch Angled Lines

View the subject with the pencil held alongside the angled line. While keeping your hand and wrist rigid, move the pencil over the drawing to transpose the angled line. You may need to do this several times and adjust the lines of your sketch to make it accurate.

What's Your Angle?

When straight, an angle ruler can be used like a standard ruler. When bent, it can be used to transpose angles with the lower portion being horizontal or vertical to better duplicate the angles of the subject.

What Lines Up?

The tops of the left and right buildings align horizontally. This information can be applied to the sketch in the same way you apply your information with proportioning and transposing angled lines.

Proportioning a Live Subject

To proportion a live subject (an actual three-dimensional subject) rather than a photograph, stretch your arm forward so that your elbow is locked straight. Hold the pencil so that the top is visible and slide your thumb down the pencil until you have determined a portion of the subject that can be used as a unit to measure by. Hold your thumb in place on the pencil to compare the unit of measurement to determine the proportions of the subject. This manner of viewing the subject with the pencil is also useful with transposing angles and aligning.

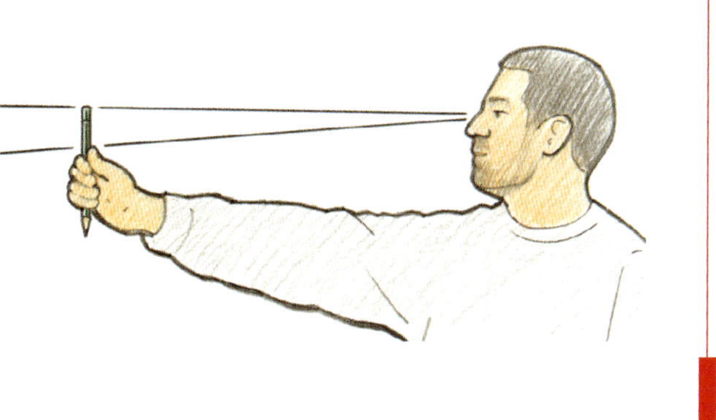

1 Linear Perspective **Basics**

Visual depth is expressed through linear perspective, atmospheric perspective and color use. With linear perspective, depth is conveyed through lines and the size and placement of forms. Learning perspective terms and principles will make the drawing process more successful.

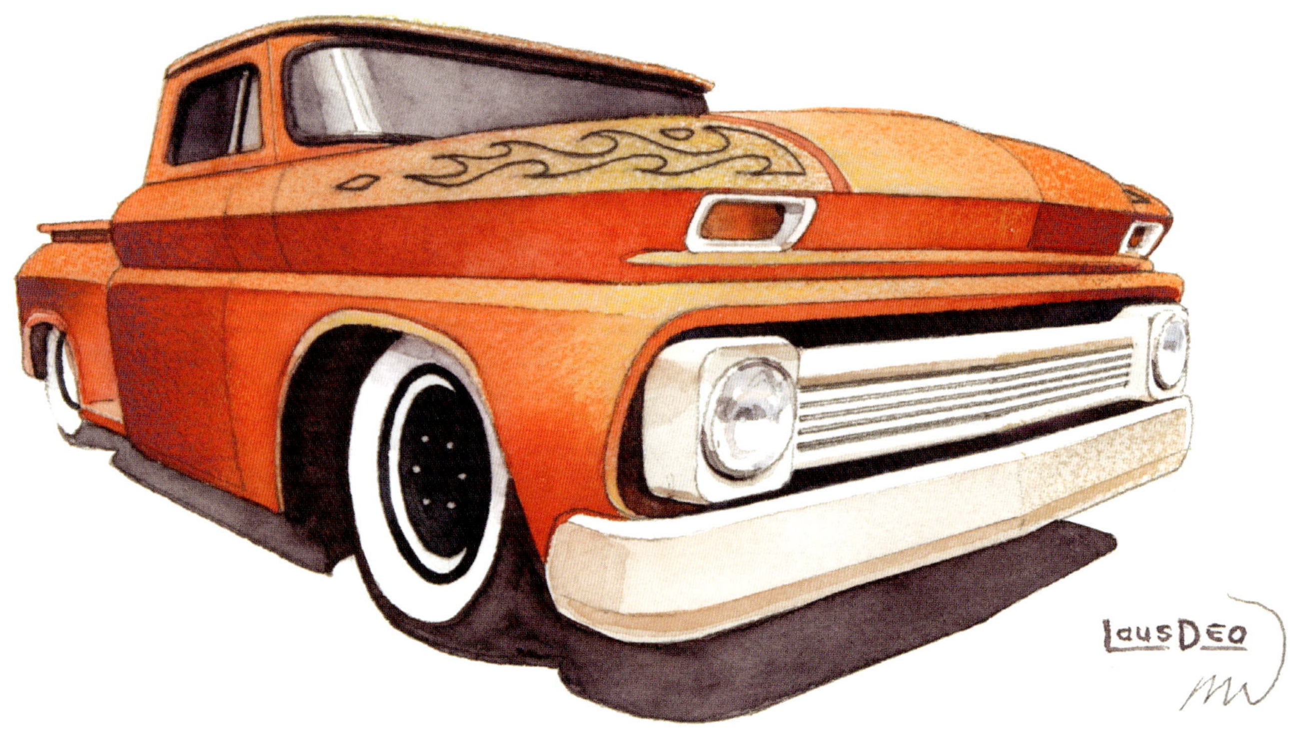

Hot Rod Truck
Watercolor and graphite pencil on watercolor paper
5" × 8" (13cm × 20cm)

Linear Perspective Terms

Though compositions may vary in complexity, the basic terms and definitions covered in this chapter are inherent to linear perspective drawings. These terms are used throughout the book.

Horizon

The horizon is the line where the sky meets land or water. The height of the horizon will influence the placement of the vanishing points and the eye level of the scene.

Vanishing Point

A vanishing point is the place where parallel lines appear to meet in the distance. With the example below, the parallel lines of the road recede and visually merge to create a single vanishing point on the horizon. There is no limit to the number of vanishing points a scene may have.

Ground Plane

The ground plane is the horizontal surface below the horizon. It may be land or water. In the example below, the ground plane is level. If the ground plane were sloped or hilly, the vanishing point, which is created by the path's parallel lines, may not rest on the horizon and may appear as if it's on an inclined plane.

Orthogonal Lines

These are lines that are directed to a vanishing point such as the parallel lines of railroad tracks. Orthogonal means right angle. It refers to right angles that are formed by lines such as the corner of a cube shown in perspective.

Vantage Point

Not to be confused with vanishing point, the vantage point is the place from which a scene is viewed. The placement of the horizon and the vanishing points affect the vantage point.

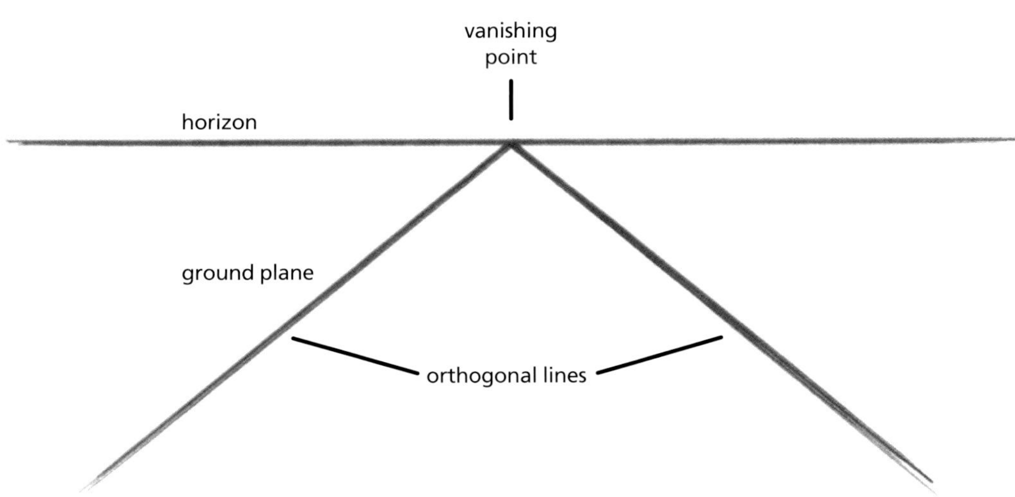

Linear Perspective Principles

Four principles that characterize how depth is conveyed in linear perspective are size of forms, overlap of forms, placement of forms and convergence of lines. Let's explore how all four principles can be used together to best interpret perspective.

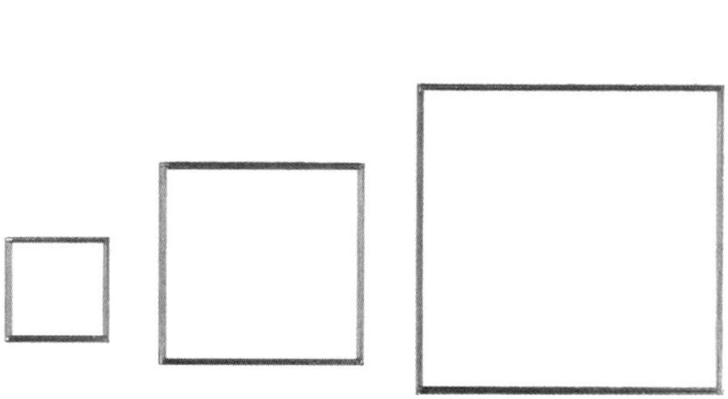

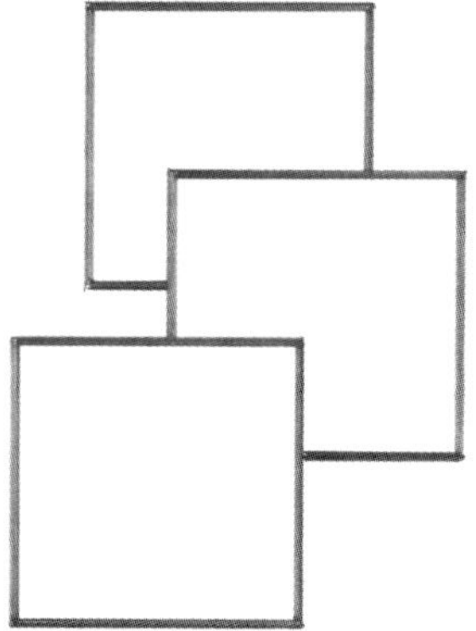

Size of Forms
One way to express depth is through the size of the forms. The largest of similar forms will appear closest to the viewer. With this scene, the square on the right appears closest because it is the largest of the three. The square on the left appears to be the most distant because it is the smallest.

Overlap of Forms
Depth can also be expressed by overlapping forms. The square at the bottom appears closest because it is overlapping the square in the middle.

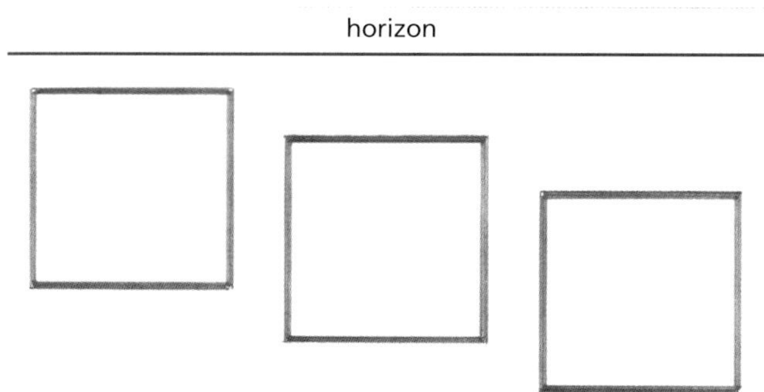

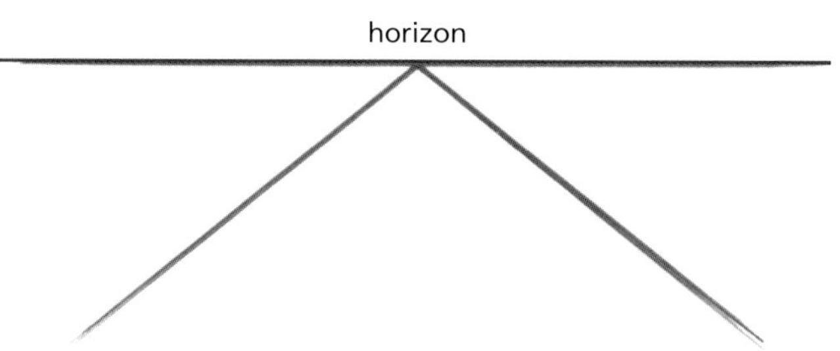

Placement of Forms
Another way of expressing depth is through placement of forms in relation to the horizon. Forms placed farthest from the horizon will appear closest to the viewer.

The square on the far right is farther away from the horizon than the other two squares, causing it to look closer to the viewer. The other squares are closer to the horizon, making them appear more distant.

Convergence of Lines
Parallel lines converge in the distance. In this scene, the road lines (orthogonal lines) meet as they recede into the distance, giving the appearance of depth. Vanishing points are formed where the orthogonal lines meet. The principle of convergence of lines shares the concept of depth expressed through size in that the width of the path decreases with distance.

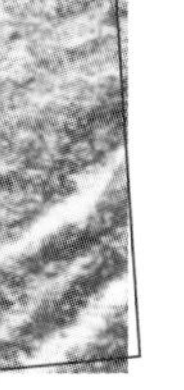

One-Point Perspective

One-point perspective is linear perspective with just one vanishing point. The vanishing point will typically appear in the center part of the scene.

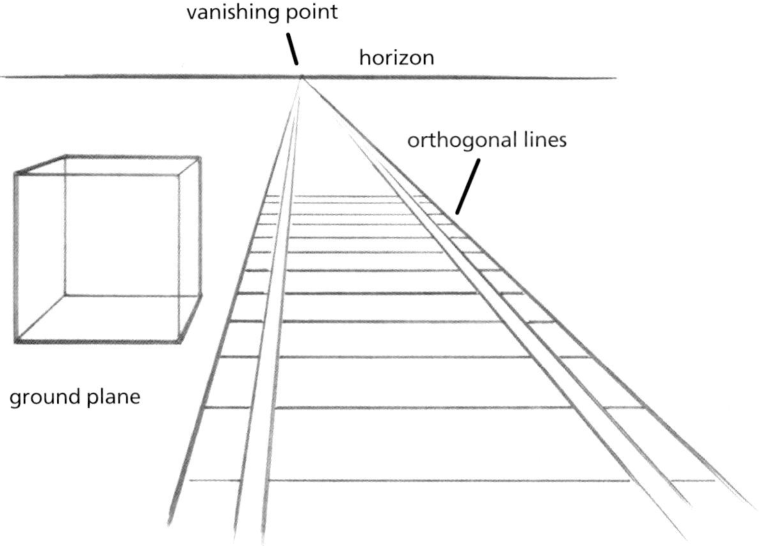

Viewing a One-Point Perspective Scene

From this vantage point, you are looking across the ground plane to the horizon in the distance. The parallel lines of the railroad tracks converge at a vanishing point on the horizon. If the lines of the box were drawn to go back to the horizon, they would converge at the same vanishing point as the railroad tracks because the lines of the box are parallel with the railroad tracks.

Notice that all of the lines in this scene either converge at the vanishing point or are vertical (perpendicular to the ground plane) or horizontal (parallel to the horizon).

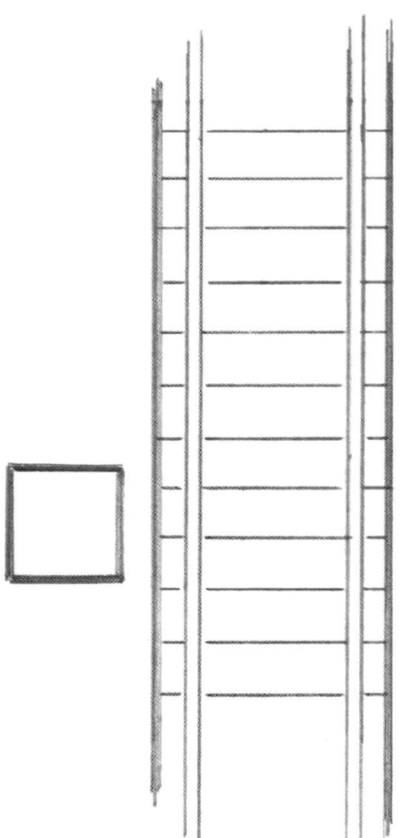

The Same Scene From Above

Changing the vantage point to look directly down onto the ground plane, it can be observed that the left and right sides of the box are parallel with the railroad tracks. When planning a linear perspective drawing, consider what lines are parallel and would share the same vanishing point.

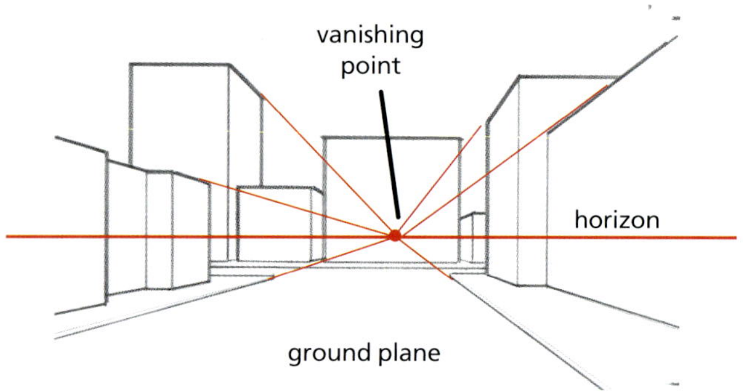

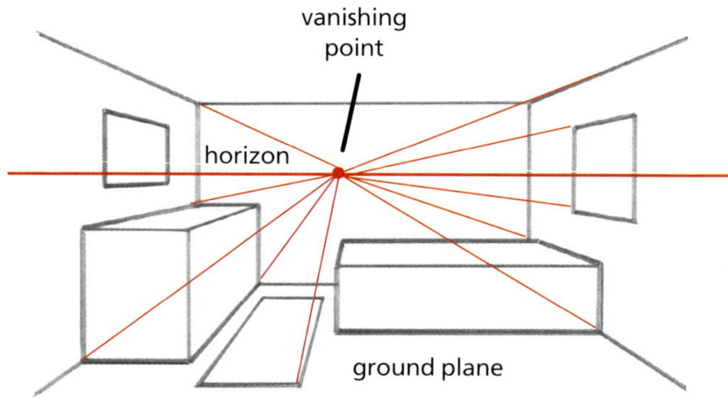

Exterior One-Point Perspective
The buildings of this urban scene can be thought of as individual boxes. Their orthogonal lines all converge at a single vanishing point.

Interior One-Point Perspective
The features in this room are drawn as boxes. As with the exterior scene, orthogonal lines converge at a single vanishing point.

Foreshortening

Foreshortening causes a subject to appear short because of the angle from which it is viewed while also giving the impression of depth.

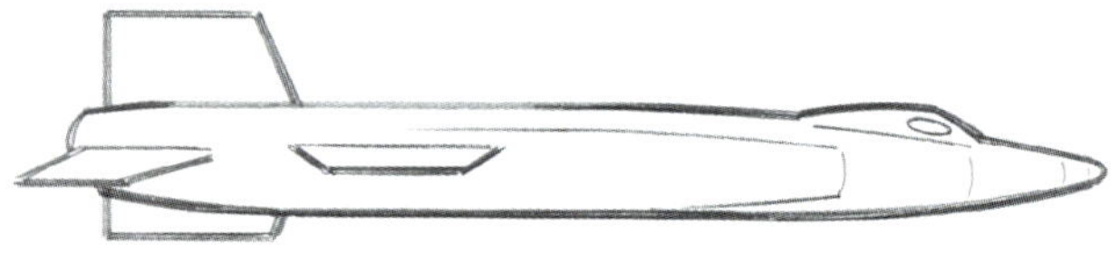

Side View of the Subject
From the side, the full length of the subject is visible.

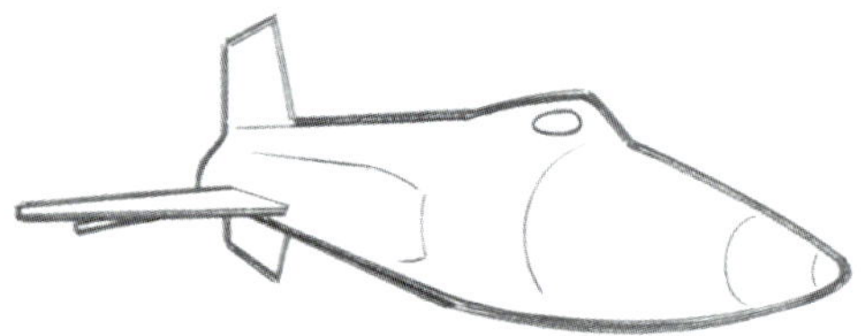

Foreshortening the Subject
Foreshortening adds depth by changing the angle of the subject so that less of the side is visible.

MINI-DEMONSTRATION

One-Point Perspective Boxes

The box is the basic building block of linear perspective. With this demonstration you can sketch as many as you want, starting with a single box. If you find freehand lines difficult to keep straight, try sketching the subject lightly by freehand, then darken by drawing over the image using a T-square and triangle.

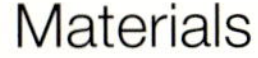

Materials

Paper
medium-texture drawing paper

Pencils
2B

Other
kneaded eraser

Optional
drawing board; masking tape; triangle; T-square

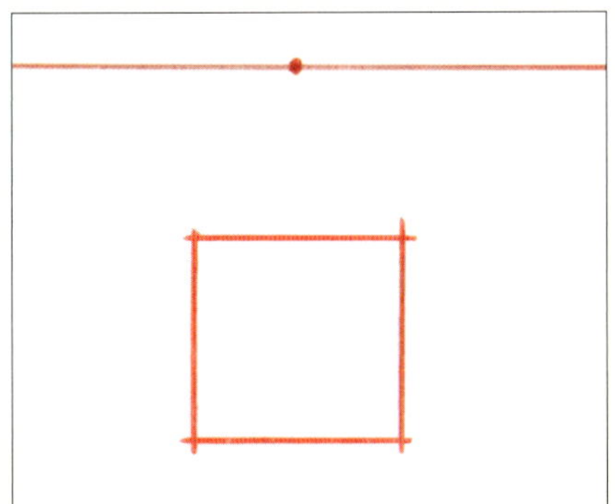

1 Sketch the Horizon, Vanishing Point and Square
Sketch a horizontal line across the top portion of the paper for the horizon. Near the center of the horizon, place a dot for the vanishing point. In the lower foreground, sketch a square that will form the front of the box.

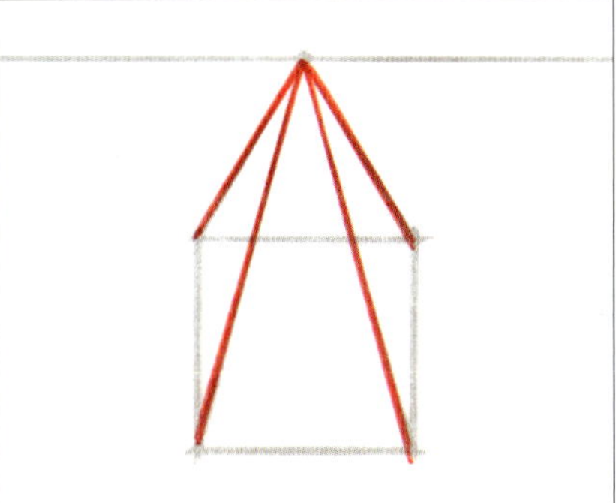

2 Add Orthogonal Lines
Add orthogonal lines from each of the four corners of the square to recede to the vanishing point. Note that all of the lines of this one-point perspective drawing are horizontal or vertical, or go to the vanishing point.

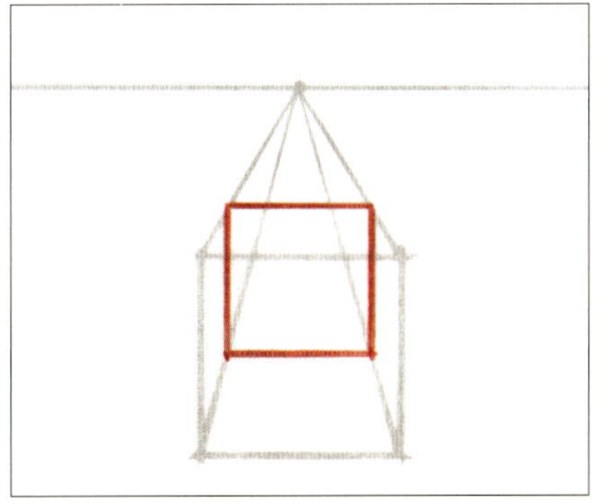

3 Add the Back Square
Sketch a square that will form the back of the box.

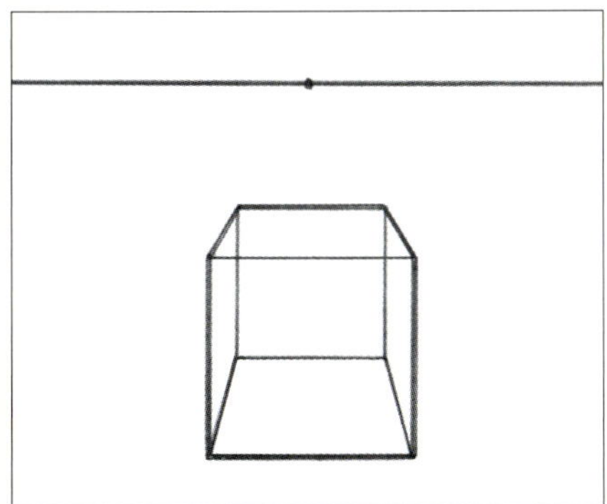

4 Erase Unwanted Lines
Erase any lines that are no longer needed, such as the orthogonal lines that receded to the vanishing point.

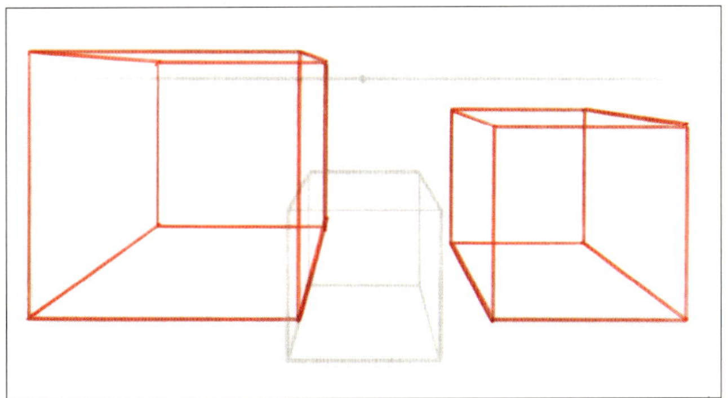

5 Add More Boxes
Sketch more boxes following the same process.

One-Point Perspective Corridor

Instead of looking at a box, this drawing looks through a box. The horizon and vanishing point will be plotted and sketched even though they would be hidden behind walls.

If you have access to observe and sketch a long corridor, such as in an office or school building, that firsthand observation would be beneficial for completing this demonstration.

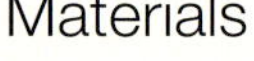

Materials

Paper
medium-texture drawing paper

Pencils
2B

Other
kneaded eraser

Optional
drawing board; masking tape; triangle; T-square

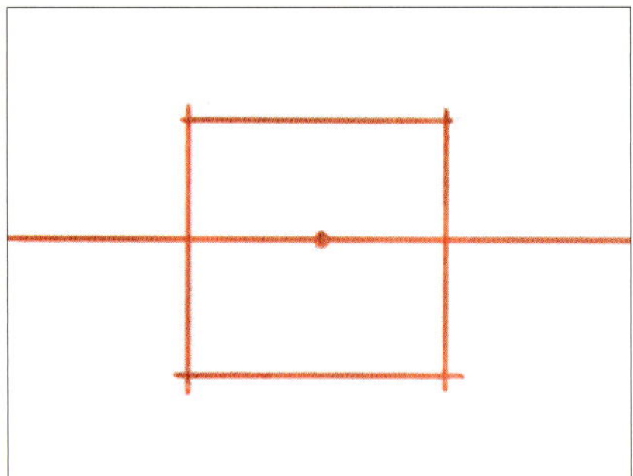

1 Sketch the Square, Horizon and Vanishing Point

Sketch a square in the middle of the paper. This will be the back wall of the corridor. Sketch a horizontal line through the center of the square for the horizon. Place a dot near the center of the square on the horizon for the vanishing point.

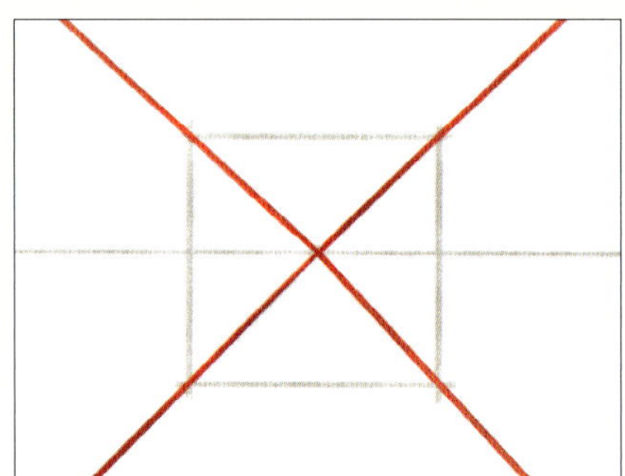

2 Add Orthogonal Lines

Add orthogonal lines that connect the vanishing point to each of the four corners of the square. Continue the lines outward from the corners of the square.

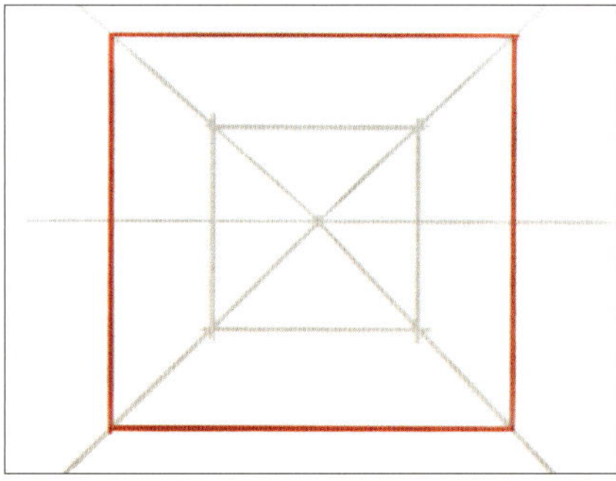

3 Sketch the Foreground Square

Sketch four lines to form a square in the foreground. The corners of the square should meet at the orthogonal lines.

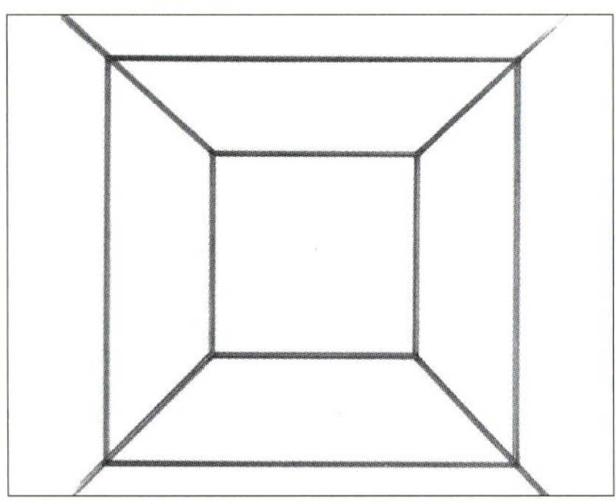

4 Erase Unwanted Lines

Erase any lines that are no longer needed, such as the horizon and orthogonal lines that recede to the vanishing point.

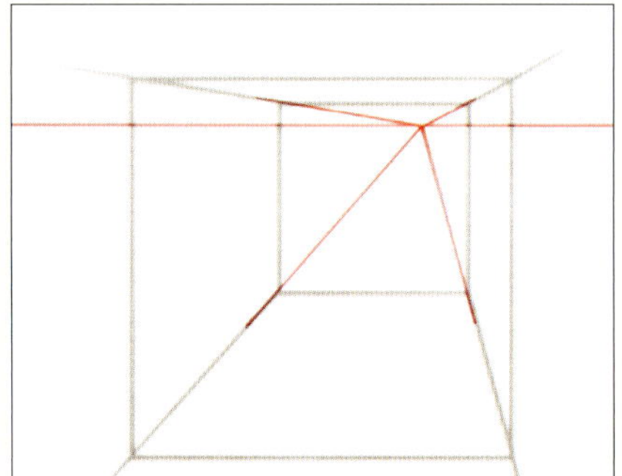

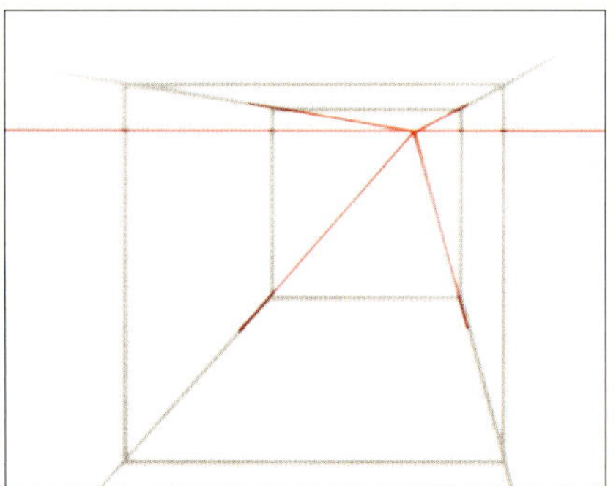

5 Try Different Vantage Points

Follow the same process to make more corridor sketches—each with a different placement of the vanishing point—thus changing the vantage point.

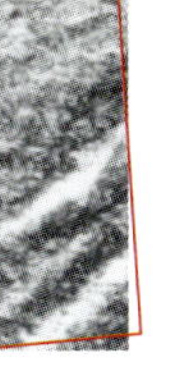

Two-Point Perspective

Two-point perspective is linear perspective that uses two vanishing points. Scenes that use two-point perspective typically have the vanishing points placed at the far left and far right.

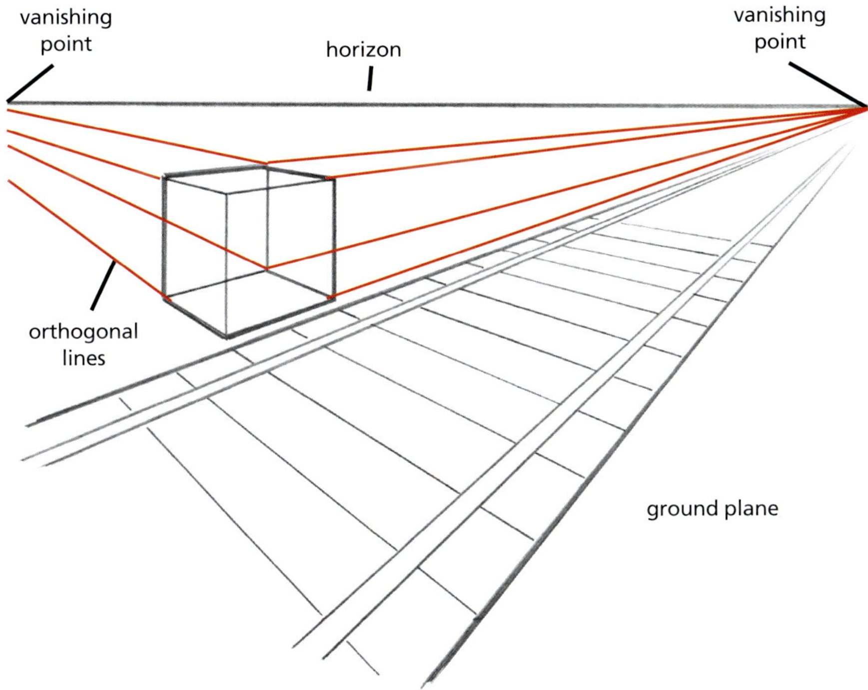

Two-Point Perspective Scene
Here is a two-point perspective scene looking across the ground plane to the horizon in the distance. The parallel lines of the railroad tracks and box converge at a vanishing point at the far right on the horizon. The other lines of the box that are parallel with the railroad ties share the same vanishing point on the far left. All of the lines of this scene converge at either the left or right vanishing point, or are vertical lines (perpendicular to the ground plane).

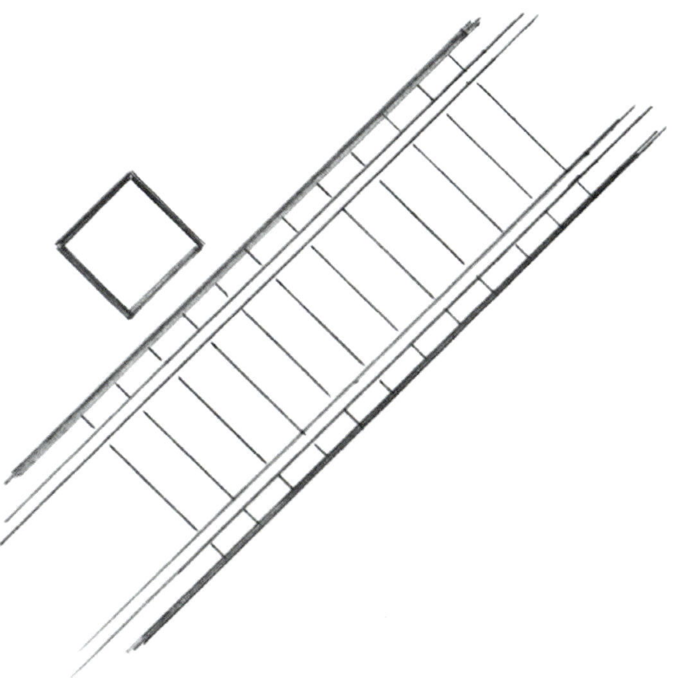

The Same Scene From Above
Changing the vantage point to look directly down on the ground plane, the lines of the box that are parallel to the railroad tracks and ties are noticeable. With this information, we know that such parallel lines will share vanishing points.

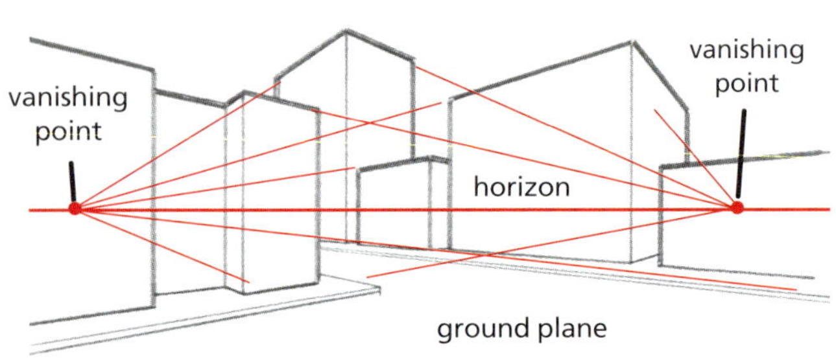

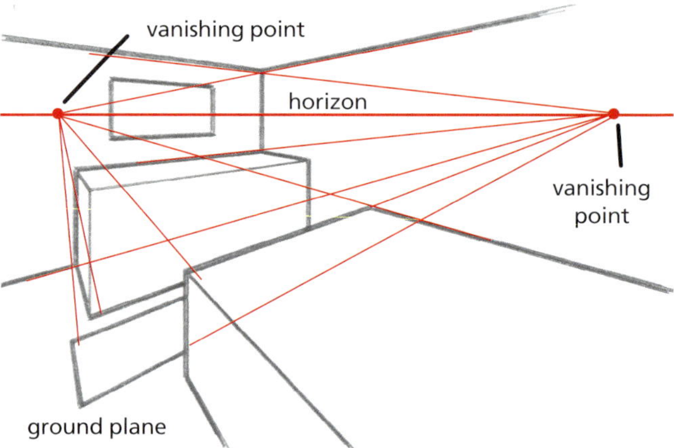

Exterior Two-Point Perspective
The boxlike forms of this urban scene are composed using two vanishing points. The many lines of the buildings are either orthogonal (going to one of the two vanishing points) or vertical.

Interior Two-Point Perspective
This interior scene is composed using two vanishing points. The lines are either orthogonal (going to one of the two vanishing points) or vertical. Both this drawing and the Exterior Two-Point Perspective drawing can be compared to their one-point perspective counterparts shown in the previous examples.

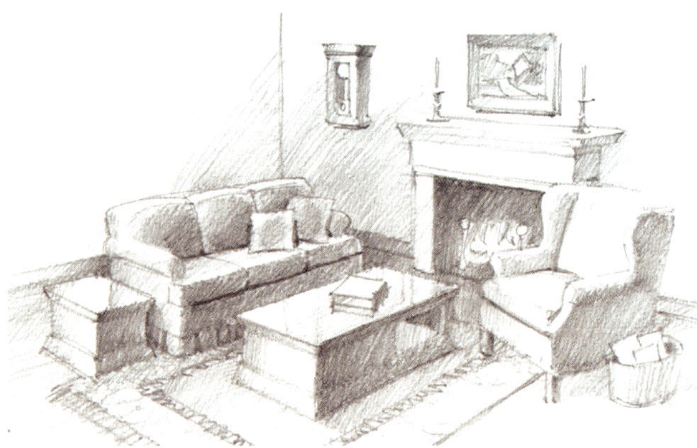

Hidden Influence
Though the horizon and vanishing points may be hidden from view, they are still influential to the scene and their placement can be plotted out.

With the drawings on this page, the horizons and vanishing points are hidden from view, either by buildings or by walls.

Different Perspectives

Oblique and isometric drawings are used for technical diagrams such as three-dimensional blueprints. They differ from linear perspective in two ways: equal-sized forms remain the same size regardless of distance, and parallel lines never converge to form vanishing points. Linear perspective, however, expresses depth and offers visual authenticity not found with oblique and isometric drawings drawings.

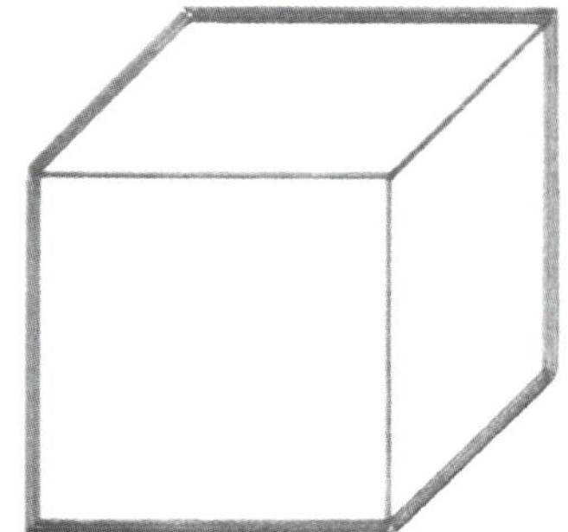

Oblique Drawing
An oblique drawing of a box has the front shown flat (as a square) with the sides angled.

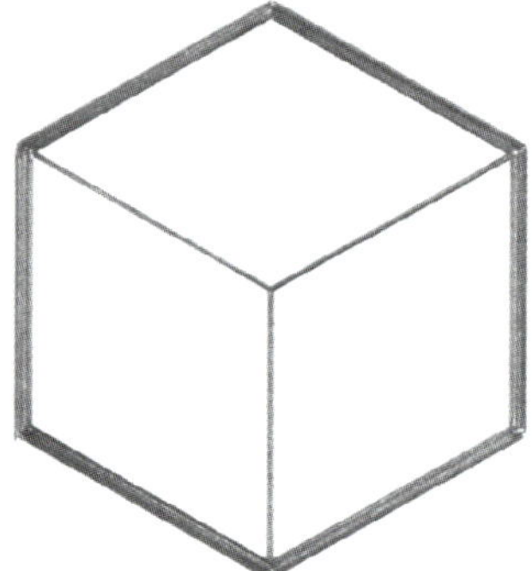

Isometric Drawing
An isometric drawing of a box has both the front and sides angled.

Two-Point Perspective Box

This demonstration involves sketching a single box using two vanishing points, then adding more boxes. The lines of these boxes either go to one of the two vanishing points or are vertical. Remember, you can draw over the lightly sketched freehand image using a T-square and triangle if you want more accurate results.

Materials

Paper
medium-texture drawing paper

Pencils
2B

Other
kneaded eraser

Optional
drawing board; masking tape; triangle; T-square

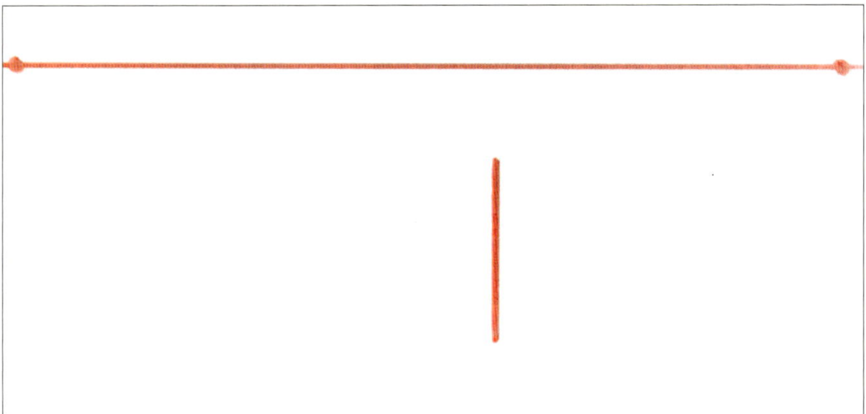

1 Sketch the Horizon, Vanishing Points and Front Corner

Sketch a horizontal line across the top portion of the paper for the horizon. Place two dots on the horizon line for the vanishing points—one on the far left and the other on the far right. In the lower foreground, sketch a vertical line for the front corner of the box.

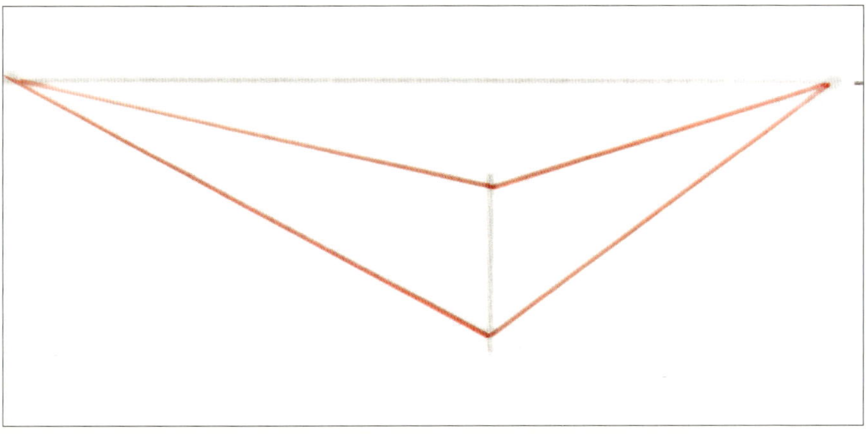

2 Add Orthogonal Lines

Add four orthogonal lines: two that connect the vertical (corner) line to the left vanishing point, and two that connect the vertical (corner) line to the right vanishing point.

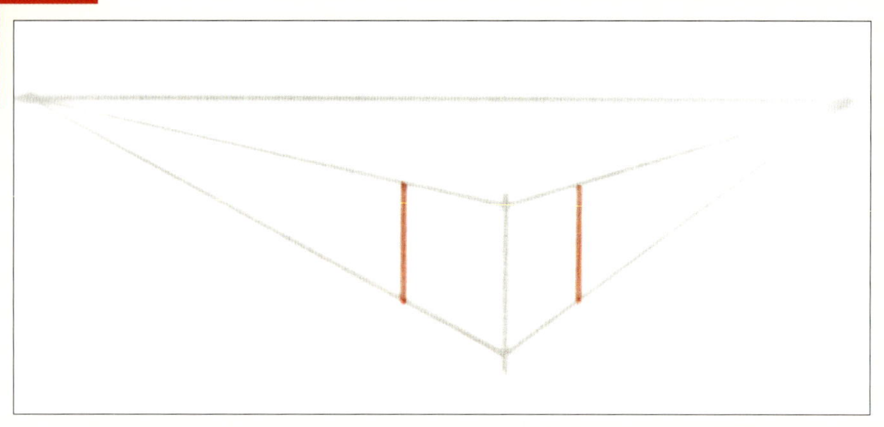

3 Add Side Corners

Add two vertical lines, one to the left of the front corner line and one to the right of the front corner line. These lines will be the side corners.

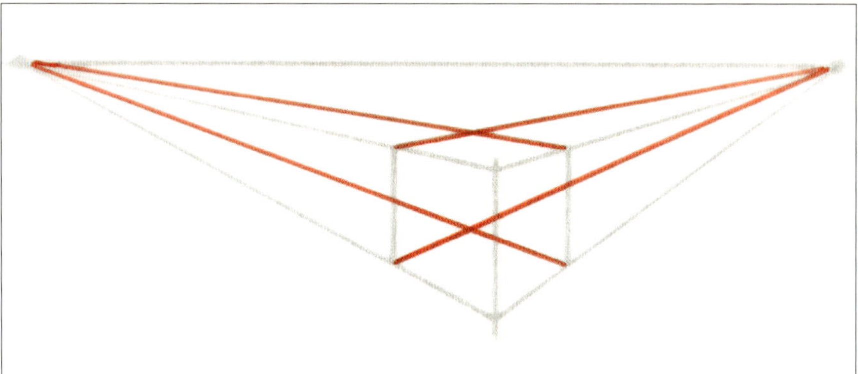

4 Add More Orthogonal Lines

Sketch four more orthogonal lines, each from the tangents where the side corner lines meet the original orthogonal lines. The lower two lines are hidden from view and are not necessary to complete the box, but are useful for checking accuracy.

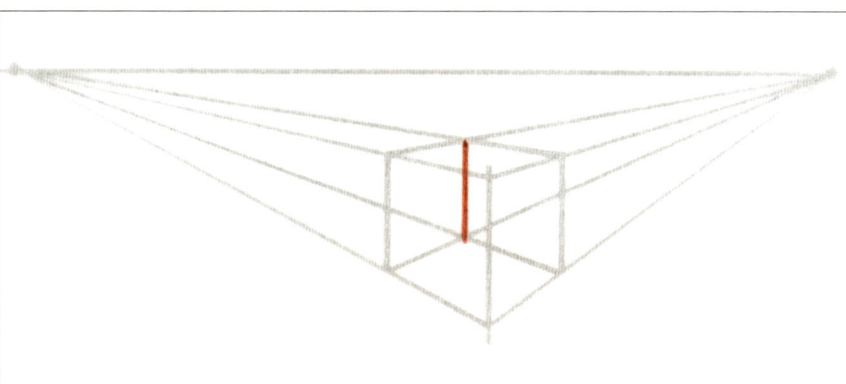

5 Add the Back Corner

Sketch a vertical line from the point where the back top orthogonal lines cross down to where the lower orthogonal lines cross.

Though this line will be hidden from view and therefore not necessary to draw, it is useful for checking accuracy.

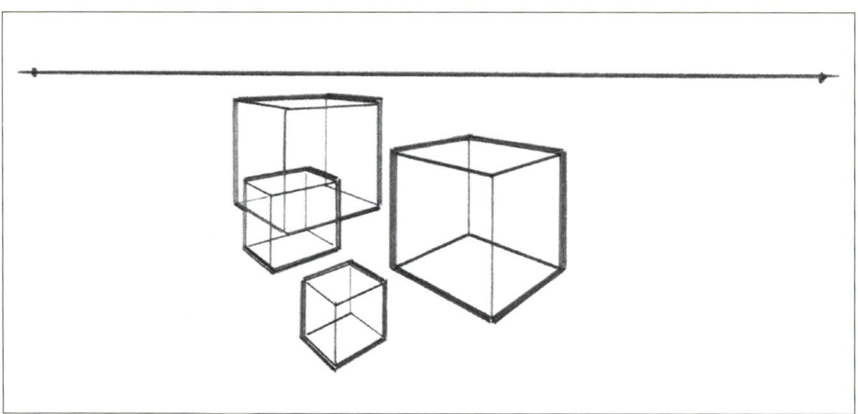

6 Erase Unwanted Lines and Add Boxes

Erase any lines that are no longer needed, such as the orthogonal lines that recede to the vanishing points. This example shows the back lines that are normally hidden from view.

Sketch more boxes following the same process.

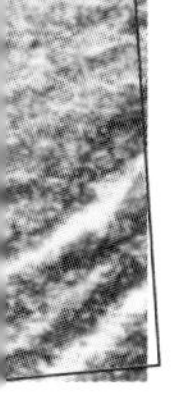

Eye Level & Distance

Eye level and distance refer to the height and depth of a scene viewed in linear perspective.

Eye Level

The eye level is the height of the vantage point. The horizon corresponds with the eye level to establish the height from which a scene is viewed. In art, it is important to be purposeful about the placement of the horizon to achieve the intended eye level.

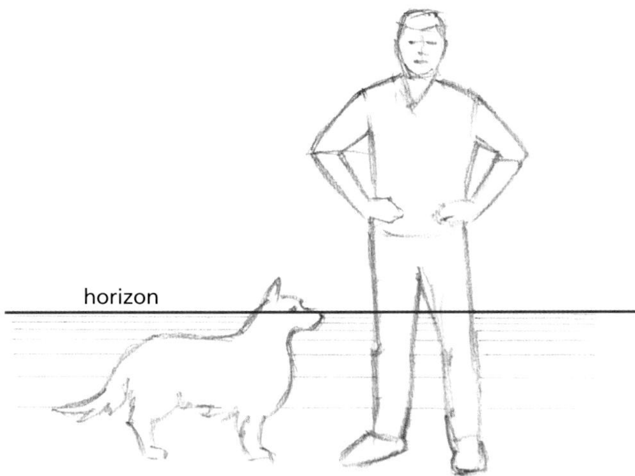

Low Horizon, Low Eye Level
With the horizon low in relation to the elements in the scene, the eye level is low, viewed from the same height as the dog.

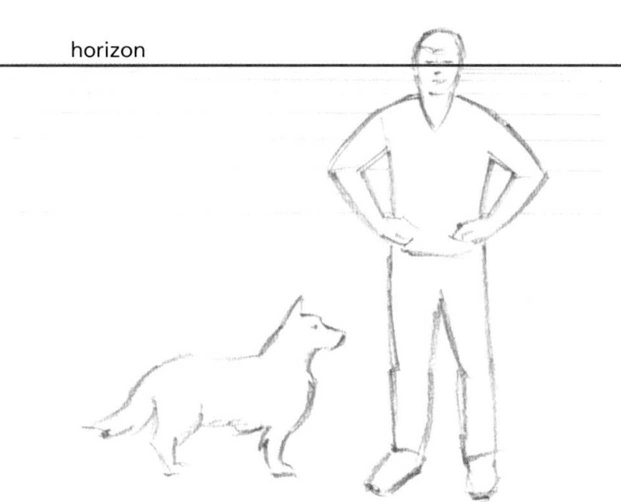

Mid Horizon, Mid Eye Level
Aligning the horizon to the height of the person's eyes, the scene is viewed from the same height as the person. This eye level should seem most familiar because this is the height we usually view the world and our surroundings.

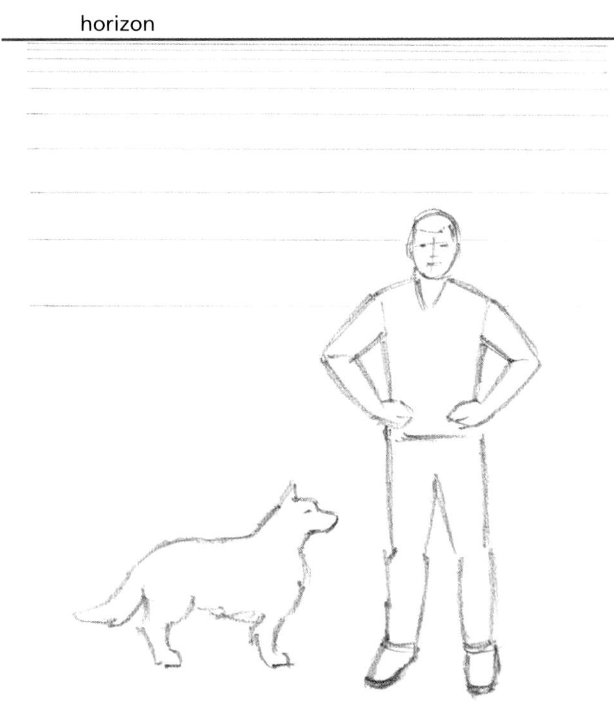

High Horizon, High Eye Level
With the horizon above the elements in the scene, the eye level is viewed from a height above the person.

First Floor Eye Level

In this first floor eye level scene, the horizon is aligned with the first floor of the buildings.

Fifth Floor Eye Level

With the horizon higher than the previous drawing, the eye level is moved to the height of the fifth floor, recognizable by the alignment of the horizon to the fifth floor of the distant buildings.

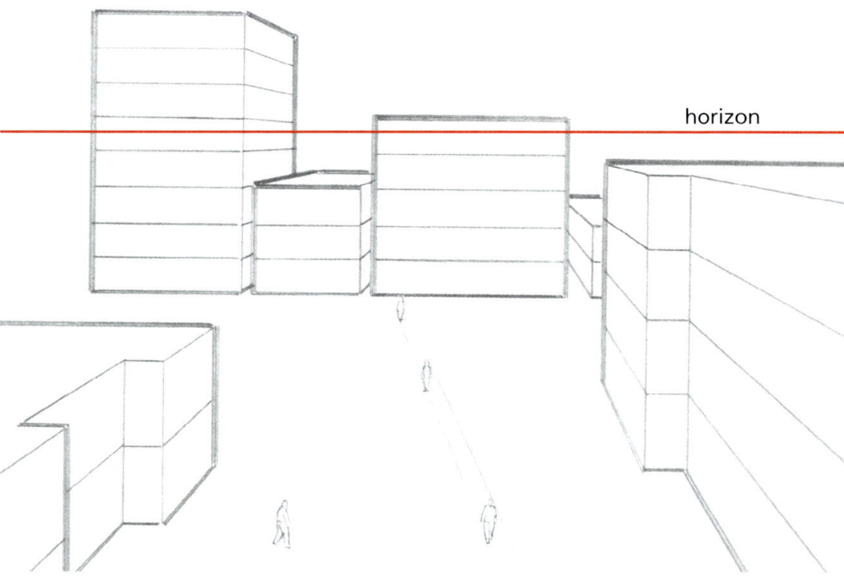

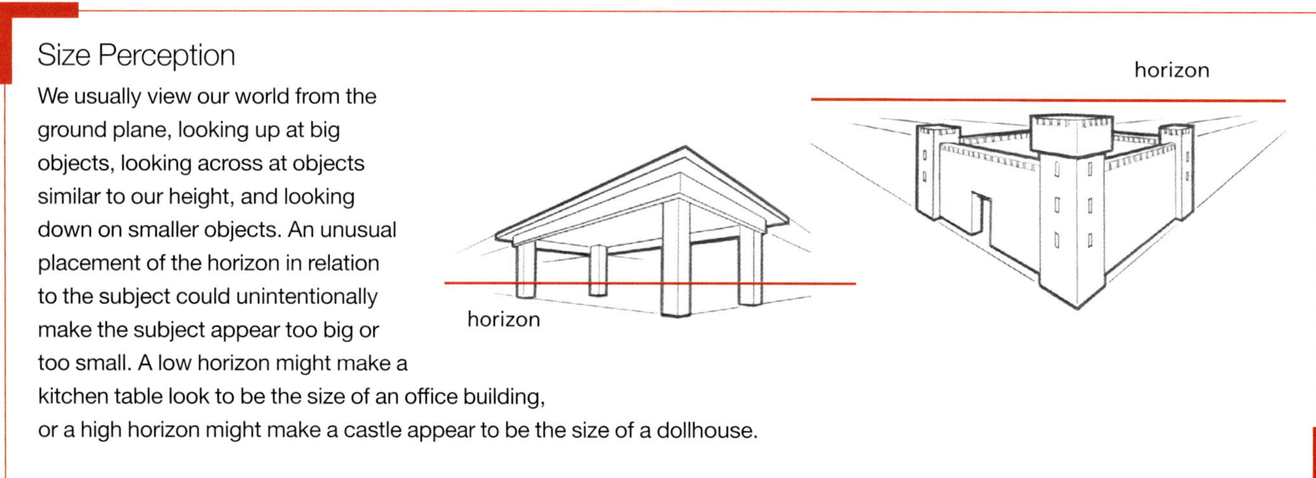

Size Perception

We usually view our world from the ground plane, looking up at big objects, looking across at objects similar to our height, and looking down on smaller objects. An unusual placement of the horizon in relation to the subject could unintentionally make the subject appear too big or too small. A low horizon might make a kitchen table look to be the size of an office building, or a high horizon might make a castle appear to be the size of a dollhouse.

Distance

Distance is how far away the vantage point appears from the subject. While the horizon determines the elevation, the vanishing points determine the distance of a scene. With two-point perspective, the farther apart the vanishing points, the more distant the vantage point will appear.

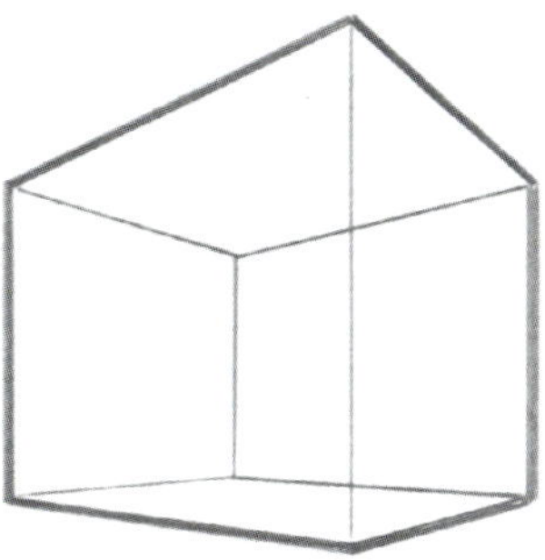

Closely Spaced Vanishing Points

By having closely spaced vanishing points, the vantage point of this scene appears close to the subject.

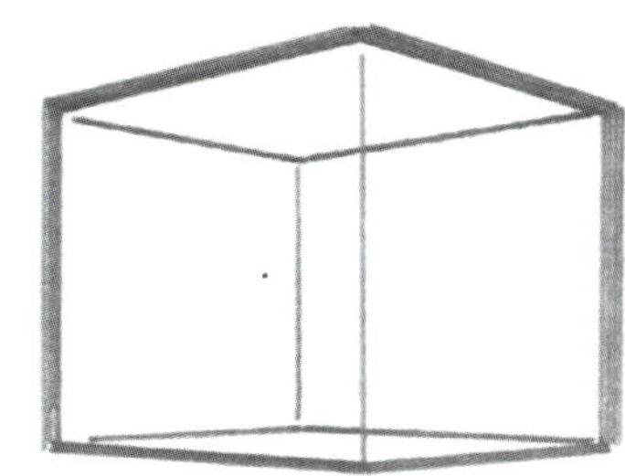

More Space Between Vanishing Points

When the vanishing points are spaced farther apart, the vantage point will appear farther from the subject.

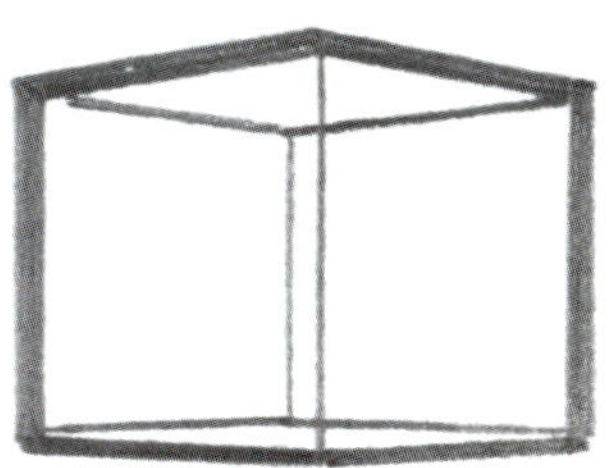

Distant Vanishing Points

When the vanishing points are moved off the page, the vantage point will appear the most distant from the subject. Far-off subjects photographed through a telephoto lens will have distant vanishing points, giving the subject a compressed appearance.

Cropping Doesn't Change Elevation or Distance

Although the placement of the horizon and vanishing points in relation to the subject does change the elevation and distance, the way the scene is cropped will not affect these components. The same scene cropped two different ways will still be viewed from the same elevation and distance.

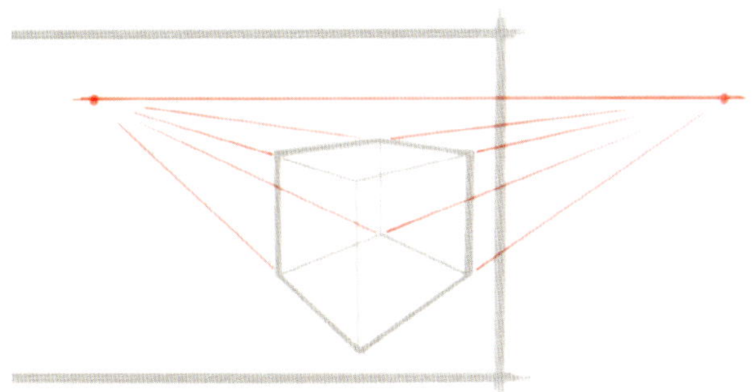

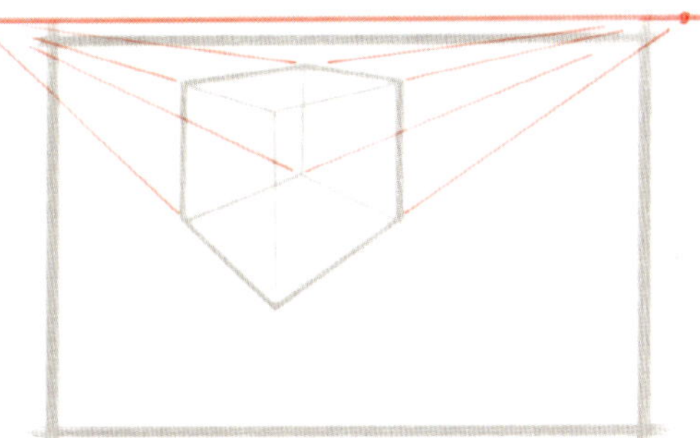

Multi-Point Perspective

Linear perspective doesn't have to be limited to one or two vanishing points. A scene may have multiple vanishing points depending on the complexity of the subject.

Three-Point Perspective

Similar to two-point perspective, three-point perspective has left and right vanishing points on the horizon. Additionally, there is a third vanishing point either below or above the horizon. With two-point perspective, these vertical lines remain straight up and down perpendicular to the ground plane. With three-point perspective, the vantage point either looks down or up at the subject. Instead of vertical lines, it has a third set of orthogonal lines that converge at a third vanishing point.

Four-Point Perspective and Beyond

While a basic subject like a box may have just two vanishing points, adding more boxes to the scene may add more vanishing points depending on whether the boxes are parallel to each other.

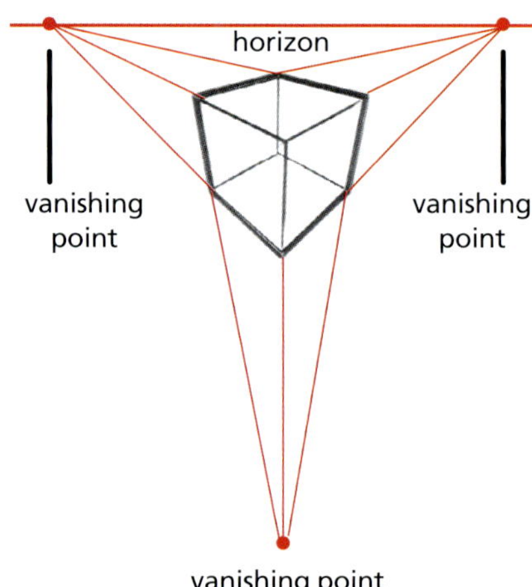

Three-Point Perspective From Above
Besides having vanishing points on the left and right, this scene has an additional vanishing point below the subject. With this drawing, the horizon is above the subject, giving a bird's-eye vantage point to the scene.

Every line of the subject is an orthogonal line and goes to one of the three vanishing points.

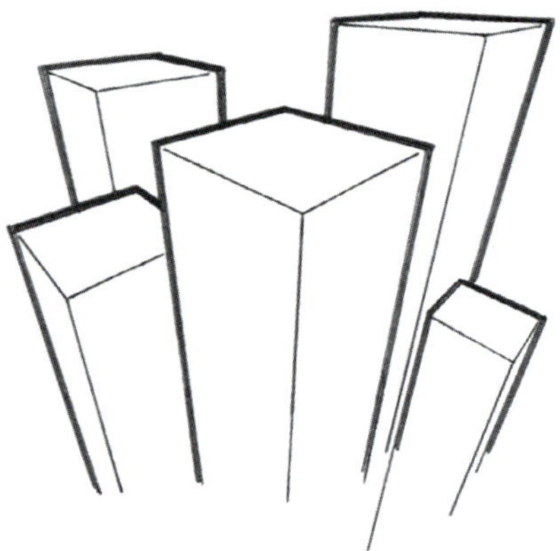

Detail of Three-Point Perspective From Above
An example of a three-point perspective drawing may be a detail of skyscrapers viewed from above.

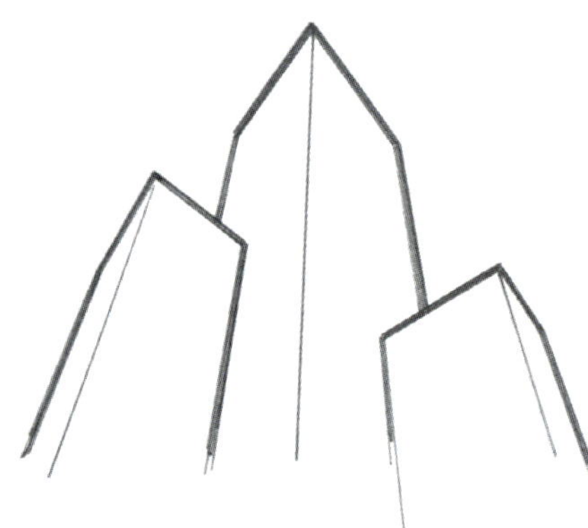

Three-Point Perspective From Below
This three-point perspective drawing has two vanishing points on a low horizon with the third vanishing point high in the sky. The vantage point appears low, and the form looks towering. As with the previous example, every line of the subject is an orthogonal line and goes to one of the three vanishing points.

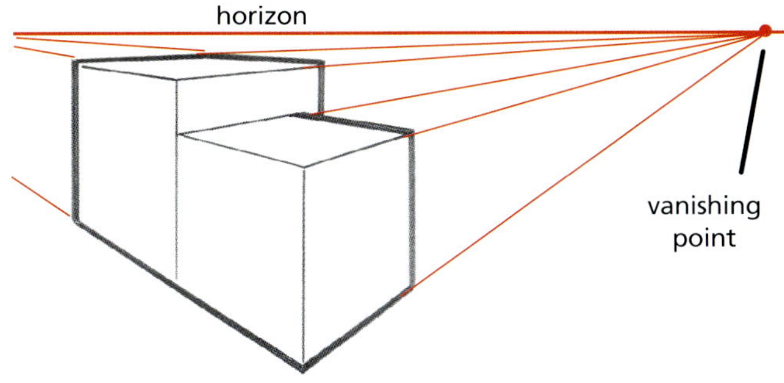

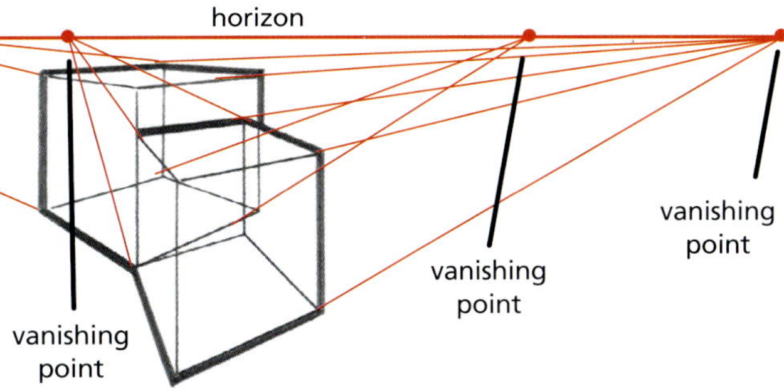

Two Subjects, Two Vanishing Points
Though different sizes, both boxes are parallel to each other and share the same two vanishing points. (In order to show this image as large as possible, the second vanishing point was cropped out.)

Two Subjects, Four Vanishing Points
By changing the angle of the foreground box, the boxes are no longer parallel to each other. Each box has its own set of vanishing points that rest on the horizon. (In order to show this image as large as possible, the fourth vanishing point was cropped out.)

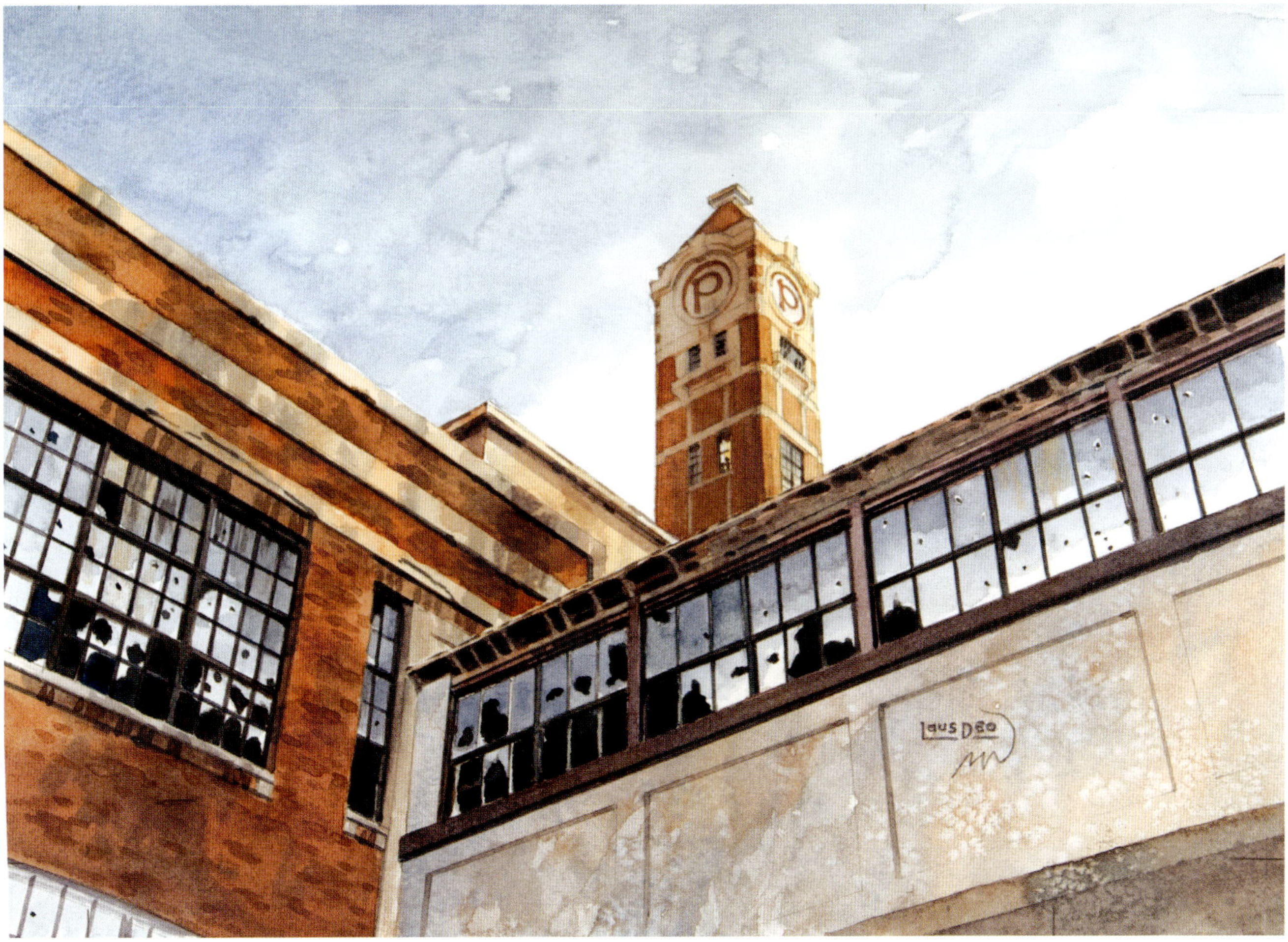

Locating Vanishing Points
The vanishing points of this three-point perspective scene can be located by continuing the lines of the buildings and windows beyond the perimeter of the scene to three places of convergence.

Peters Cartridge Factory
Watercolor on watercolor paper
9" × 11" (23cm × 28cm)

Three-Point Perspective Box

This three-point perspective demonstration has two vanishing points at the top on the horizon and a third vanishing point at the center bottom, causing the vantage point to appear above the subject. All of the lines of the box are orthogonal lines and go to one of the three vanishing points.

Materials

Paper
medium-texture drawing paper

Pencils
2B

Other
kneaded eraser

Optional
drawing board; masking tape; triangle; T-square

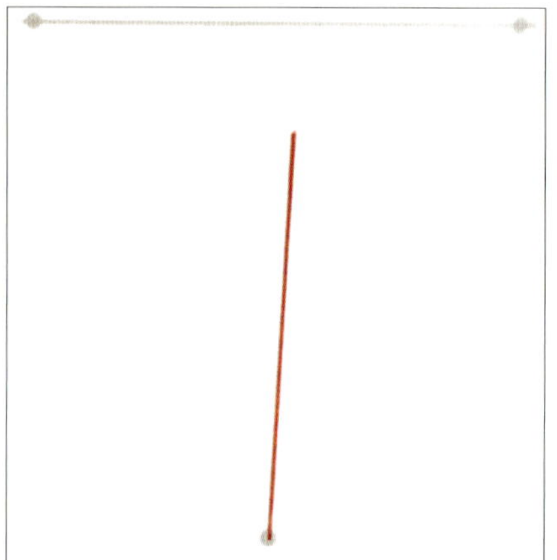

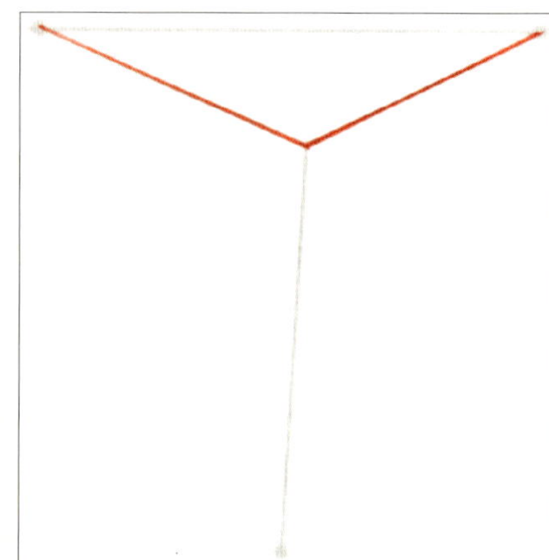

1 Sketch the Horizon and Vanishing Points

Sketch a horizontal line near the top of the paper for the horizon. Place two dots on the horizon for the vanishing points—one on the far left and one on the far right. Near the lower center portion of the paper, place another dot for the third vanishing point. This point can be in the exact center, but it doesn't have to be.

2 Sketch the Front Corner

Sketch a line coming up from the lower vanishing point to form the front corner of the box. This line can be exactly vertical but it doesn't have to be.

3 Add Top Lines

Add two lines at the top coming from the same point on the vertical line. One line goes to the left vanishing point. The other line goes to the right vanishing point to form the top forward edge of the box.

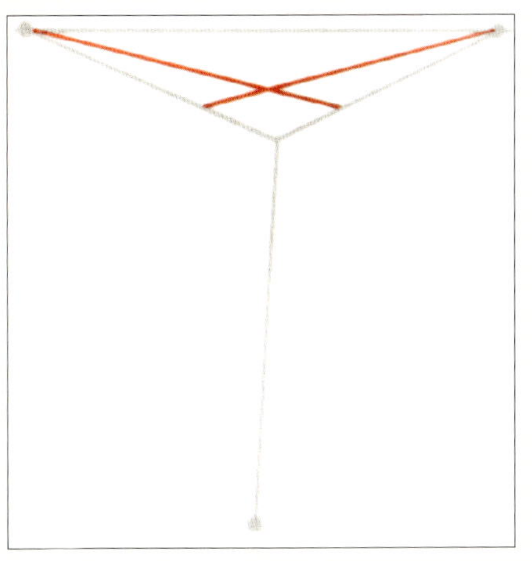

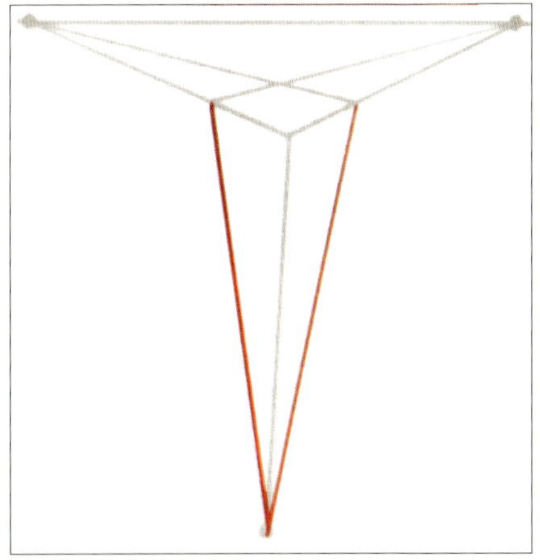

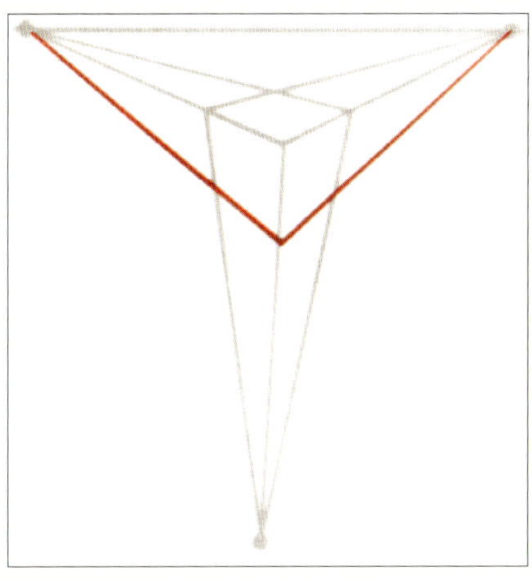

4 Continue Adding Top Lines

Add two more lines to form the top of the box. One line connects the left top edge line to the right vanishing point; the other connects the right top edge line to the left vanishing point to form the top of the box.

5 Add Side Lines

Add two lines to form the sides of the box. These lines connect the top corners (formed as tangents in the previous step) to the lower vanishing point.

6 Add Bottom Lines

Place a point below the top lines of the box on the center vertical line. From this point, sketch one line to the left vanishing point and another line to the right vanishing point to form the bottom of the box.

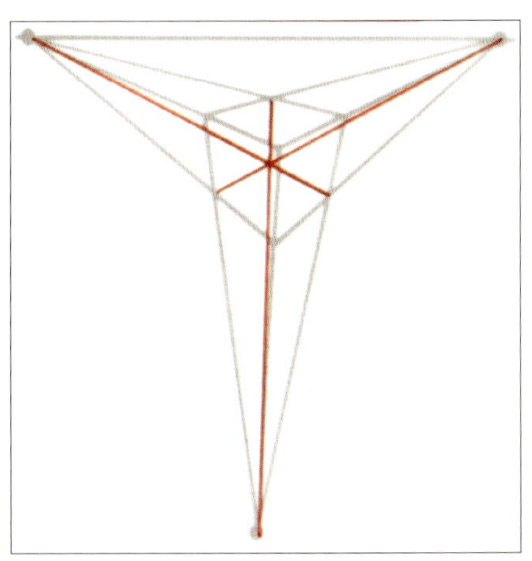

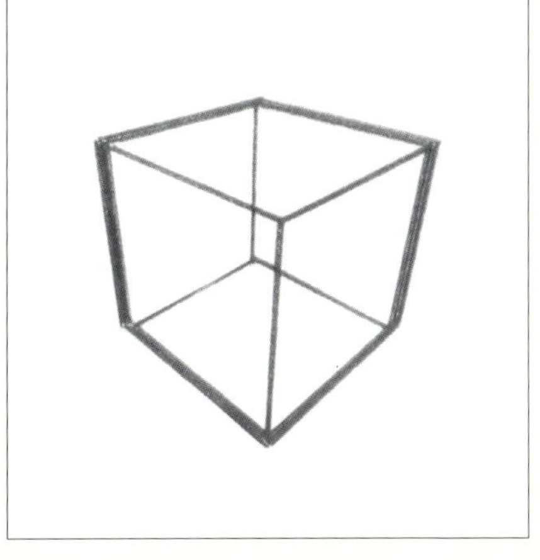

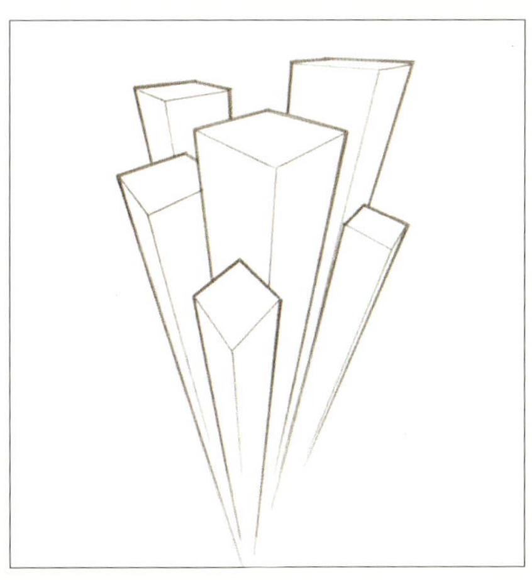

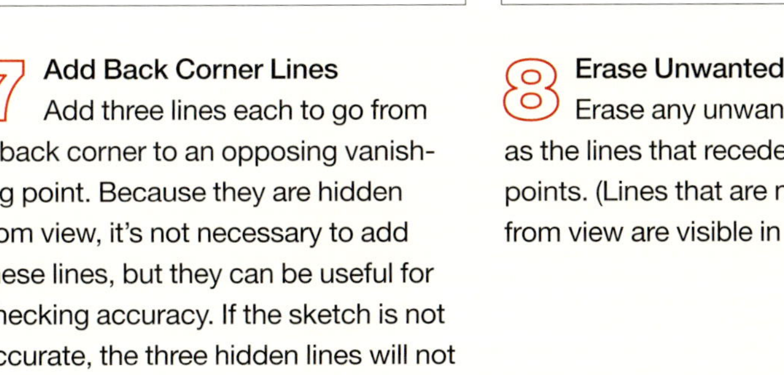

7 Add Back Corner Lines

Add three lines each to go from a back corner to an opposing vanishing point. Because they are hidden from view, it's not necessary to add these lines, but they can be useful for checking accuracy. If the sketch is not accurate, the three hidden lines will not meet at the same point.

8 Erase Unwanted Lines

Erase any unwanted lines, such as the lines that recede to the vanishing points. (Lines that are normally hidden from view are visible in this example.)

9 Add More Boxes

Follow the same set of steps to sketch more boxes, leaving out the lines that would be hidden. In this example, the bottom lines of the forms were not drawn. The effect gives the forms an appearance of skyscrapers.

2 Linear Perspective **Techniques**

When examining linear perspective in the world around us, you'll notice patterns emerge. Recognizing and utilizing these patterns will assist in creating features such as floors, roofs, staircases, ellipses and reflections.

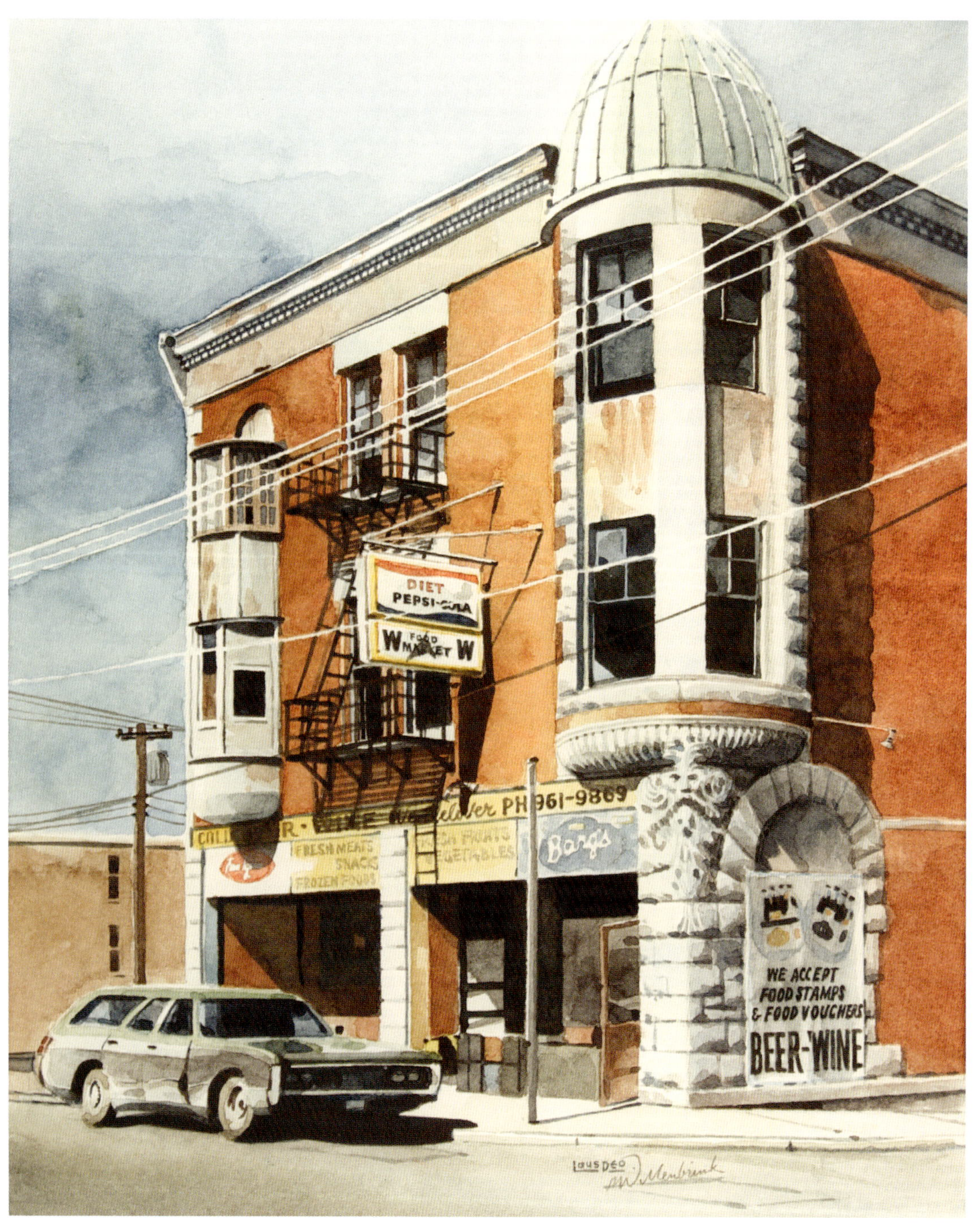

WW Market
Watercolor on watercolor paper
9½" × 7½" (24cm × 19cm)

Adding Orthogonal Lines Without Vanishing Points

Middle orthogonal lines can be added to a drawing by dividing the vertical lines and connecting them. This is especially helpful when doing a quick sketch or when vanishing points are difficult to plot because of their distance from the form being drawn.

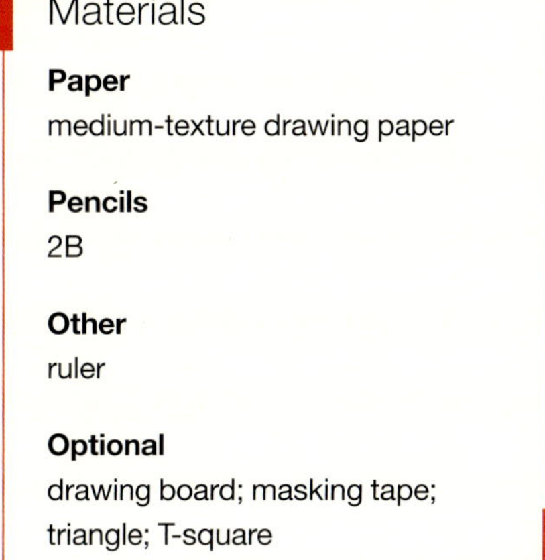

Materials

Paper
medium-texture drawing paper

Pencils
2B

Other
ruler

Optional
drawing board; masking tape; triangle; T-square

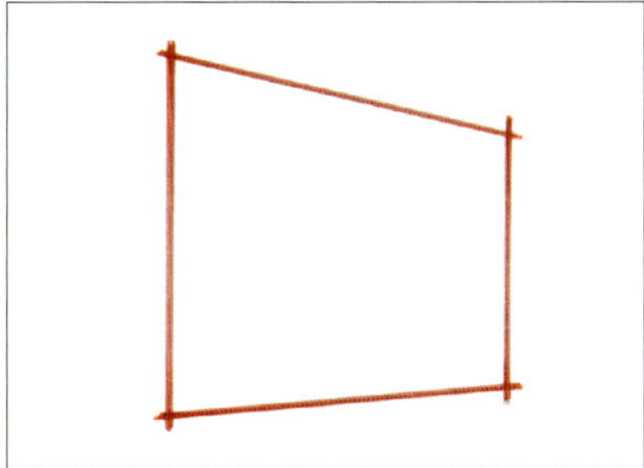

1 Sketch the Surface
Sketch the surface, such as the side of a building, by sketching lines for the top and base and two vertical lines for the corners. If working from a specific subject, transpose the angled top and base lines.

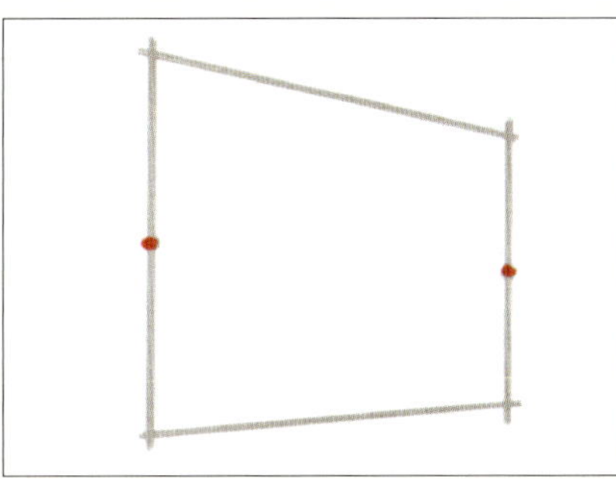

2 Divide the Vertical Lines
Place a dot halfway on the left vertical line by using a ruler to measure between the top orthogonal line and the base orthogonal line. Divide and mark the right vertical line following the same process.

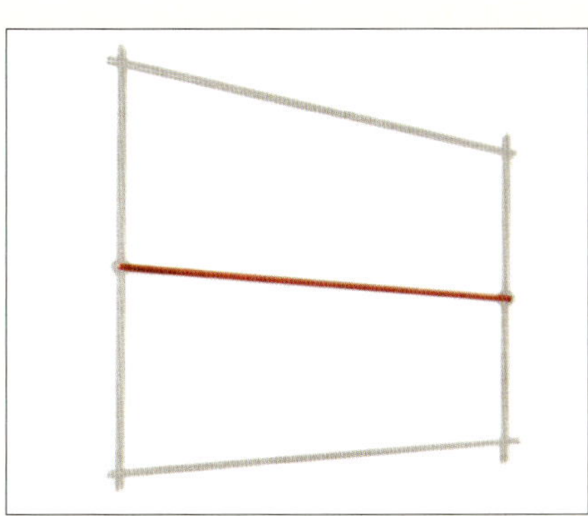

3 Connect the Dots
Add a line connecting the dots on the left and right vertical lines.

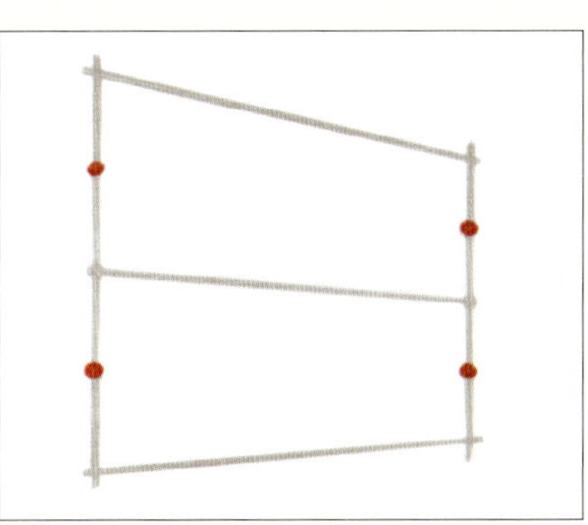

4 Divide the Vertical Lines Again
Divide the left and right vertical lines again and mark with dots.

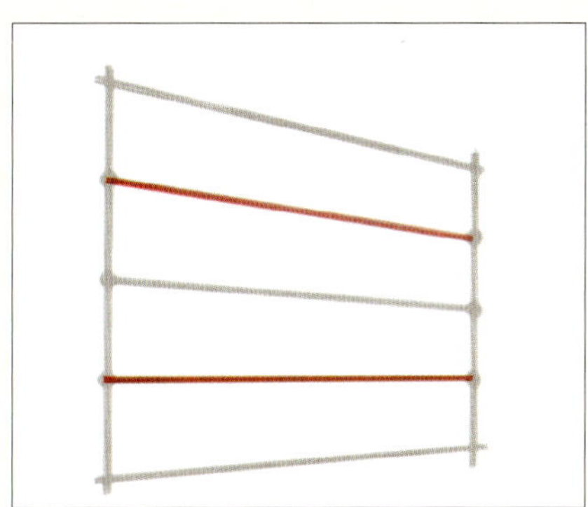

5 Connect the Dots
Add two lines connecting the dots on the left and right vertical lines.

One-Point Perspective Grid

This demonstration will use equally spaced orthogonal lines that cross lines of diminishing distances to form tiles on the ground plane. A one-point perspective grid such as this can be useful for creating architectural drawings. Specific measurements are given to help you achieve a similar result; however, the same processes can be followed using different measurements.

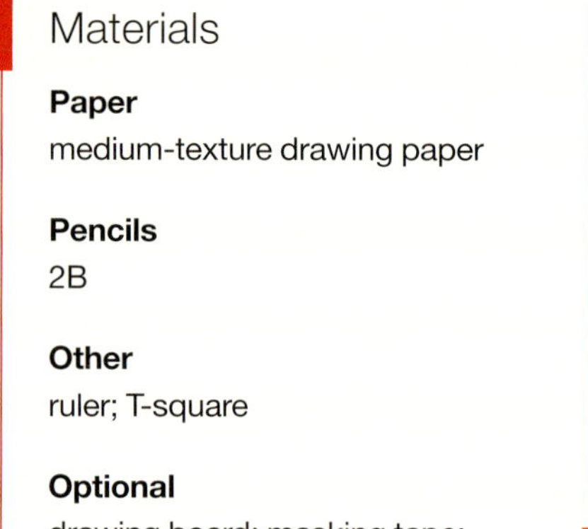

Materials

Paper
medium-texture drawing paper

Pencils
2B

Other
ruler; T-square

Optional
drawing board; masking tape; triangle

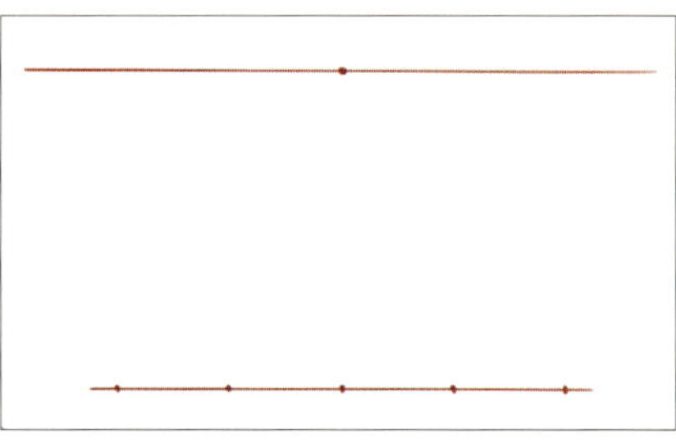

1 Sketch the Horizon, Vanishing Point and Foreground Line

Sketch a horizontal line for the horizon 2¾" (7cm) below the top edge of the paper using a T-square and 2B pencil. Place a dot at the center of the horizon as the central vanishing point. Sketch another horizontal line 5½" (14cm) below the horizon as the foreground line. Place fine marks 2" (5cm) apart along the foreground line.

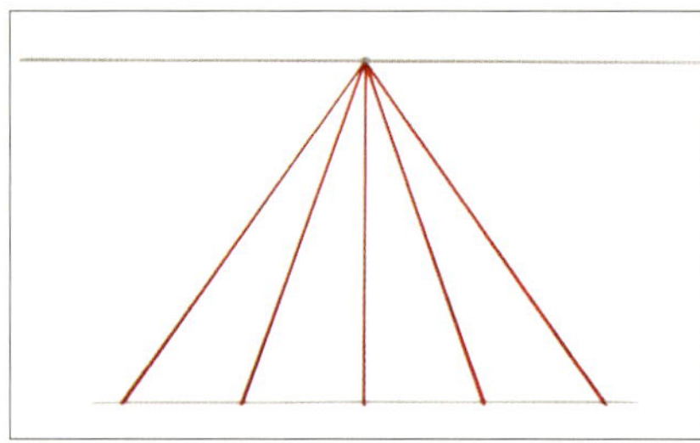

2 Add Orthogonal Lines

Sketch lines from the marks on the foreground line to the vanishing point, creating equally spaced orthogonal lines.

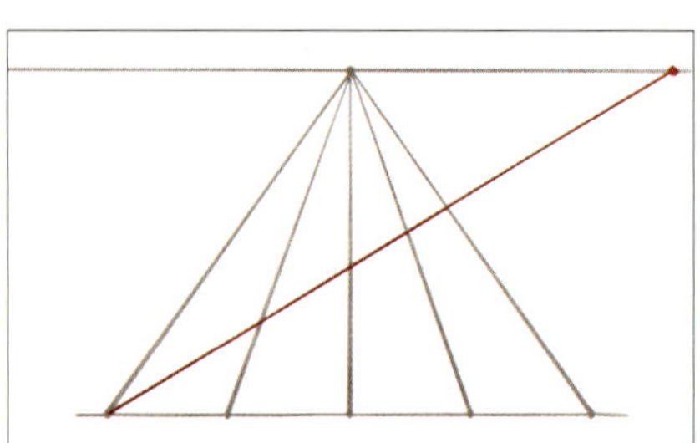

3 Add a Vanishing Point and Diagonal Line

Place another dot on the right side of the horizon 5½" (14cm) to the right of the central vanishing point. From the point where the foreground line meets the far left orthogonal line, sketch another orthogonal line to the far right vanishing point.

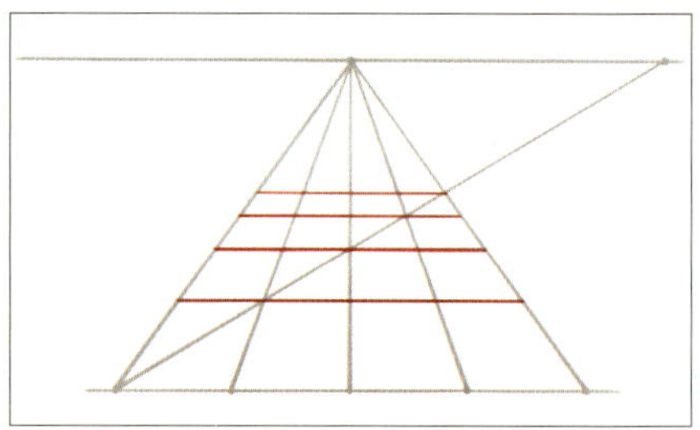

4 Add Horizontal Lines

Sketch horizontal lines from where the newly created orthogonal line meets the central vanishing point orthogonal lines. Diminishing in distance, these horizontal lines create a grid when placed with the orthogonal lines.

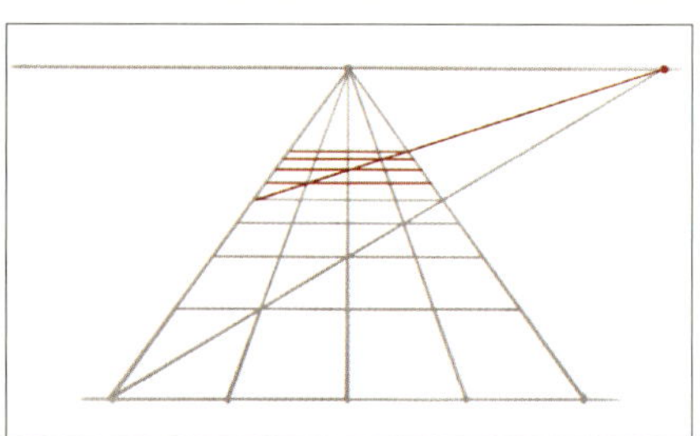

5 Continue the Grid

Repeat steps 3 and 4 to continue sketching the grid farther into the distance by using the same vanishing point to plot the diagonal line.

Continuing Lines & Grids

Picking up where the previous demonstration left off, these steps demonstrate how to create walls and other surfaces by continuing the lines and grids.

Materials

Paper
medium-texture drawing paper

Pencils
2B

Other
kneaded eraser; ruler; T-square

Optional
drawing board; masking tape; triangle

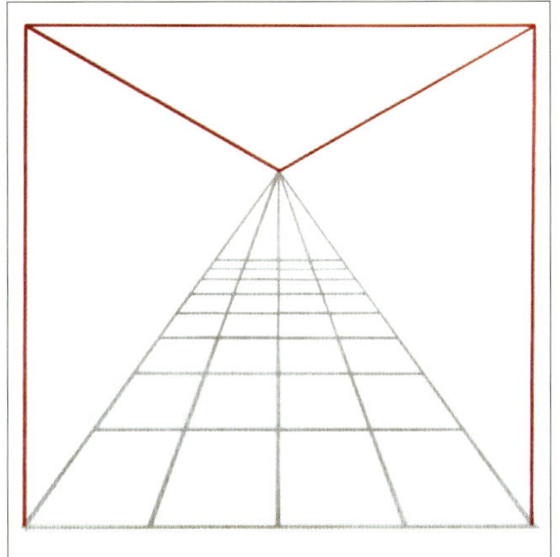

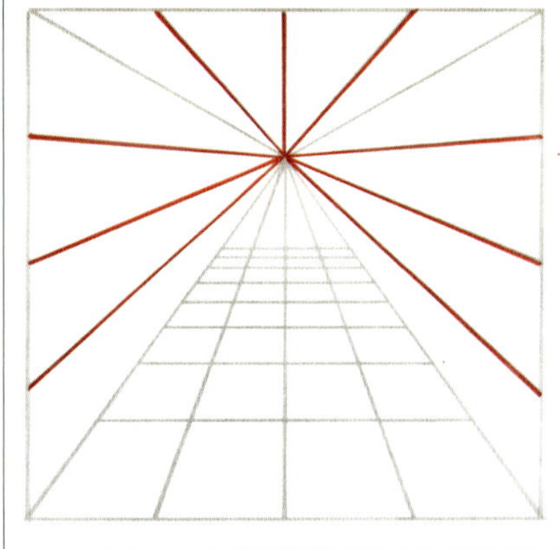

1 Sketch a Square and Corner Lines

Erase lines that are no longer needed, including the left and right portions of the horizon and the orthogonal lines that lead to the far right vanishing point. Add two 8" (20cm) vertical lines at the far ends of the foreground line, both the same length as the foreground line. Add a horizontal line connecting the tops of the vertical lines to form a square. Sketch orthogonal lines from the top two corners of the square to the central vanishing point.

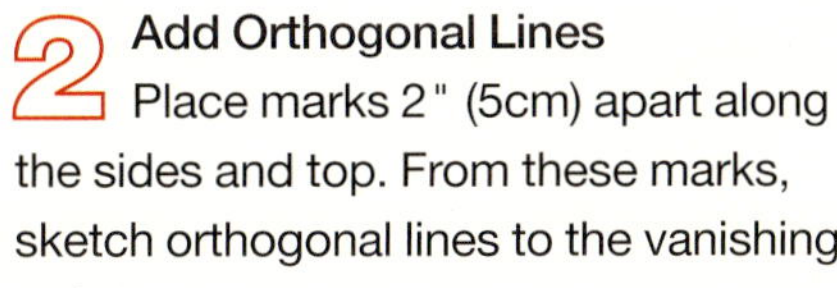

2 Add Orthogonal Lines

Place marks 2" (5cm) apart along the sides and top. From these marks, sketch orthogonal lines to the vanishing point.

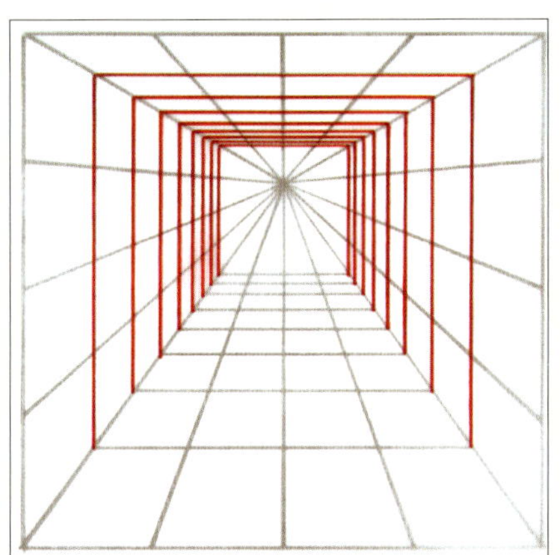

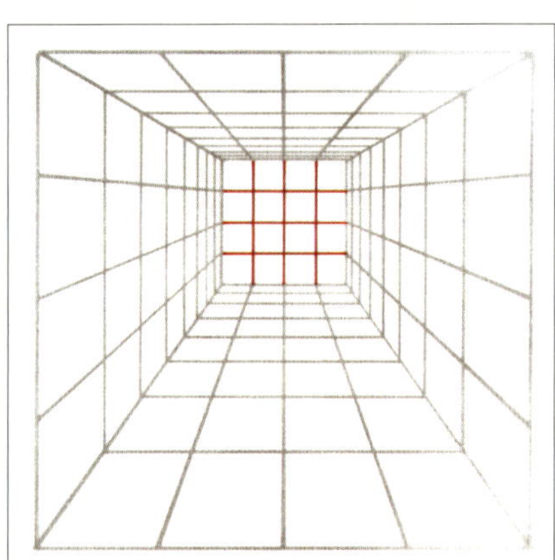

3 Add Vertical and Horizontal Lines

Sketch vertical lines where the lower horizontal lines meet the lower corner lines. Sketch horizontal lines where those vertical lines meet the upper corner lines.

4 Grid the Distant Square

Erase unwanted lines within the center square. Sketch vertical and horizontal lines from where the orthogonal lines meet the center square to form the distant grid.

MINI-DEMONSTRATION

Fence Posts

While the previous demonstration involved making lines of diminishing distances, this technique creates diminishing distances without plotting out a complete grid.

Materials

Paper
medium-texture drawing paper

Pencils
2B

Other
ruler; triangle

Optional
drawing board; masking tape; T-square

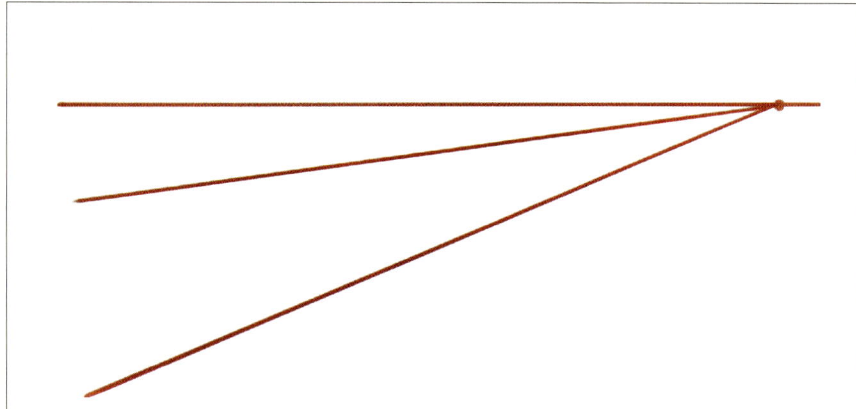

1 Sketch the Horizon, Vanishing Point and Orthogonal Lines
Sketch a horizontal line for the horizon 4" (10cm) below the top edge of the paper using a T-square and 2B pencil. Place a dot on the horizon 1" (2.5cm) from the right edge of the paper as the vanishing point. Sketch an orthogonal line from the lower left corner of the paper to the vanishing point. Sketch another orthogonal line 3" (8cm) above the lower left corner of the paper to the vanishing point.

Secure Your Success

For consistent results when using a T-square and triangle, secure the paper to the drawing board with masking tape.

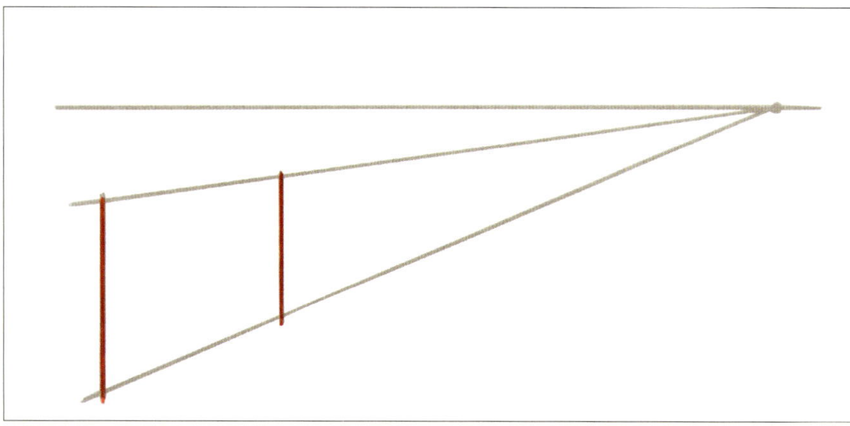

2 Sketch Two Fence Posts
Sketch a vertical fence post 1" (2.5cm) from the left edge of the paper. Sketch another fence post 3½" (9cm) from the left edge of the paper. For accuracy, these lines need to be perpendicular to the horizon.

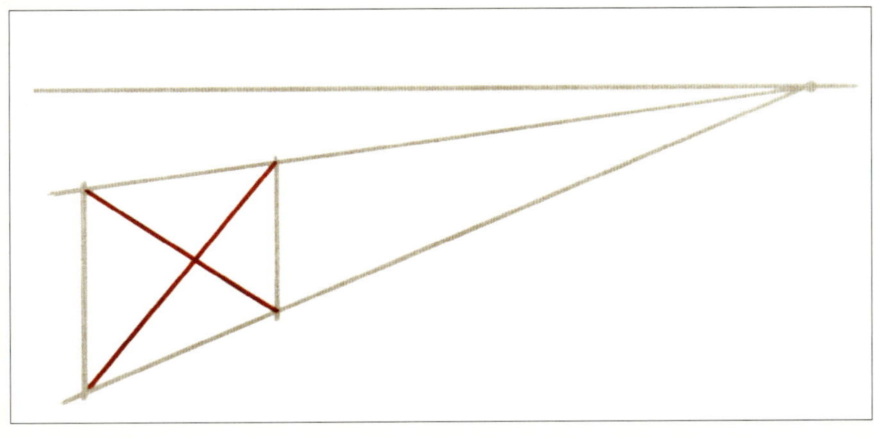

3 Sketch Diagonal Lines

Sketch two diagonal lines connecting the opposite corners of the fence posts to form an X.

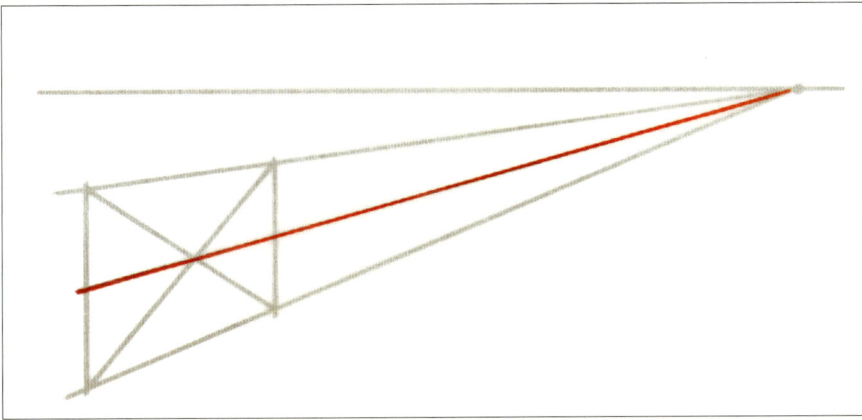

4 Add a Third Orthogonal Line

Sketch the third orthogonal line to the vanishing point from the tangent that is the center of the X.

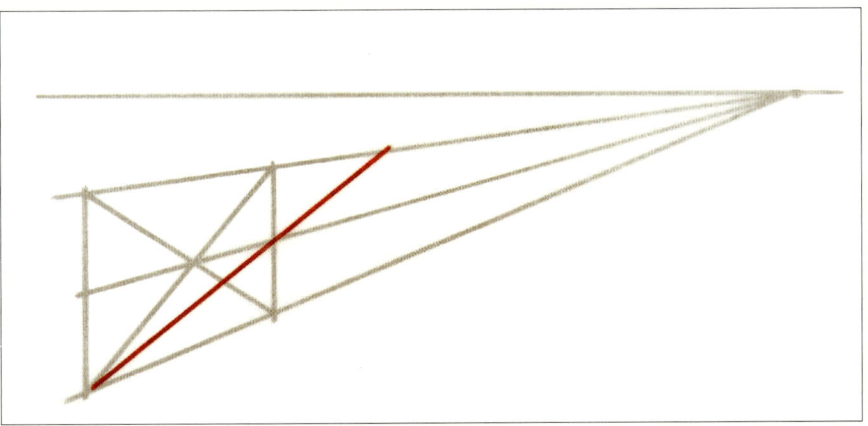

5 Sketch a Connecting Line

Sketch a line from the lower left fence post connecting where the right fence post and the center orthogonal line meet, passing through to the top orthogonal line.

If the connecting lines are continued, they act as orthogonal lines that meet at a vanishing point. This is covered further in the Accidental Vanishing Points section later in this chapter.

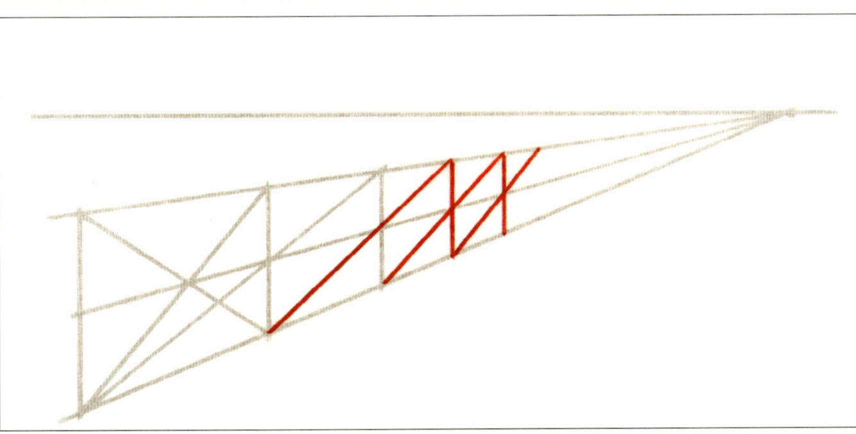

6 Continue Adding Posts

Sketch the third fence post down from the tangent of the connecting line and the top orthogonal line. Repeat the previous two steps to add more fence posts.

Try rotating the paper 90°. The lines for the fence post now appear to be on the ground plane and the line that was perpendicular to the vanishing point is the horizon.

MINI-DEMONSTRATION

Two-Point Perspective Grid

This demonstration involves creating two sets of orthogonal lines, each going to a different vanishing point, that cross each other. This results in a grid that can be used as a foundation for two-point perspective drawings.

Materials

Paper
medium-texture drawing paper

Pencils
2B

Other
ruler; triangle; T-square

Optional
drawing board; masking tape

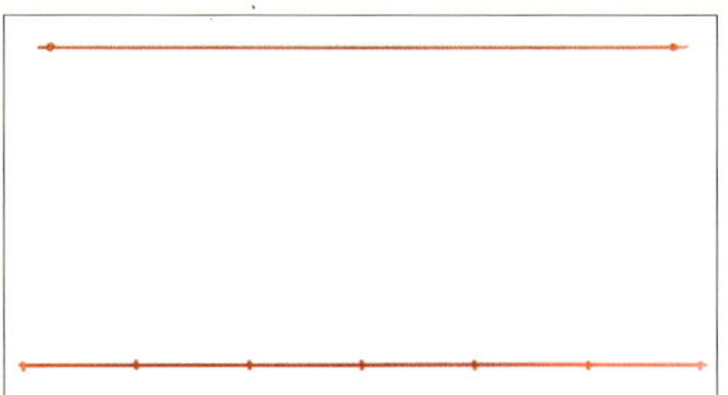

1 Sketch the Horizon, Vanishing Points and Foreground Line

Sketch a horizontal line for the horizon 2" (5cm) below the top edge of the paper using the T-square and 2B pencil. Place a dot on the far left of the horizon and another on the far right as the vanishing points. Sketch another horizontal line 1" (2.5cm) above the lower edge of the paper as the foreground line. Place equally spaced marks on the foreground line, 2" (5cm) apart starting from the left edge of the paper and then working to the right.

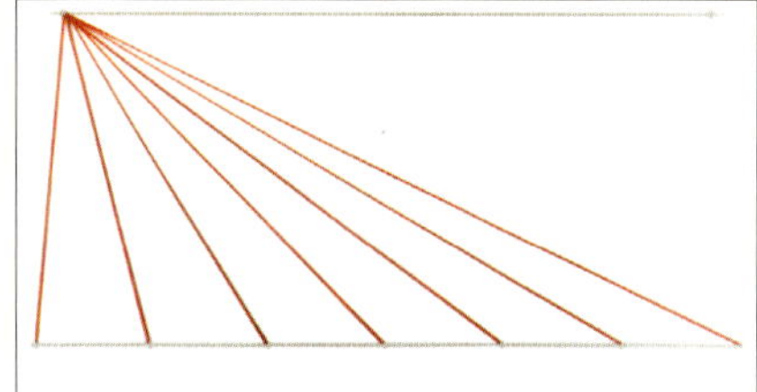

2 Add Left Orthogonal Lines

From the marks on the foreground line, add orthogonal lines to the left vanishing point using the triangle or straightedge.

3 Add Right Orthogonal Lines

From the same marks on the foreground line, add orthogonal lines to the right vanishing point to create a grid.

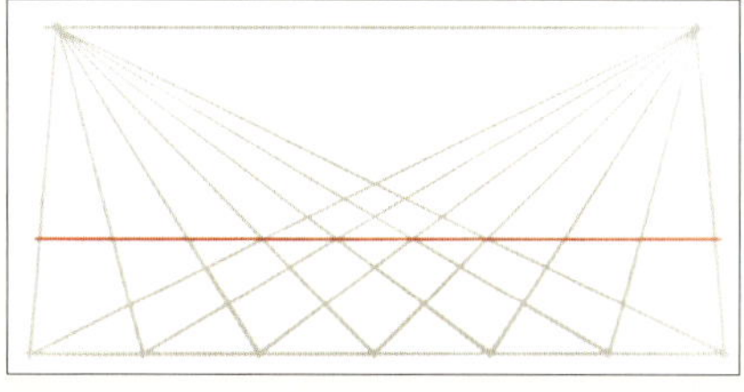

4 Sketch a Horizontal Line to Further the Grid

To start the process of furthering the grid, sketch a horizontal line through the corners of the distant grid tiles.

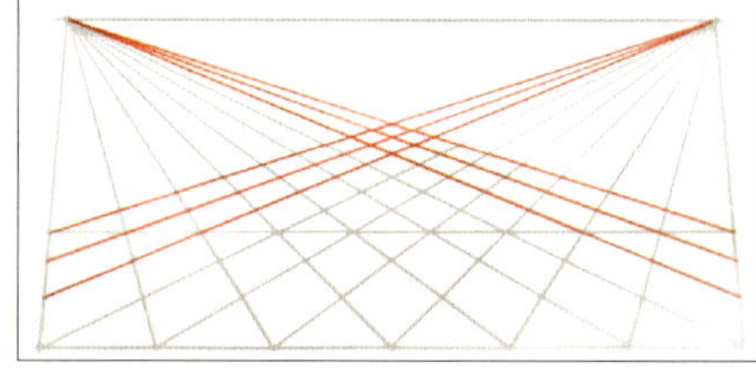

5 Add More Orthogonal Lines

From the tangents created by the previous horizontal lines intersecting the former orthogonal lines, add new orthogonal lines that connect to the left vanishing point, and then to the right vanishing point. A different process that would provide similar results is to start with wider paper, then lengthen the foreground line with more marks. From these marks, more orthogonal lines can be added, creating a bigger grid.

Draw an Accurate Square

Drawing an accurate square in two-point perspective can be done without having to work up a grid. This process ensures that the sides are equally sized and in perspective.

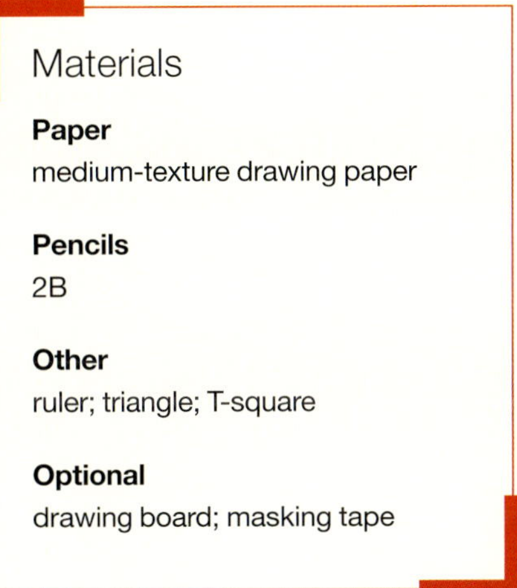

Materials

Paper
medium-texture drawing paper

Pencils
2B

Other
ruler; triangle; T-square

Optional
drawing board; masking tape

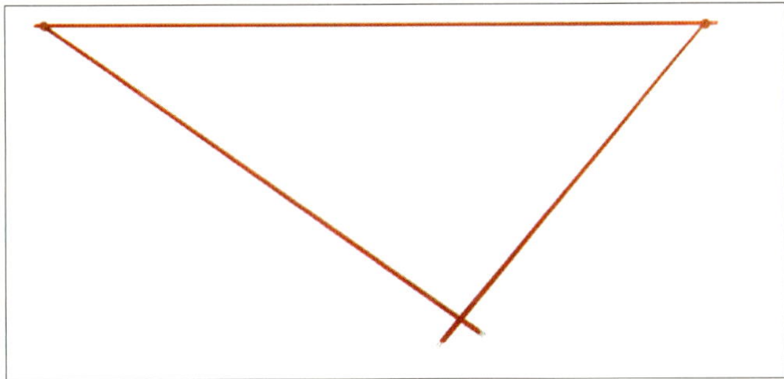

1 Sketch the Horizon, Vanishing Points and Two Orthogonal Lines

Sketch a horizontal line for the horizon using the T-square and 2B pencil. Place a dot on the far left of the horizon and another on the far right as the vanishing points. Sketch two orthogonal lines that cross each other using the triangle or straightedge.

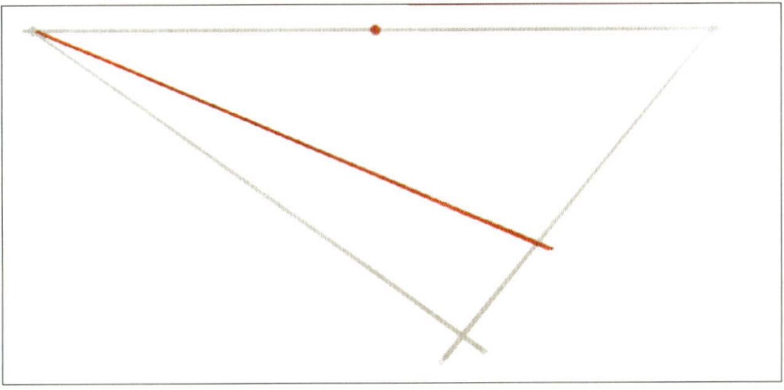

2 Add a Third Orthogonal Line and Vanishing Point

Add a third orthogonal line that crosses the right line and recedes to the left vanishing point. For accuracy, use a ruler to measure and place a dot as the third vanishing point, which is centered between the two vanishing points.

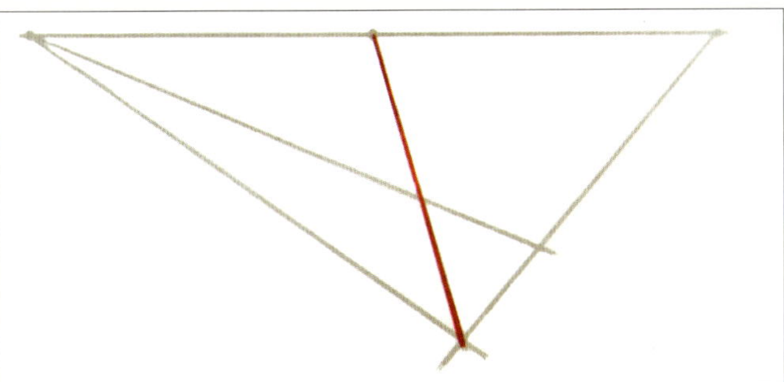

3 Sketch a Line to the Center Vanishing Point

From the lowest tangent of the orthogonal lines, sketch a line to the center vanishing point.

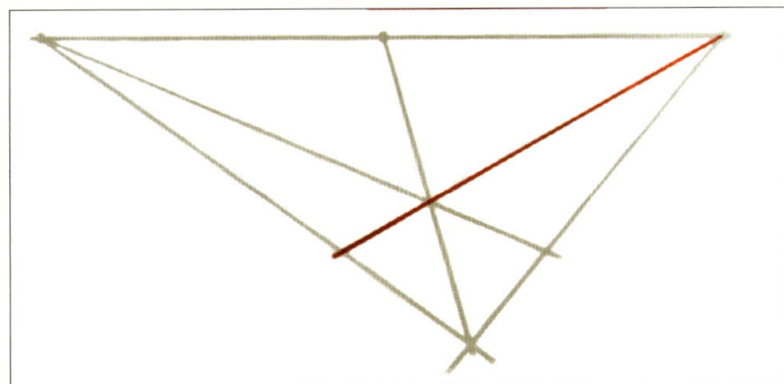

4 Sketch the Fourth Orthogonal Line to Form the Square

From the tangent of the previous line crossing the third orthogonal line, sketch a line that extends from the foreground orthogonal line to the right vanishing point. The resulting form is an accurately proportioned square in perspective.

MINI-DEMONSTRATION

Centerpoints & Subdivisions

Forms such as pyramids, roof peaks and arches are drawn by first establishing their centerpoint. Determining a centerpoint in linear perspective is done through the drawing process, not by measuring with a ruler. Using a ruler to determine a centerpoint may give an inaccurate result.

The process of drawing sometimes requires not just finding the centerpoint of a square or rectangle, but finding the centerpoint for a subdivided square or rectangle. This demonstration details how to find the centerpoint of a square or rectangle as well as how to subdivide a square or rectangle to proportionally smaller units.

Materials

Paper
medium-texture drawing paper

Pencils
2B

Optional
drawing board; masking tape; ruler; triangle; T-square

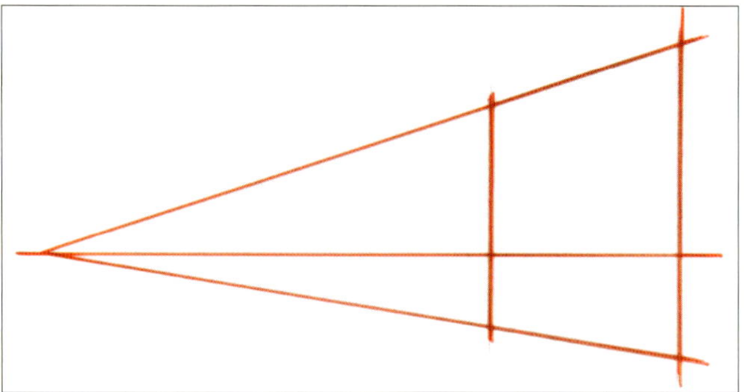

1 Sketch a Square or Rectangle

Sketch the form of a square or rectangle in linear perspective, which includes a vanishing point and horizon.

2 Form an X

Connect the opposite corners of the square or rectangle to form an X. The intersection of the lines of the X is the centerpoint of the square or rectangle.

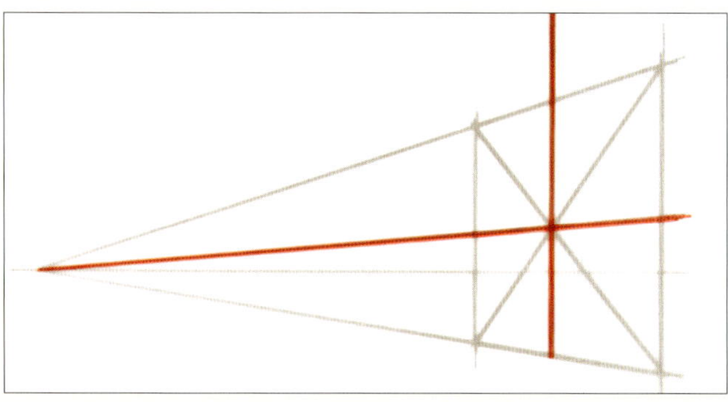

3 Add Horizontal and Vertical Bisections

Add a horizontal bisection by sketching a line through the centerpoint to the vanishing point. Add a vertical bisection by sketching a vertical line through the centerpoint. Notice four sections have been created from the original unit.

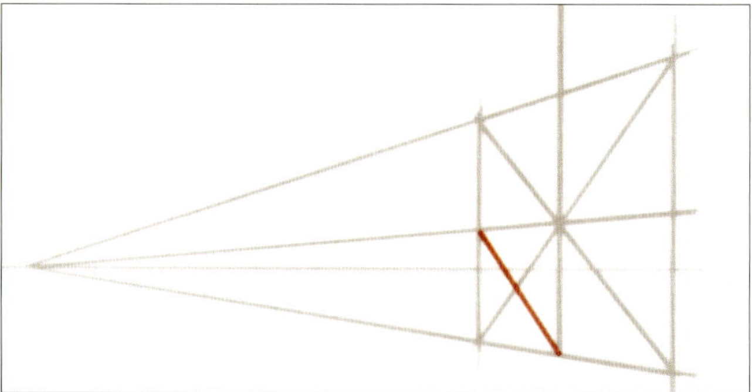

4 Form a Smaller X

Sketch a diagonal line from the back horizontal bisection to the bottom vertical bisection to form an X that is half the height of the original X. This process can be used to make even smaller units.

MINI-DEMONSTRATION

Pyramid

The basic form of the pyramid can be accurately drawn by finding the centerpoint and then sketching the centerline.

Materials

Paper
medium-texture drawing paper

Pencils
2B

Optional
drawing board; masking tape; ruler; triangle; T-square

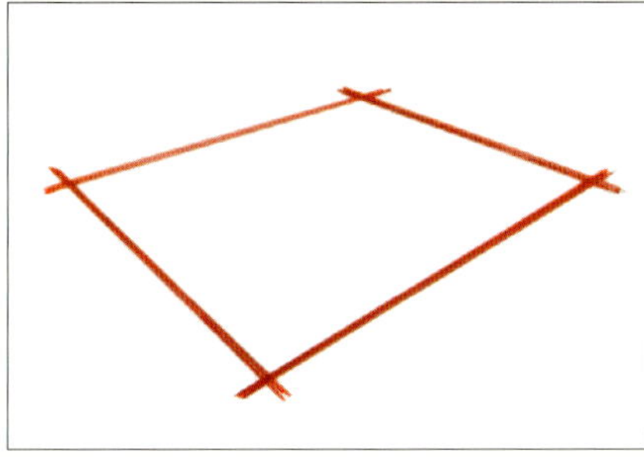

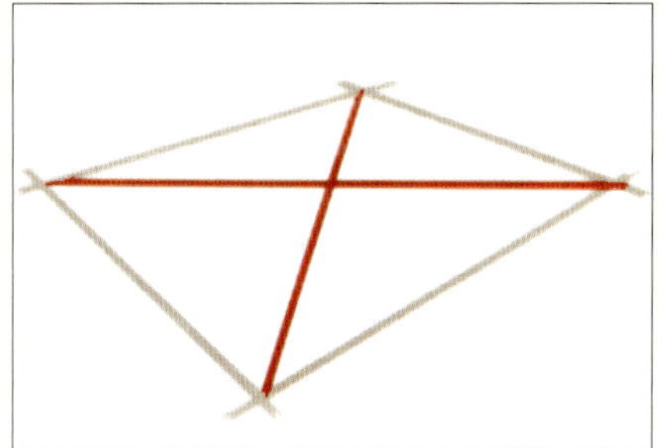

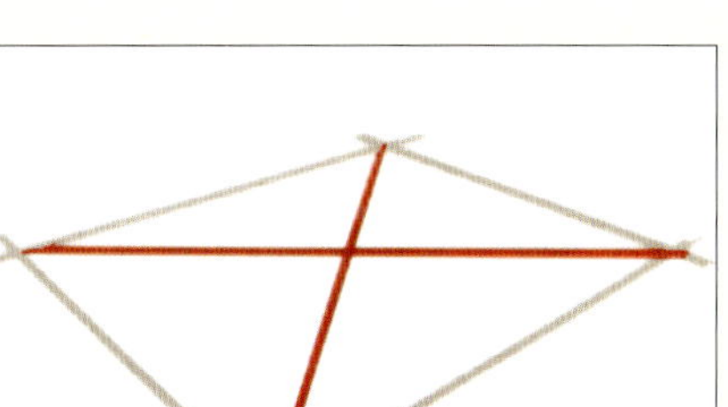

1 Sketch a Square

Sketch the form of a square on the ground plane in linear perspective. The horizon and vanishing points are not shown for this demonstration.

2 Form an X

Connect the opposite corners of the square to form an X. The intersection of the X is the centerpoint.

X Marks the Spot

Finding the centerpoint is as easy as making an X created by connecting the opposite corners of a square or rectangle.

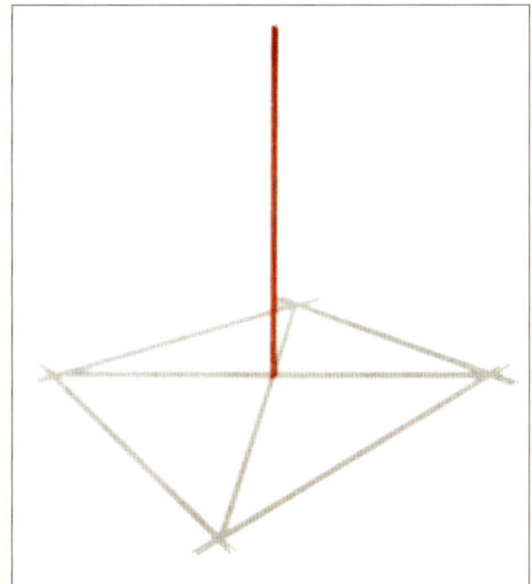

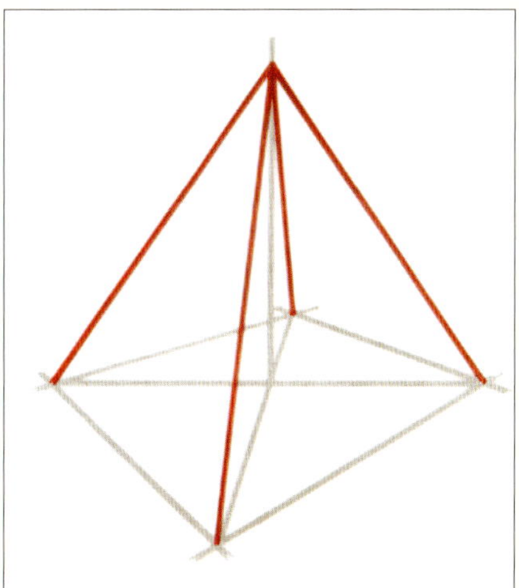

3 Sketch the Centerline

Sketch a vertical line up from the centerpoint as the centerline.

4 Add Four Lines

Form a common point along the centerline, then add four lines that connect to the four corners of the square to form a pyramid.

MINI-DEMONSTRATION

Roofs

Roofs are inclined planes (slanted flat areas) on top of box forms. Roofs can be drawn symmetrically by determining the centerline on the side of the box. Inclined planes will be discussed more in depth throughout the following pages.

This demonstration details how to draw a symmetrical roof on a box. The same process for establishing the centerpoint and centerline that is used to create a roof peak can be used to draw arches and other structural forms.

Materials

Paper
medium-texture drawing paper

Pencils
2B

Optional
drawing board; masking tape; ruler; triangle; T-square

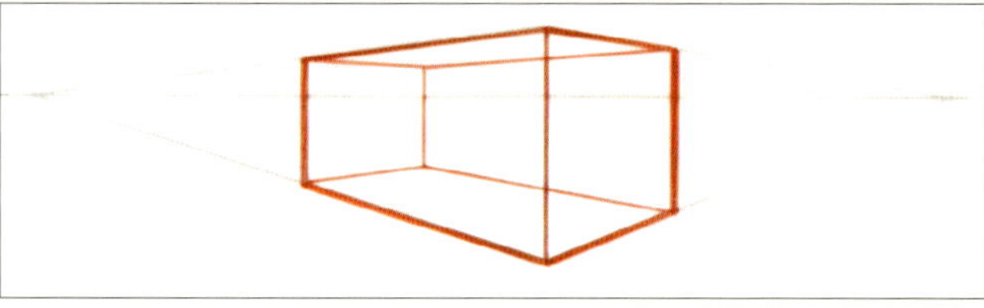

1 Sketch a Box

Sketch a box following the steps outlined in the Two-Point Perspective Box demonstration in Chapter 1.

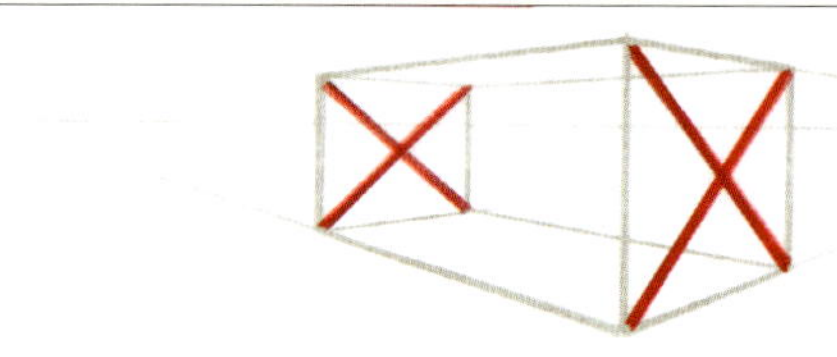

2 Find the Centerpoint

Connect the opposite corners of the sides of the boxes to form an X. These Xs establish the centerpoints.

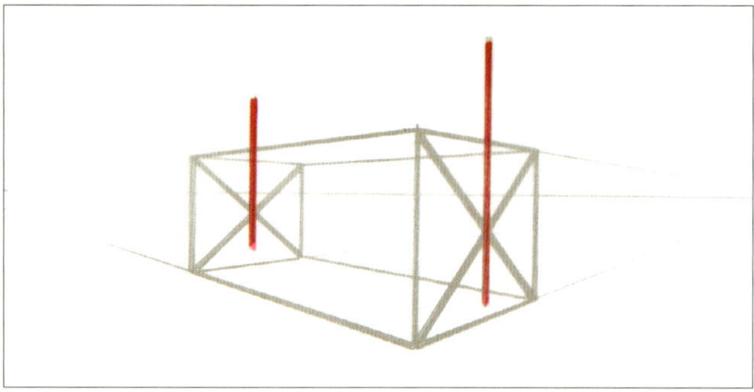

3 Add Centerlines

Sketch centerlines up through the centerpoints.

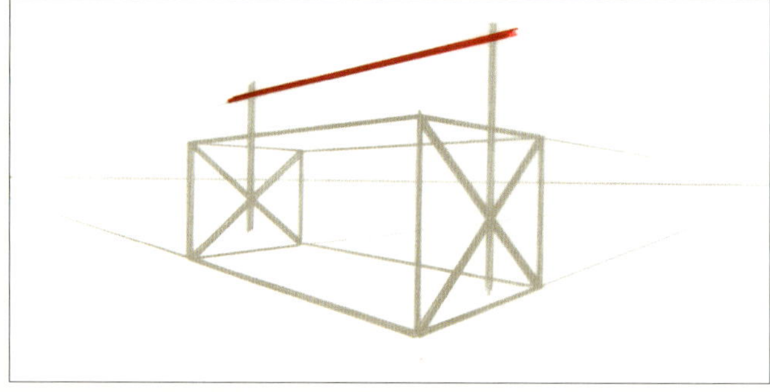

4 Sketch the Roof Ridge

Sketch a line that connects the centerlines to form the roof ridge. Check for accuracy by making sure the roof ridge line continues to the left vanishing point.

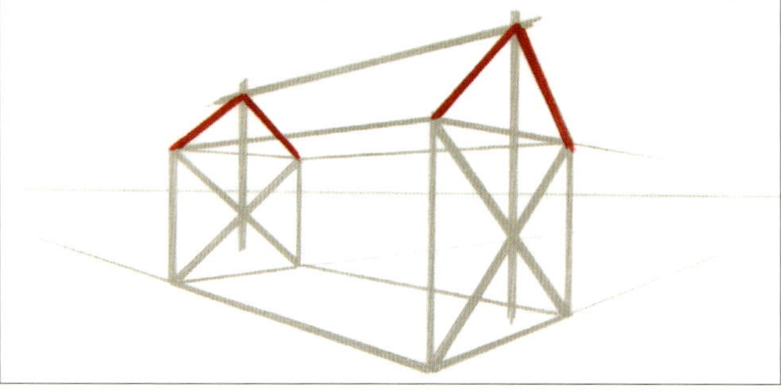

5 Add the Roof Peaks

Connect the top corners of the box to the roof ridge to form the roof peaks.

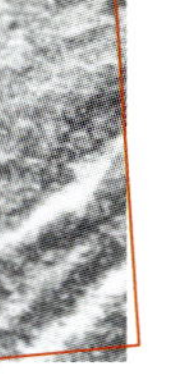

Accidental Vanishing Points

Located directly above or below the vanishing point for a box form, accidental vanishing points are used when drawing roofs and inclined planes.

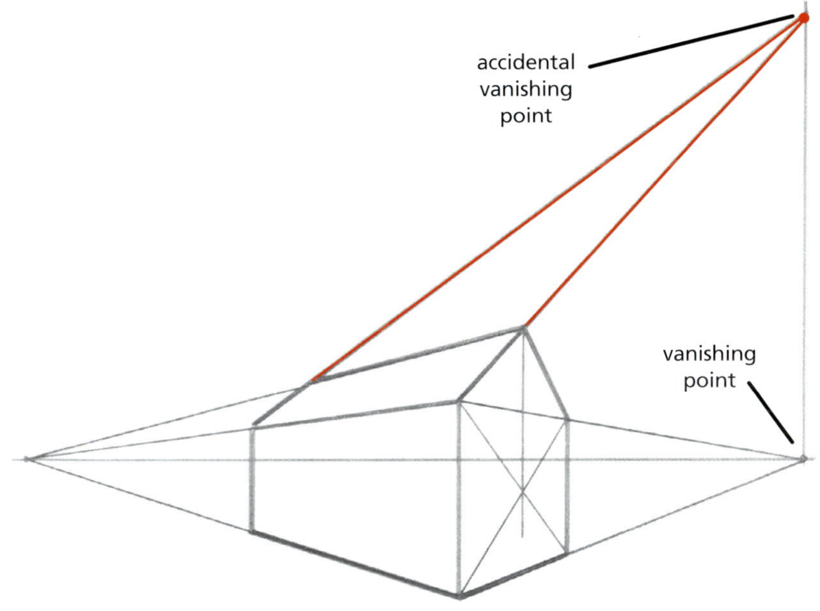

Accidental Vanishing Point for a Gable Roof

A gable roof has its accidental vanishing point directly above the vanishing point of the box form. If plotted out, the accidental vanishing point of the back side of the roof would lie equal in distance below the horizon as the accidental vanishing point of the front side of the roof lies above the horizon.

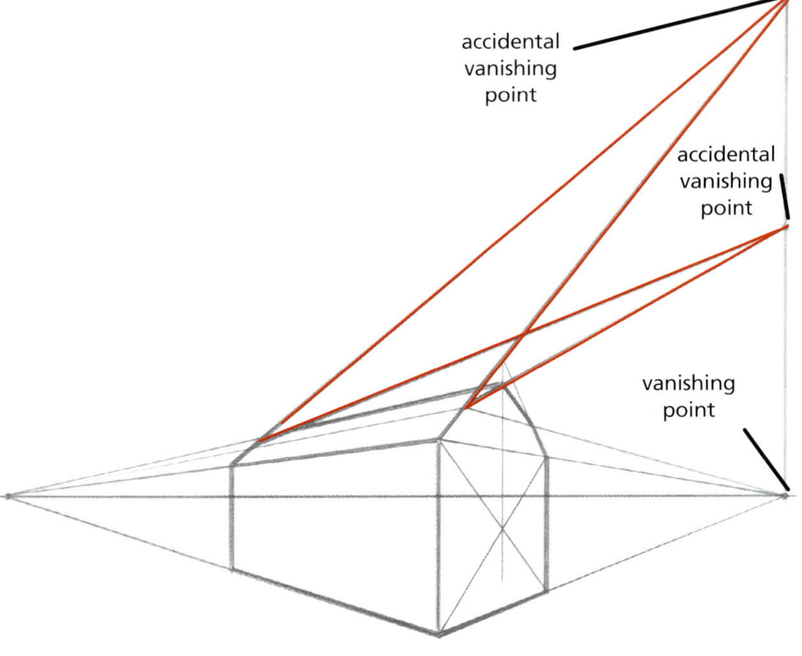

Accidental Vanishing Points for a Gambrel Roof

Because a gambrel roof has two inclined planes per side, it has two accidental vanishing points per side. Both accidental vanishing points are located directly above the vanishing point of the box form.

MINI-DEMONSTRATION

Stairs

Stairs can be drawn as boxed forms stacked on top of one another. The same principle used when drawing inclined planes can be used for drawing stairs by aligning the boxed forms as they recede. This places the accidental vanishing point above the vanishing point on the horizon.

While this demonstration teaches how to draw three steps, an unlimited number of steps may be drawn by following the same procedure. If stair rails are to be added, they would use the same accidental vanishing point.

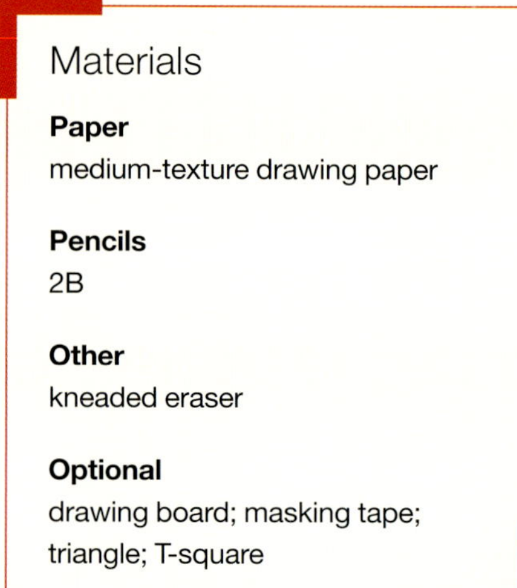

Materials

Paper
medium-texture drawing paper

Pencils
2B

Other
kneaded eraser

Optional
drawing board; masking tape; triangle; T-square

1 Sketch the Horizon, Vanishing Points and Vertical Line

Sketch a horizontal line through the middle portion of the paper for the horizon. Place two dots on the horizon line, one on the far left and the other on the far right to represent the vanishing points. In the lower foreground, sketch a vertical line. This line will be the front corner of the foremost step and will be used to establish the height of all the steps.

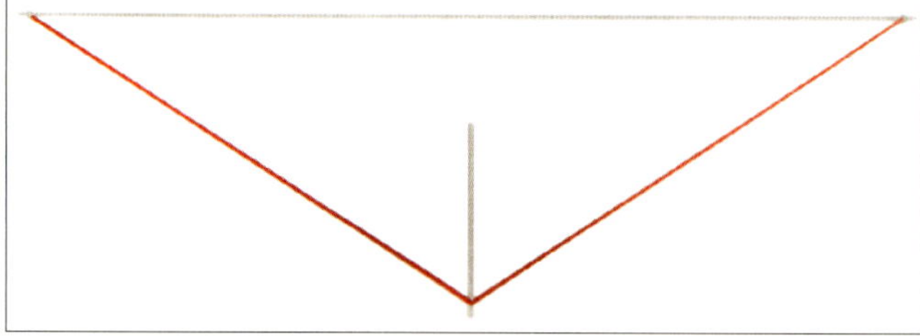

2 Sketch Orthogonal Lines

From the base of the vertical line, sketch two orthogonal lines that go to each of the vanishing points.

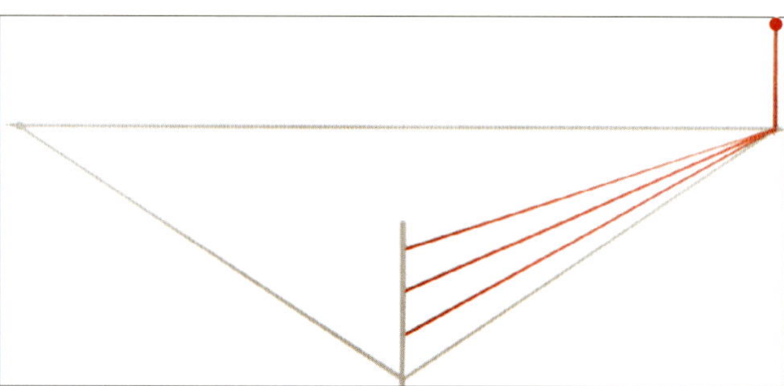

3 Add Orthogonal Lines and Place the Accidental Vanishing Point

Place three evenly spaced marks on the vertical line. From the three marks, sketch orthogonal lines that converge at the right vanishing point. Sketch a vertical line up from the right vanishing point, perpendicular to the horizon. Place a dot at the top as the accidental vanishing point.

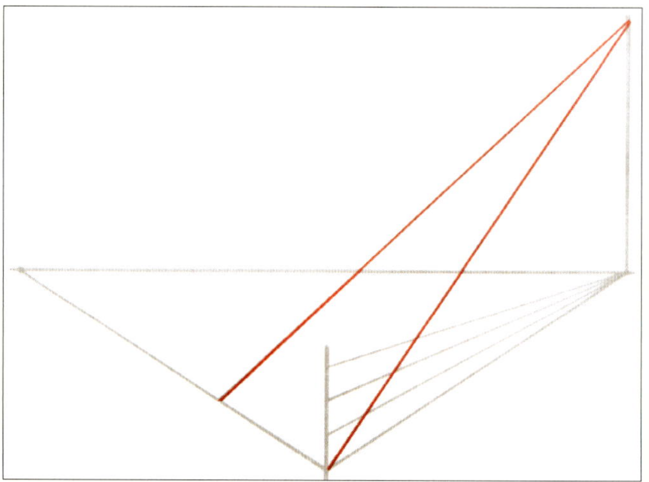

4 Sketch Orthogonal Lines to the Accidental Vanishing Point

From the base of the vertical line, sketch an orthogonal line to the accidental vanishing point. From a point along the left orthogonal line, sketch another orthogonal line to the accidental vanishing point.

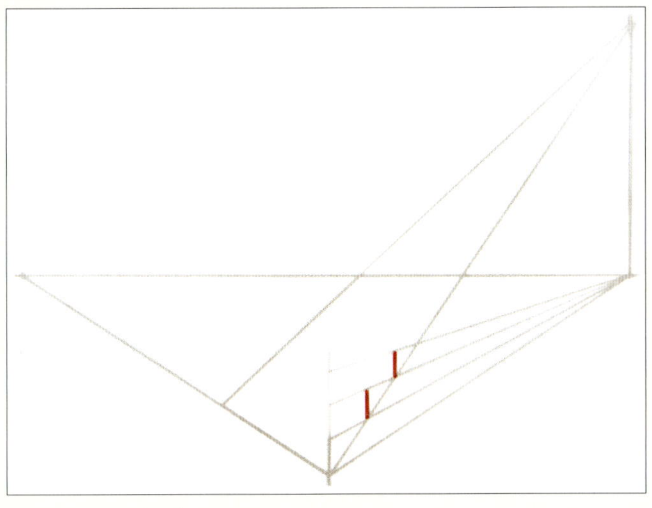

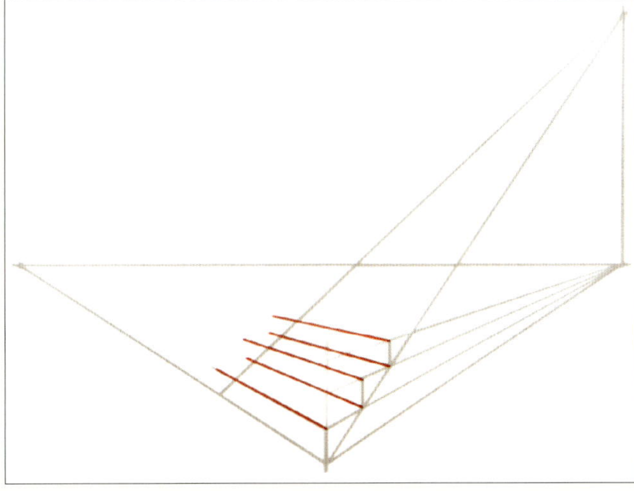

5 Sketch Short Vertical Lines

Sketch two short vertical lines up from the tangents of the orthogonal lines. These will be the corners of the top two steps. Erase unwanted lines throughout the demonstration.

6 Sketch Orthogonal Lines to the Left Vanishing Point

From the corners of the steps, add orthogonal lines that converge at the left vanishing point.

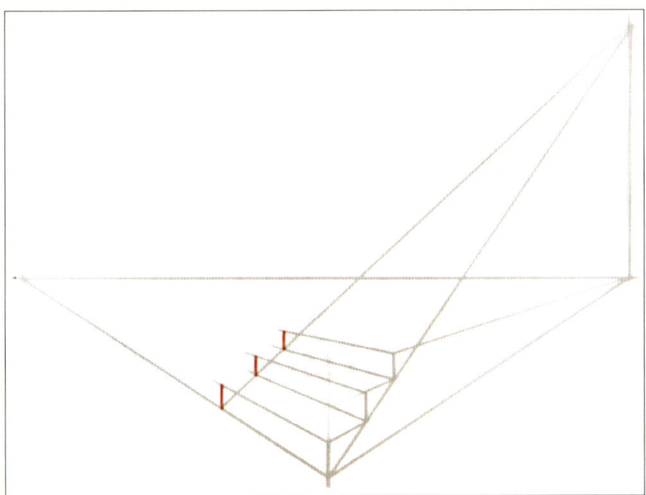

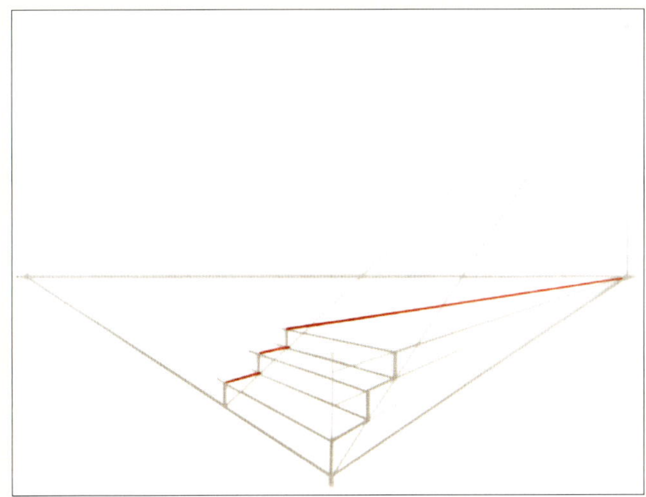

7 Add More Vertical Lines

From the tangents of the orthogonal lines on the left, sketch three short vertical lines.

8 Sketch Orthogonal Lines to the Right Vanishing Point

From the tops of the short vertical lines on the left, sketch orthogonal lines to the right vanishing point.

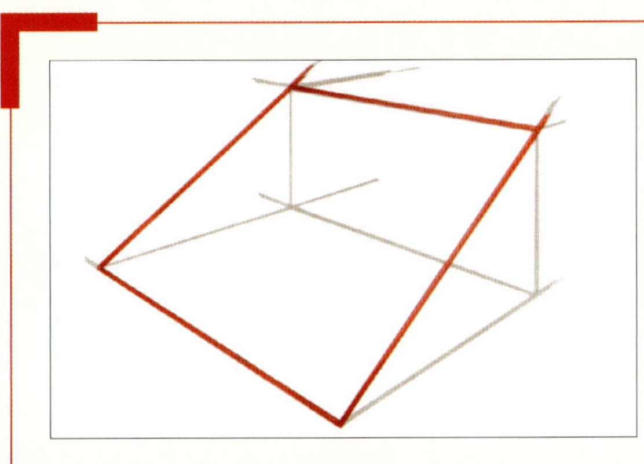

Drawing Inclined Planes

In the same manner that accidental vanishing points are used to draw roofs and stairs, they are also used to draw basic inclined planes. The accidental vanishing point is directly above the vanishing point that rests on the horizon. The combined lines form a wedge shape and an inclined plane.

Circles

As with straight forms, circles may be expressed through linear perspective. When circles are viewed in perspective, they will take on an elliptical shape. Some circles in perspective are true ellipses, which are symmetrical side to side and top to bottom. However, many circles drawn in perspective will not be symmetrical, but they will take on a unique appearance. An ellipse template may be used for oblique and isometric drawings.

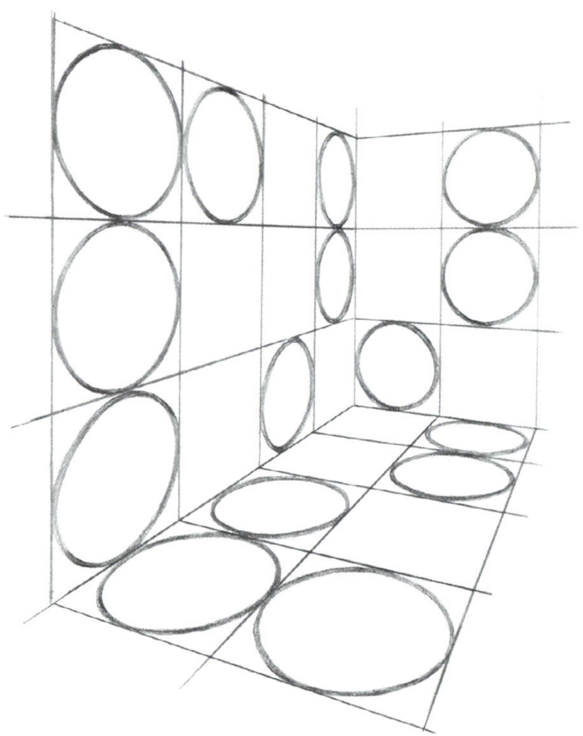

The Many Forms of Circles
Circles in perspective take on many different forms. When drawing circles in perspective, it is beneficial to first draw a square in perspective. If you are drawing many circles, a grid pattern can be used.

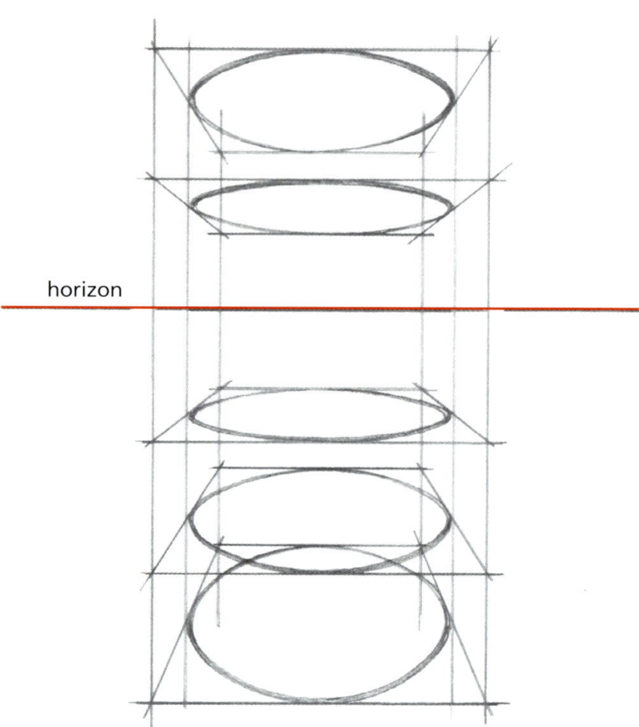

Circles in Perspective
Circles in perspective that are level with the ground plane will flatten out the closer they appear to the horizon. Their forms become more circular and round the farther above or below they are from the horizon.

Completing the Circle

When drawing circles in perspective, it is helpful to draw their complete form even if a portion of that circle is hidden from view. This will ensure that the circle is drawn accurately.

Start with a Square

Just as a circle evenly fills a square, a circle in perspective can be drawn by first drawing a square in perspective, then sketching in the circle.

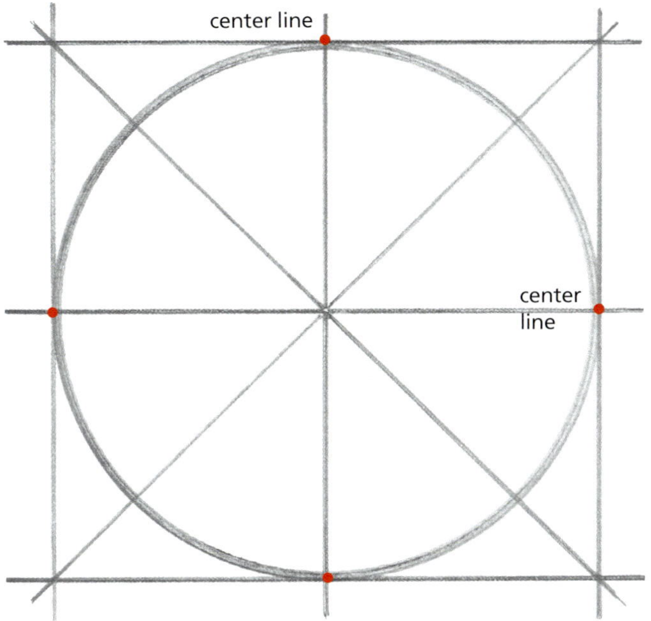

Circle and Square Straight On

Looking straight on, a circle in a square has four contact points, one on each side of the square. These contact points meet at the vertical and horizontal centerlines. The diagonal lines that are visible are used to determine the centerlines.

minor axis
center line
center line
major axis

Circle and Square in Perspective

Viewing the circle and square in perspective, the contact points of the circle and square are at the vertical and horizontal centerlines, just as observed with the straight-on view.

The Round Ends of Circles

Circles in perspective have round ends even when they're long and narrow, such as when they are close to the horizon.

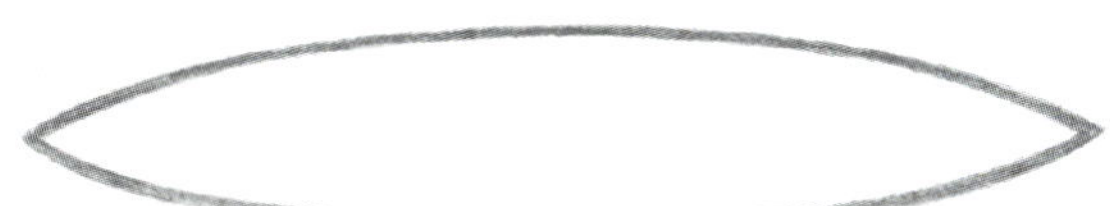

Don't Make a Point of It

Circles in perspective don't have pointy ends.

Major and Minor Axes

A circle in perspective has a major and a minor axis. The major axis is the widest distance and the minor axis is the narrowest distance. Understanding their characteristics will assist in drawing accurate circles in perspective.

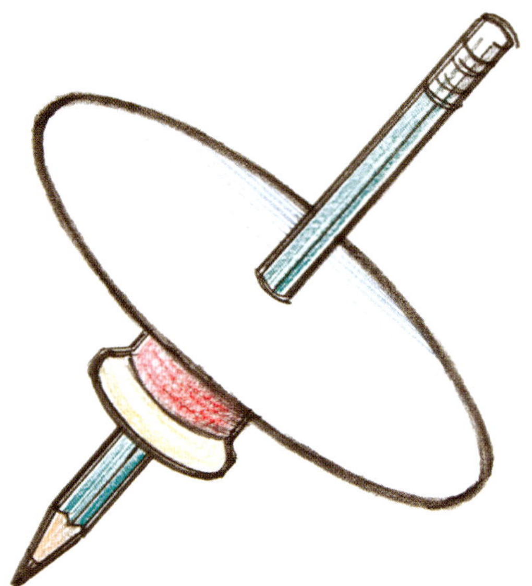

Observe the Perpendicular Nature of a Minor Axis

You can use a pencil, paper plate and thread spool to observe the perpendicular nature of a minor axis.

Find and mark the center of the paper plate with a ruler and pencil. Following the inner circle of the paper plate, use scissors to cut the outer portion away so that the circle of the plate is flat. With a craft knife, carefully cut a very small X in the center of the circle. Push a pencil through the center of the paper plate. Place two-sided tape to the top of the spool, slip it over the pencil and adhere the spool to the flat cardboard circle.

Hold the pencil from underneath, tilting the circle at different angles. Observe that the minor axis, represented by the pencil, is perpendicular to the surface of the circle (or ellipse). Also note that the minor axis appears perpendicular to the major axis—the widest distance of the ellipse.

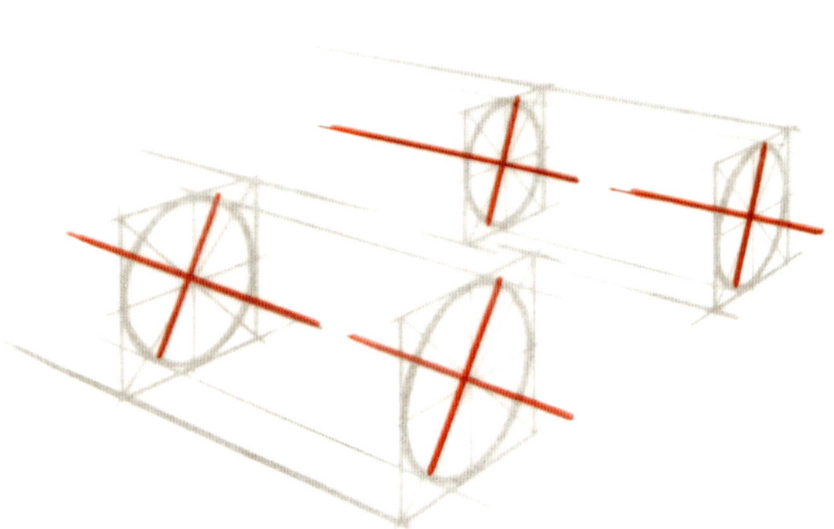

Finding the Axes

Minor axes are perpendicular to the flat surface of the circles represented and typically will share the same vanishing point as the square form that surrounds a circle. Another principle is that major and minor axes are perpendicular to each other. By first placing the minor axis, the major axis can be positioned by drawing a perpendicular line in relation to the minor axis. These principles are generalizations and distortion will occur with extreme perspective. Note that the closer the circle is to the horizon, the more aligned its minor axis will be with the horizon, and the major axis becomes more perpendicular to the horizon.

MINI-DEMONSTRATION

Draw a Circle in Perspective

This circle demonstration starts by drawing the surrounding square to ensure proper perspective.

Materials

Paper
medium-texture drawing paper

Pencils
2B

Optional
drawing board; masking tape; ruler; triangle; T-square

1 Draw a Square

Draw an accurate square, following the demonstration from earlier in this chapter. Include the horizon, vanishing points and orthogonal line although they are not fully shown with this demonstration.

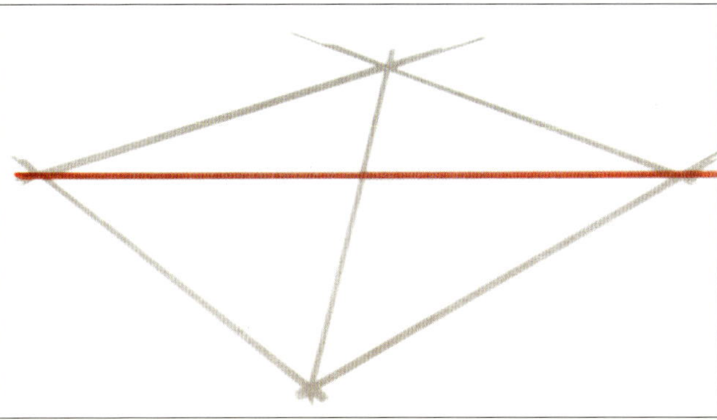

2 Add a Diagonal Line

Add a diagonal line by connecting the opposite corners of the square. There are now two diagonals. The centerpoint of the square is where they meet.

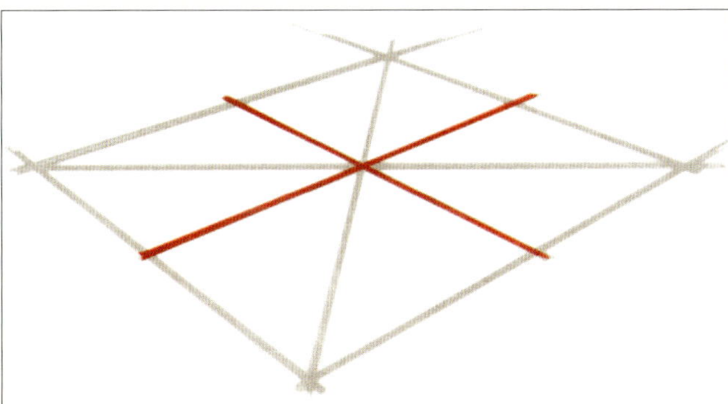

3 Add Centerlines

From the centerpoint add one line that goes to the left vanishing point and another that goes to the right vanishing point to represent the centerlines.

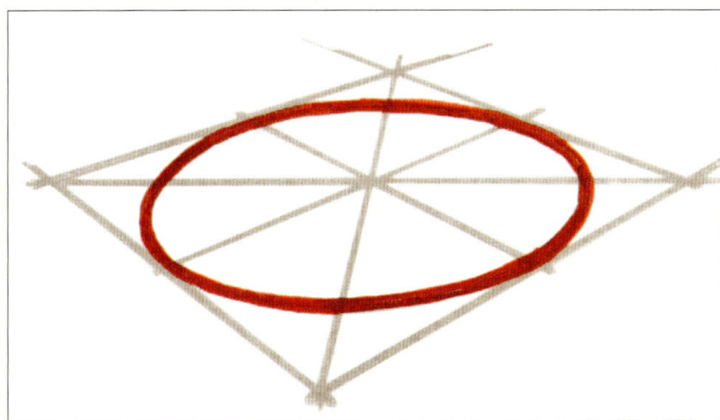

4 Draw a Circle in the Square Area

The contact points of the circle and square are where the centerlines touch the lines of the square. Using these contact points, draw a circle that fills the area of the square.

Drawing Cylinders

To make a cylinder, sketch a box using a square as the base. Add vertical lines up from the contact points. Add another circle in perspective at the top.

Reflections

Reflections are images cast on a surface. A reflection is made up of its primary object, the reflecting surface and the reflection base.

The image of the primary object is cast onto the reflecting surface to create the reflection. The reflecting surface may be anything reflective, such as a mirror, water or a metallic surface. The reflection base is the point at which the primary object reflects off the reflecting surface.

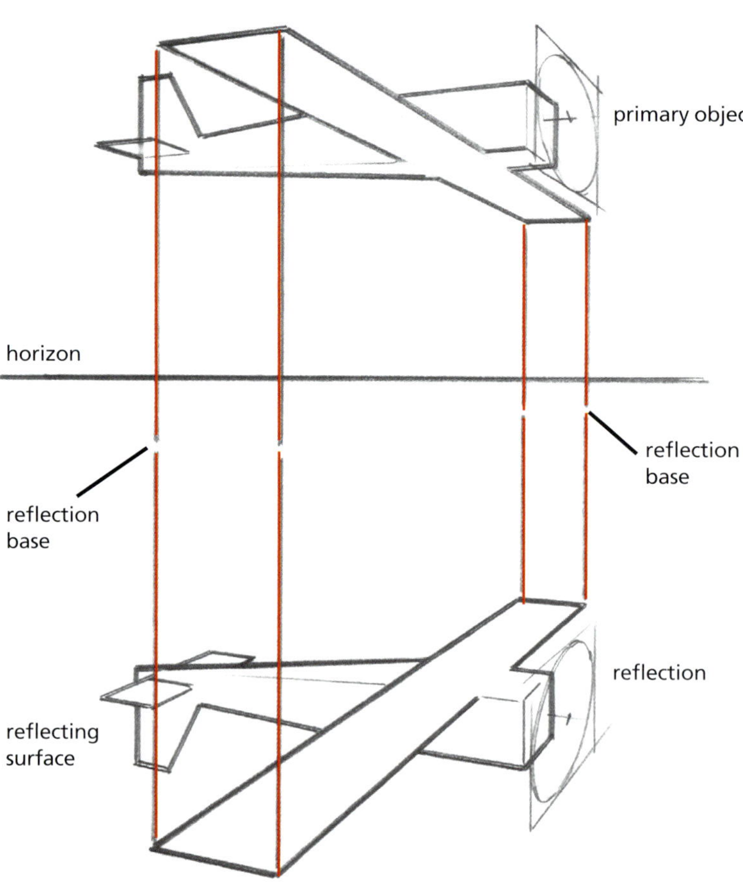

Reflections Are Perpendicular to Reflecting Surface

The reflection of the primary object is perpendicular, or straight up and down, to the reflecting surface. This is easier to observe with a flat, horizontal reflecting surface that continues to the horizon. However, it remains true even with a contoured reflecting surface such as waves. The reflections still reflect perpendicularly, but the reflecting surface is not flat, which makes the reflections appear to be at different angles.

Equal Distance for Reflections and Primary Objects

Reflections and primary objects are the same distance from the reflecting surface. The reflection is the same distance below the reflecting surface as the primary object appears above the reflecting surface.

Mirror, Mirror

Using a mirror, observe the reflective characteristics of different items around the home such as cardboard cereal boxes, metal soup cans, glass bowls and cloth towels.

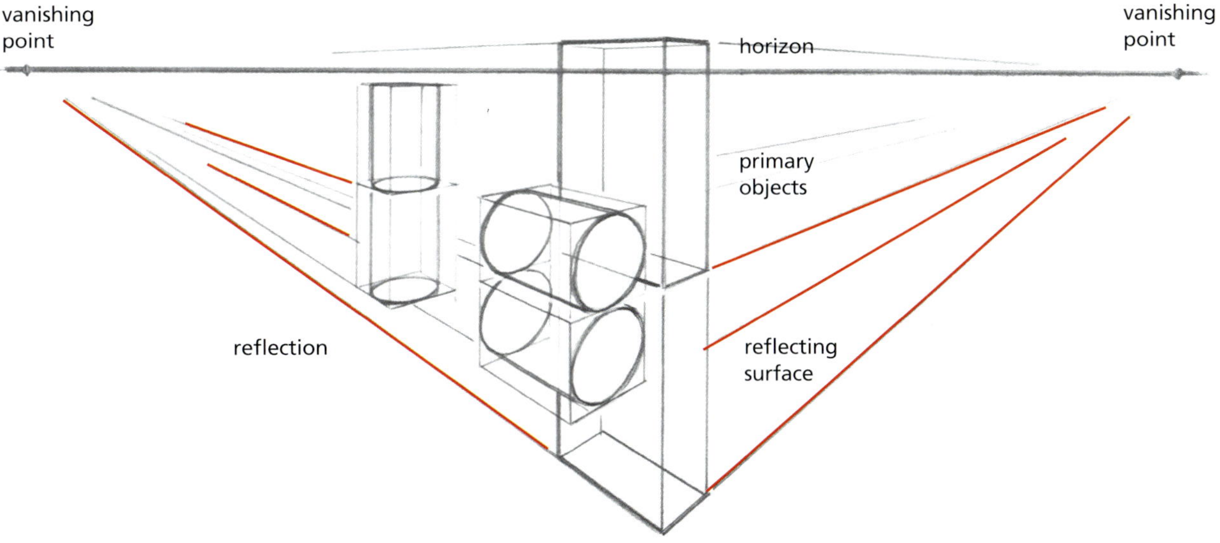

Sharing Perspective

The reflection is bound to use the same horizon and vanishing points as the primary objects, thus sharing the same perspective. The reflecting images can be thought of as a continuation of the primary objects rather than repeated or reversed.

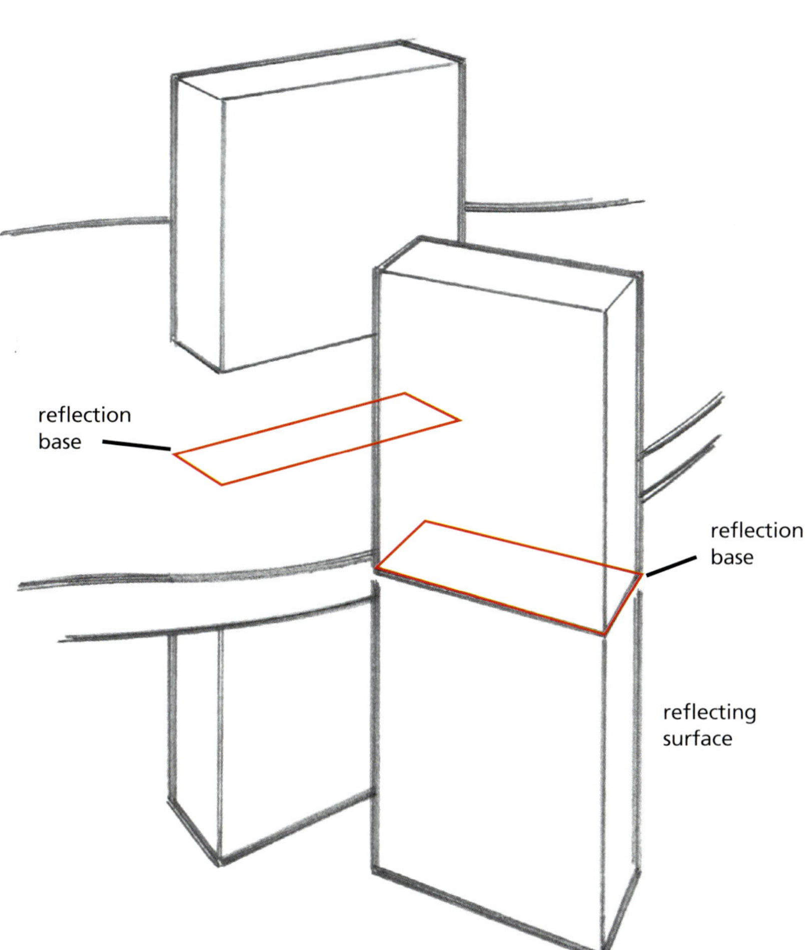

Finding the Reflection Base

The reflection base of some objects can be easy to identify, such as where the foreground box rests on the reflecting surface. However, sometimes the reflection base is harder to identify and may be hidden from view. Even though the taller box looks distant from the reflecting surface, the reflection acts as if the reflecting surface continues under the taller box. The reflection base is where the rear box would make contact with the reflecting surface, although it is hidden from view.

Reflecting Surfaces

The reflection of a scene may be mirrorlike or distorted depending on the reflecting surface.

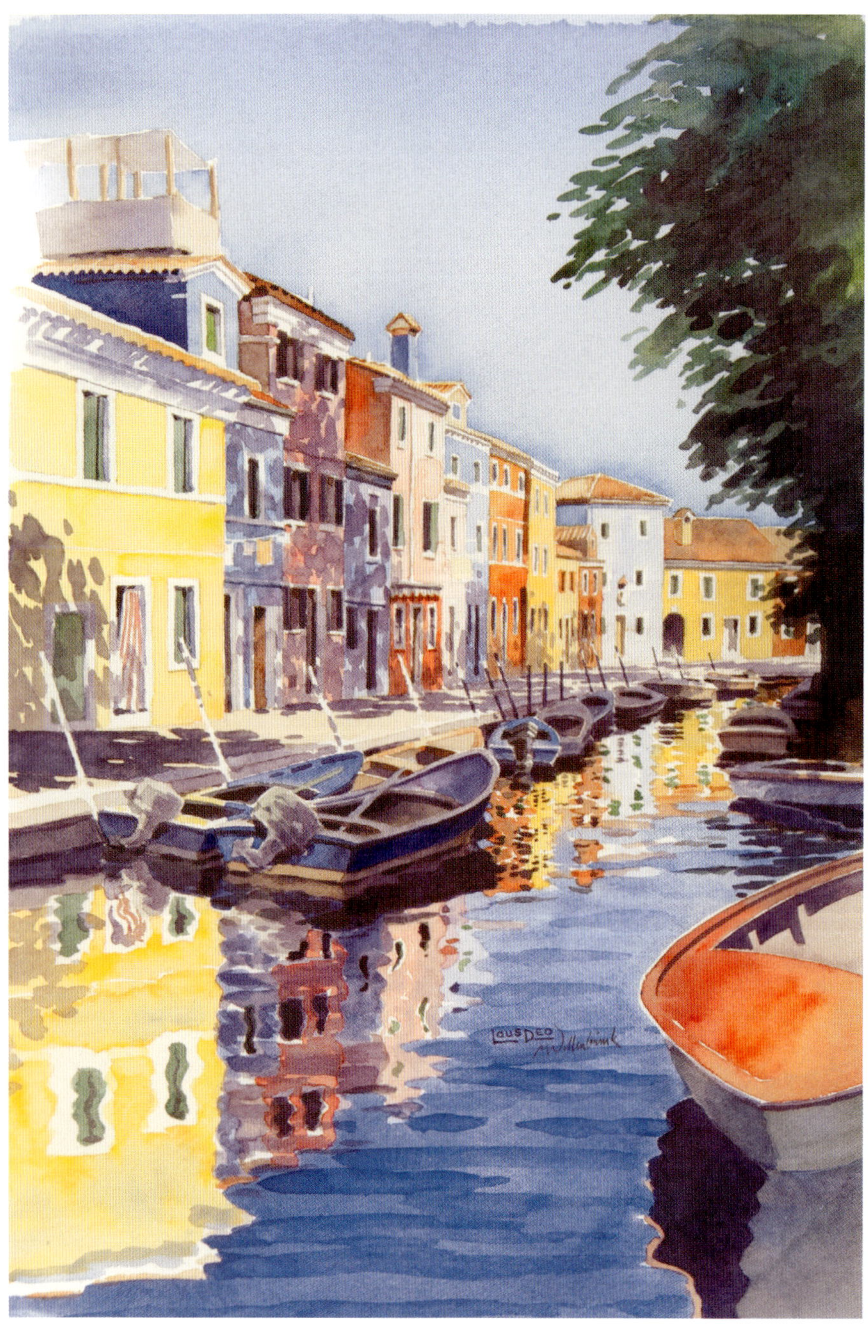

Rippled Reflecting Surface

A rippled water surface can create convex and concave forms that reflect the primary objects with subtle distortions. The principles of reflections covered earlier are noticeable in this painting of Burano, Italy.

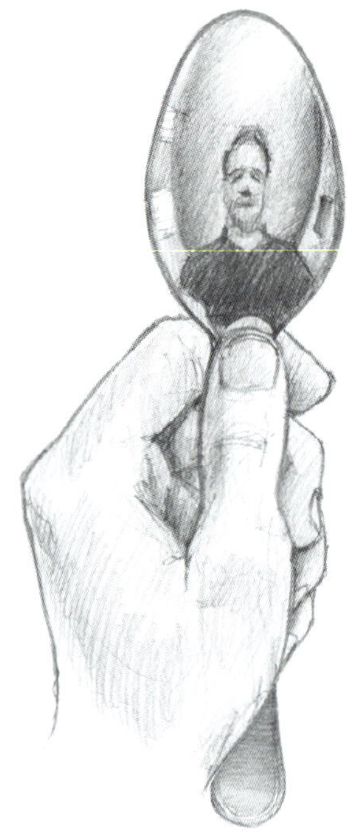

Convex Reflecting Surface

A spoon held with the curved bowl toward you provides a convex reflecting surface. The round surface of the spoon reflects straight lines as curved lines and distorts the size and proportions of the scene.

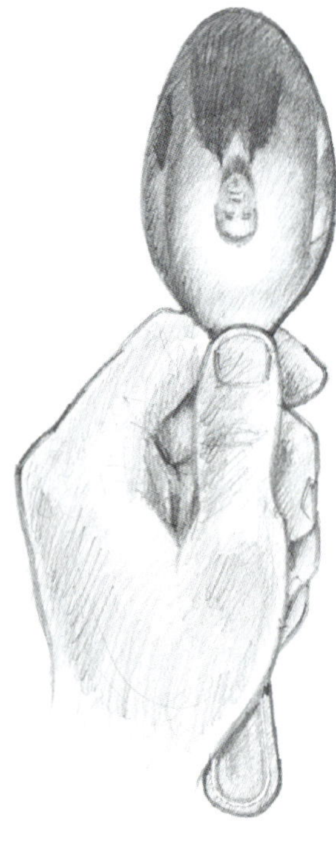

Concave Reflecting Surface

A concave reflecting surface is observable by turning the curved bowl of the spoon away from you. Not only are the lines and proportions distorted, but the reflection image is turned upside down and reversed as well.

Distortion & Peripheral Vision

Within the field of vision, distortion can occur when a scene goes beyond the central viewing area to include the peripheral area. Distortion can also occur when a subject is viewed in extreme closeup. With either case, the results may appear unusual, unnatural or dramatic.

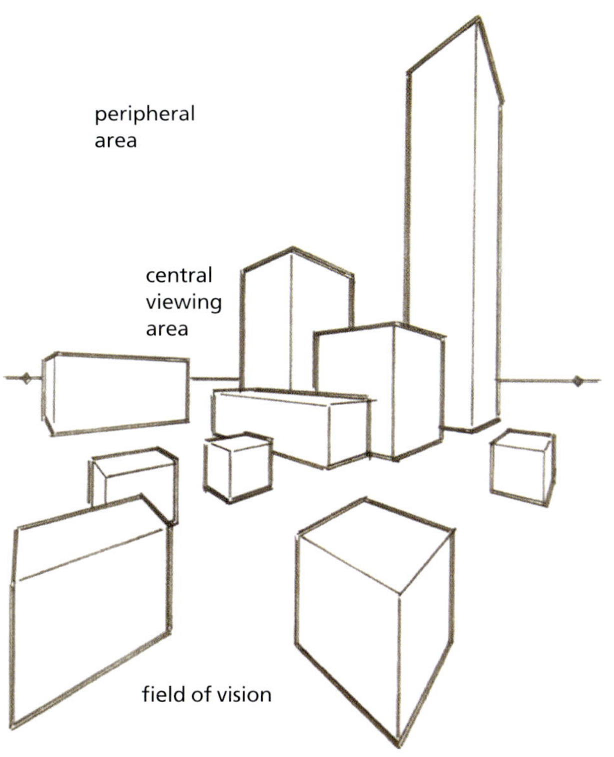

Field of Vision
The field of vision includes the central viewing area and the peripheral area. By limiting a scene to the central viewing area, distortion may be avoided. Some drawings, however, may be enhanced with a dramatic tone when the peripheral area is included.

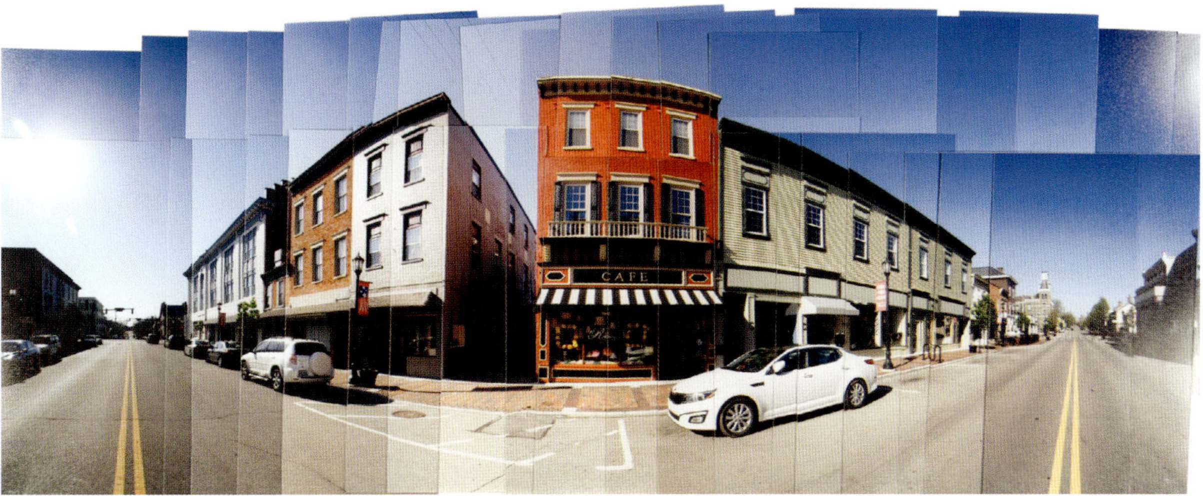

Create a Peripheral Photo Montage
Create a photo montage that includes the peripheral area by taking many different photos at different angles from a single vantage point. Splice the photos together and observe the panoramic effect. Cameras with fish-eye lenses can shoot photos similar to a montage with their broad field of vision.

3 Atmospheric Perspective, Color & Everyday **Subjects**

In addition to linear perspective, depth can also be expressed through atmospheric perspective and the use of color. Combining all three will produce optimal results. This chapter explores how to apply the principles of atmospheric perspective and color when working with a variety of subjects.

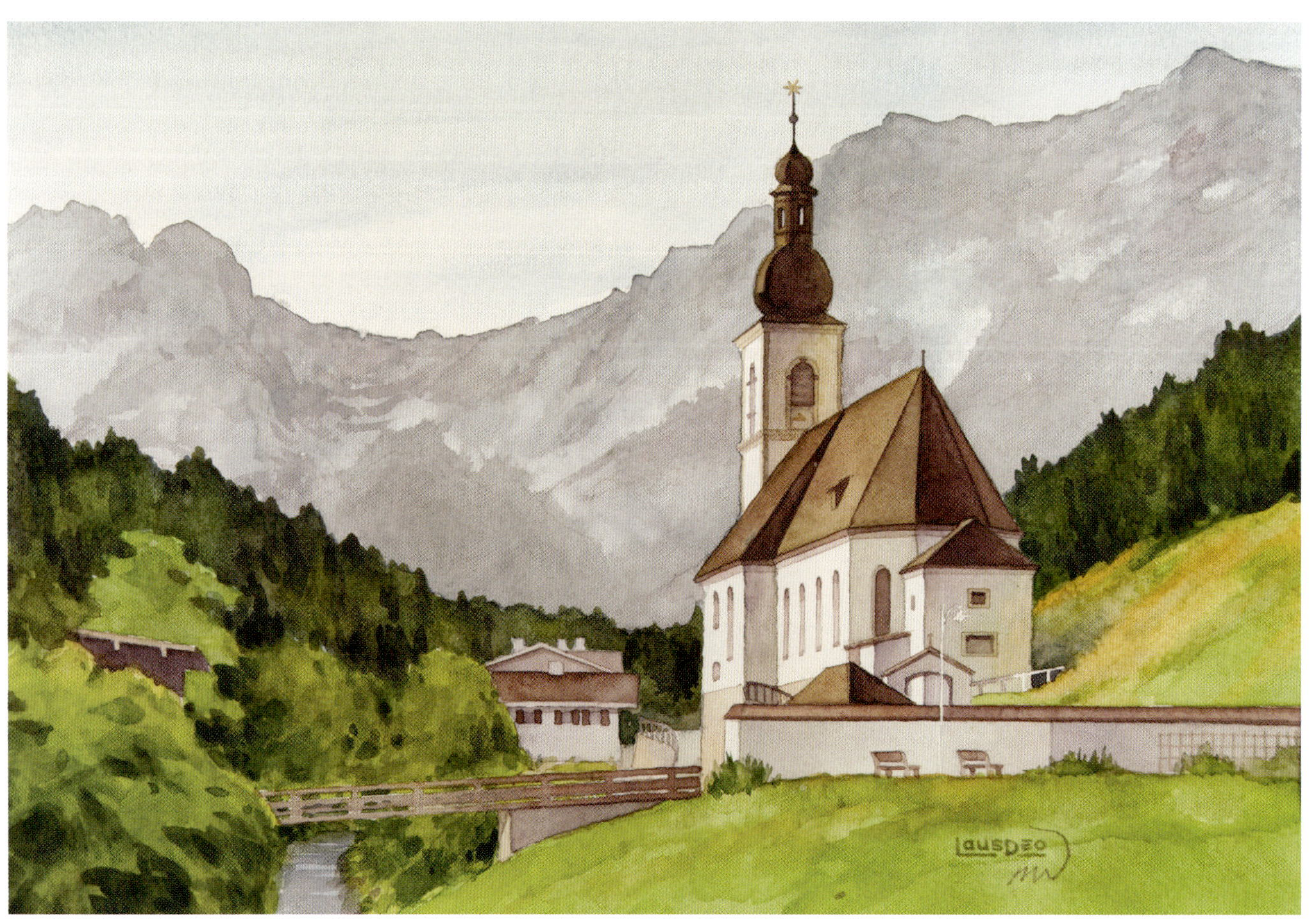

Ramsau Church
Watercolor on watercolor paper
12" × 17" (30cm × 43cm)

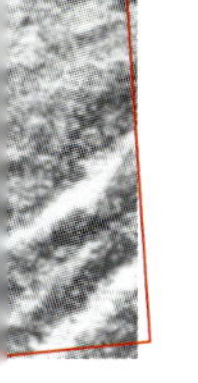

Atmospheric Perspective Basics

Atmospheric perspective, also called aerial perspective, conveys depth through variations of values (lights and darks), colors and clarity of elements. Foreground elements in a composition have greater value contrasts, more intense colors and greater definition of details. With distance, the values and colors become neutral, the details are less defined and the elements take on a dull blue-gray appearance.

Atmospheric perspective occurs because particles in the air, such as water vapor and smog, affect what is seen. Forms viewed from a distance are not as defined and have less contrast because there are more particles in the atmosphere between the forms and the viewer. Likewise, the wavelengths of color are affected by distance. Blues bounce around, whereas the longer color wavelengths are not affected by particles in the same way. The result is that the blues remain more visible than the other colors in the spectrum.

Values

Values are the lights and darks of a composition. Intrinsic to atmospheric perspective, values can influence the impression of depth in a scene. Highly contrasting values tend to appear forward of values with little contrast.

Lighting

The lighting of a scene affects shadows and values of forms. It can also affect how those forms are perceived.

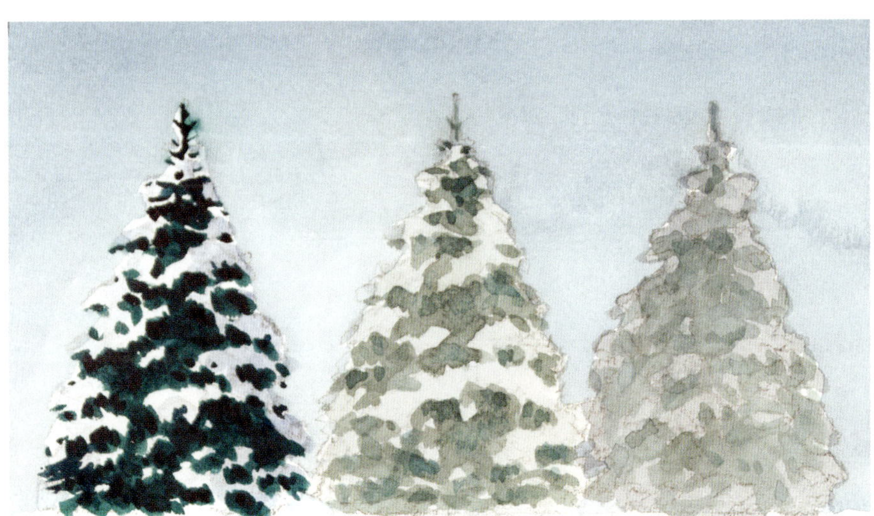

Dulling with Distance
By putting atmospheric perspective to use, forms in the foreground will have greater clarity than background forms. The hazy blue-gray appearance of the tree on the right, with its dull colors and values, suggests that it is the most distant of the three trees.

Observe Atmospheric Perspective

Find a location with a view of scenery including such forms as hills, trees or buildings. From this vantage point, note the changes in atmospheric perspective during different times of day and in different weather conditions. Forms will appear muted on a misty morning and will have more clarity on a bright, sunny afternoon.

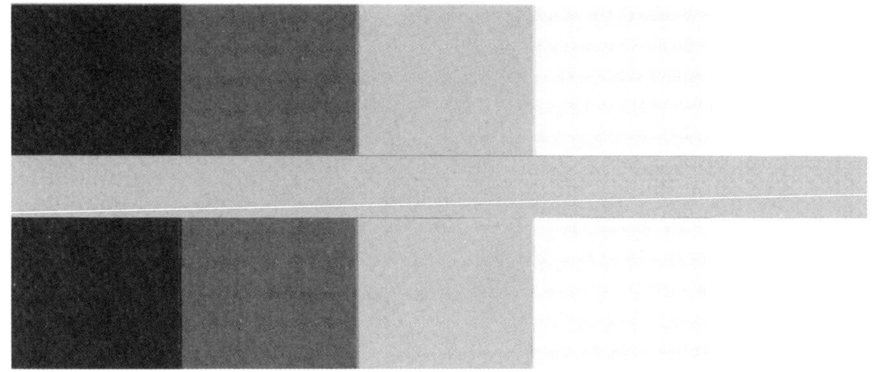

It's All Relative

Values may appear lighter or darker depending on their surroundings. When viewing the horizontal gray stripe, it may appear lighter where it is surrounded by dark values and darker where it is surrounded by light values, but the gray stripe itself is the same value throughout its length.

Depth of Values

Generally speaking, the brighter the values, the more forward they appear, whereas the dark values appear more distant. White may appear larger and closer than black, which can appear heavy, smaller and more distant.

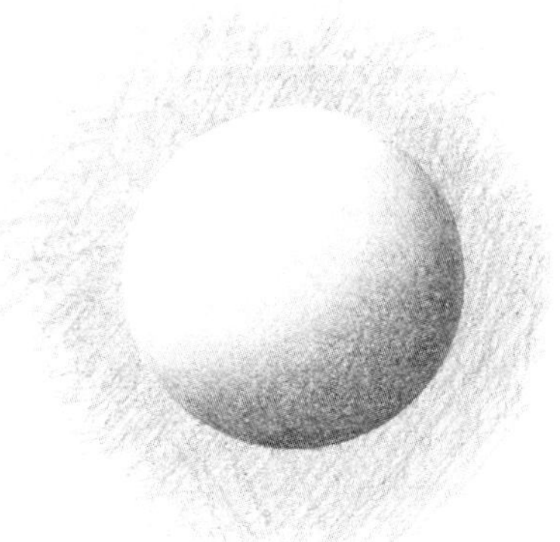

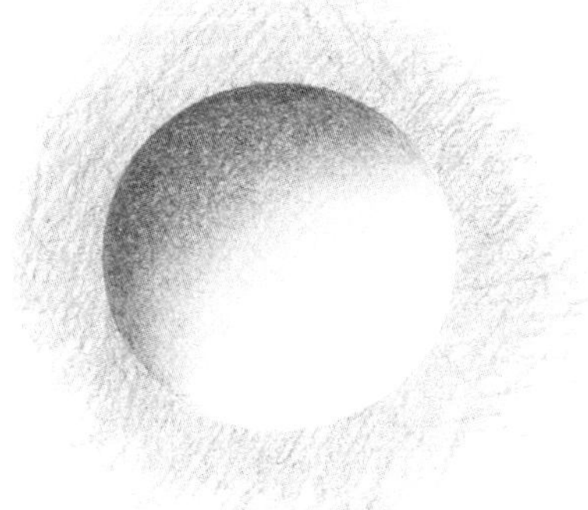

Convex or Concave?

When comparing these two forms, both are the same, but because they are positioned differently on the page, one appears convex while the other appears concave. The placement of the light influences how these forms are perceived. Because it is most common to have the light source coming from above, the left form appears to bulge outward while the right form appears inset.

Foreground Shadow

This demonstration plots a foreground shadow that is created by a light source coming from the background.

Materials

Paper
medium-texture drawing paper; medium-texture sketch paper

Pencils
2B

Other
kneaded eraser; lightbox or transfer paper

Optional
drawing board; masking tape; ruler; triangle; T-square

1 Sketch a Box

On sketch paper, sketch a box following the steps in the Two-Point Perspective Box demonstration in Chapter 1. Include the back side, along with the horizon and vanishing points.

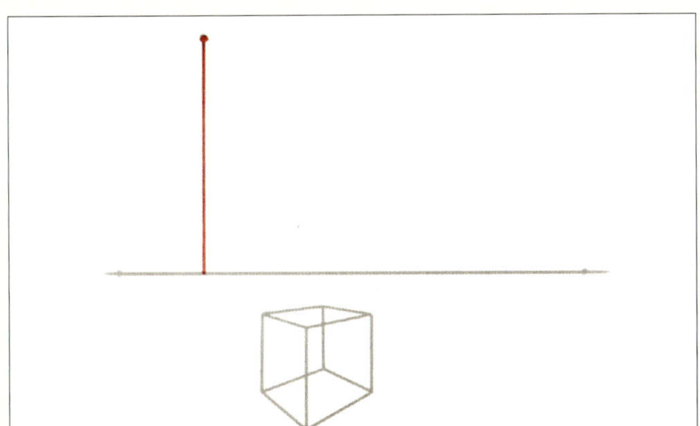

2 Add the Light Source and Light Source Vanishing Point

Place a dot above the horizon as the light source. Add a vertical line down from the light source to the horizon. Add another dot where the vertical line meets the horizon as the light source vanishing point.

3 Add Shadow Direction Lines

Add three orthogonal lines from the light source vanishing point that pass through the three forward corners of the box on the ground plane. These lines determine the direction of the shadow.

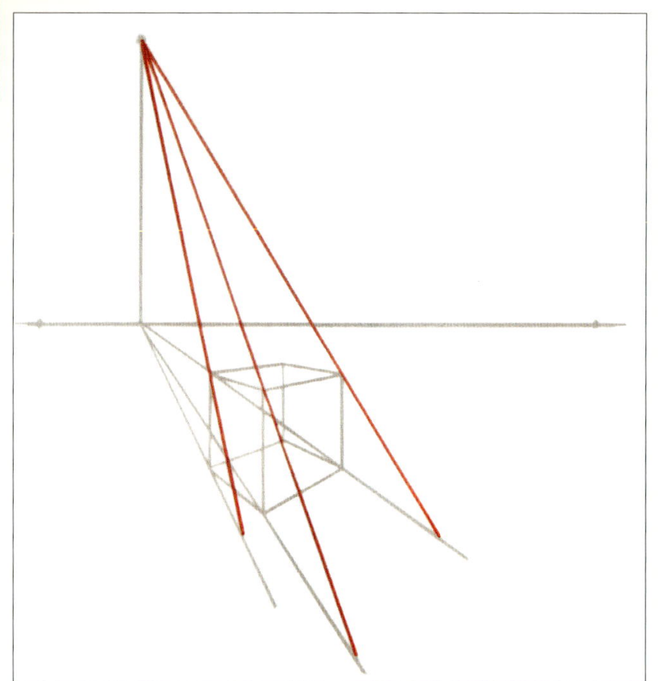

4 Add Shadow Length Lines

Add three orthogonal lines from the light source that pass through the three top forward corners of the box. These lines determine the length of the shadow.

5 Add Lines to Form the Shadow

Add lines that connect the tangents that were created by intersecting the direction lines with the length lines. Connect these lines to the direction lines to form the shadow.

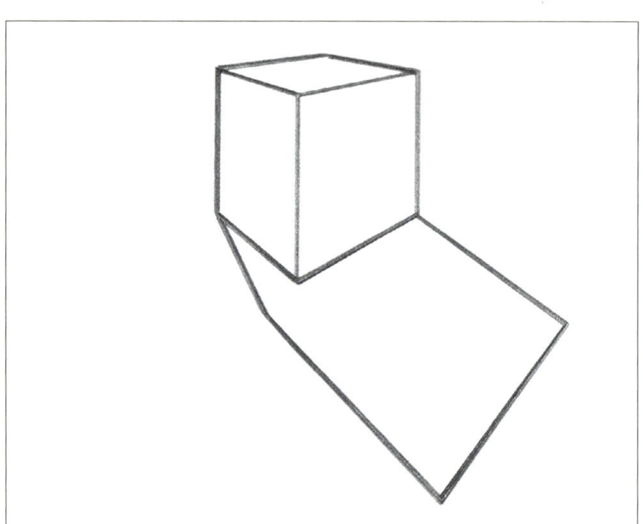

6 Erase Unwanted Lines

Erase all the lines except the visible lines of the box and the outer form of the shadow.

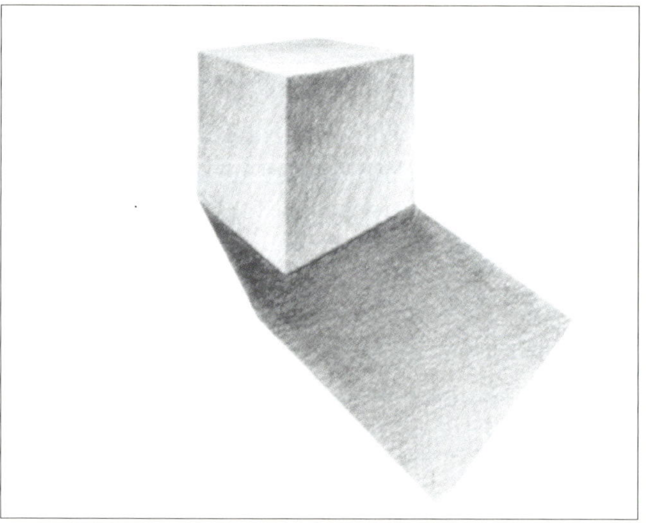

7 Add Shading to Complete the Drawing

Trace or transfer the sketch onto drawing paper and add values. The cast shadows on the ground plane should be darker than the form shadows, which are on the box.

MINI-DEMONSTRATION

Background Shadow

This demonstration plots a shadow that is in the background from an unseen light source that is behind the viewer. Because the light source cannot be placed in the scene, the process is different than determining a foreground shadow.

Materials

Paper
medium-texture drawing paper; medium texture sketch paper

Pencils
2B

Other
kneaded eraser; lightbox or transfer paper

Optional
drawing board; masking tape; triangle; T-square

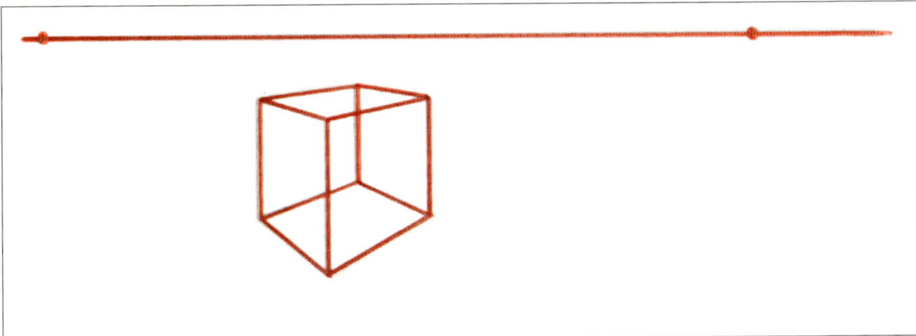

1 Sketch a Box

On sketch paper, sketch a box following the steps in the Two-Point Perspective Box demonstration in Chapter 1. Include the back side, along with the horizon and vanishing points. Extend the line for the horizon beyond the right vanishing point.

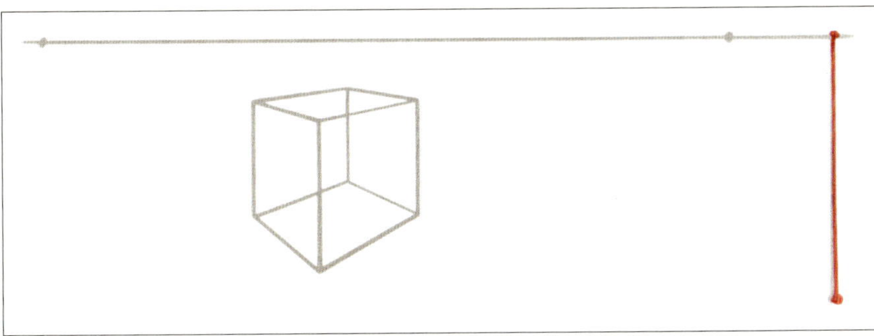

2 Add the Shadow Vanishing Point and the Construct Vanishing Point

Place a dot on the horizon as the shadow vanishing point. Add a vertical line down from the shadow vanishing point and place a dot as the construct vanishing point. This is done on the opposite side of the scene from where the light is coming from.

3 Add Shadow Direction Lines

Add three orthogonal lines from the bottom corners of the box to the shadow vanishing point. These lines determine the direction of the shadow.

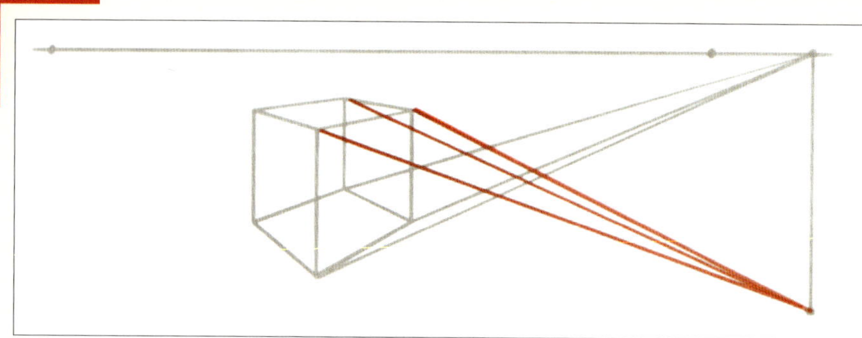

4 Add Shadow Length Lines

Add three lines from the top right corners of the box to the construct vanishing point. These lines determine the length of the shadow.

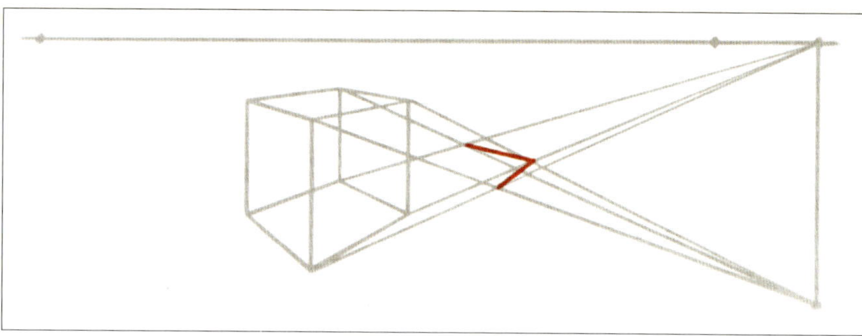

5 Add Lines to Form the Shadow

Add lines that connect the tangents that were created by intersecting the direction lines with the length lines. Also connect these lines to the direction lines to form the shadow.

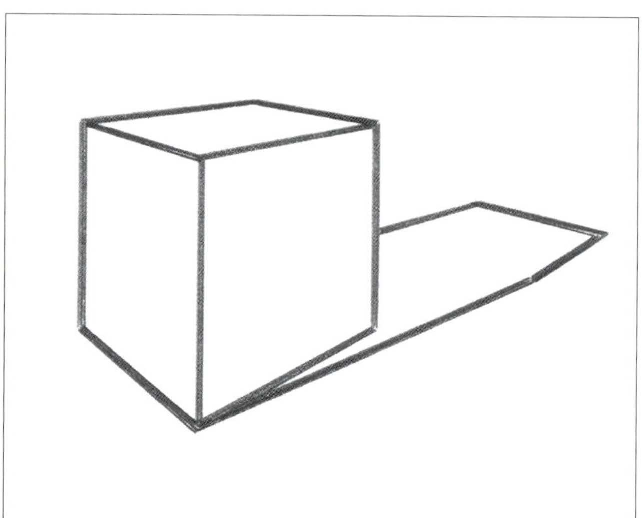

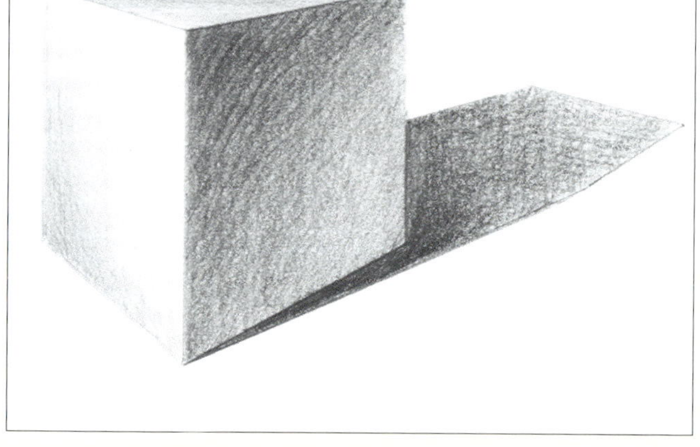

6 Erase Unwanted Lines

Erase all the lines except the visible lines of the box and the outer form of the shadow.

7 Add Shading to Complete the Drawing

Trace or transfer the sketch onto drawing paper and add values. The lightest part of the box is where it is most directly placed in the light.

Color Basics

Colors can enhance depth and suggest emotion. Depth in art as a visual experience can be enhanced through the proper use of warm and cool colors. Colors can be categorized and their characteristics better understood through the use of a color wheel.

- **Primary colors:** Red, yellow and blue are the three primary colors. All of the other colors on the color wheel are derived from two or more of these three colors.
- **Secondary colors:** Orange, green and violet are the three secondary colors. These colors are created by combining two primary colors.
- **Tertiary colors:** Tertiary colors are created by combining a primary color with an adjacent secondary color. These colors include red-orange, yellow-orange, yellow-green, blue-green, blue-violet and red-violet.
- **Complementary colors:** Any combination of two colors that are opposite each other on the color wheel are complementary colors. Red and green are an example of a set of complementary colors.
- **Neutral colors and grays:** Neutral colors and grays are created by combining any combination of complementary colors. This would be the same as mixing all three primary colors together.
- **Warm colors:** Reds, oranges and yellows make up the range of warm colors. These colors can feel energetic and appear to come forward. An example of this is an area bathed in sunlight.
- **Cool colors**: Greens, blues and violets make up the range of cool colors. These colors can feel calming and appear to recede. An area darkened by shadows is an example of cool colors.

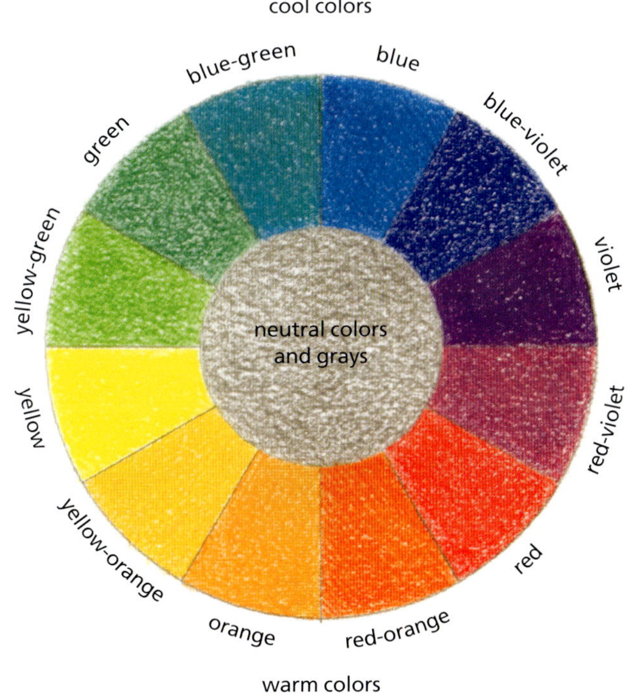

Color Wheel Categories
Colors can be categorized and their characteristics better understood through the use of a color wheel. A color wheel is an essential tool when creating colored artwork. Manufactured color wheels are available at most craft and art supply stores. They provide information regarding terms and definitions along with a mixing guide and color combinations.

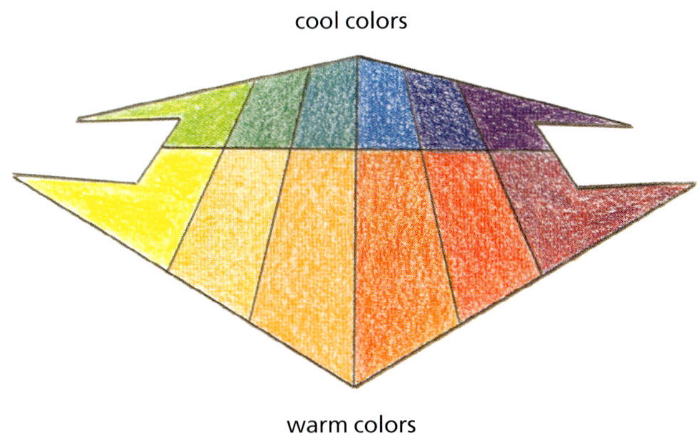

Warm Colors Advance, Cool Colors Recede
Warm colors can feel active and appear to come forward, whereas cool colors tend to feel passive and appear to step back or recede.

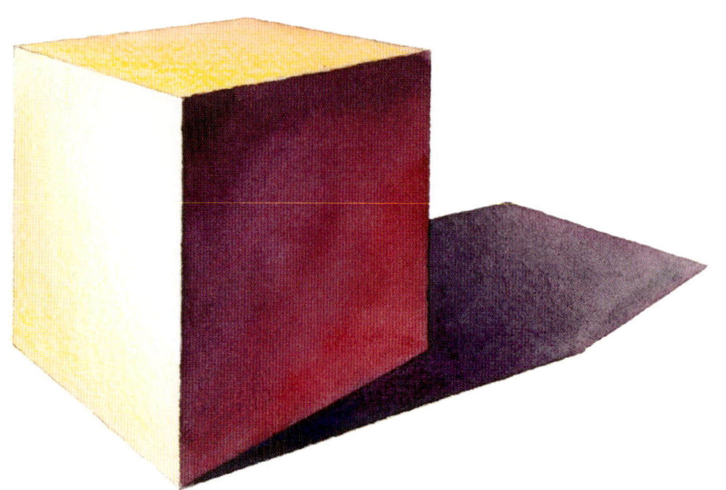

Sunlight Is Warm, Shadows Are Cool

Colors can also be used to emphasize light and shadow. To place the colors properly, consider sunlight as being warm and shadows as being cool.

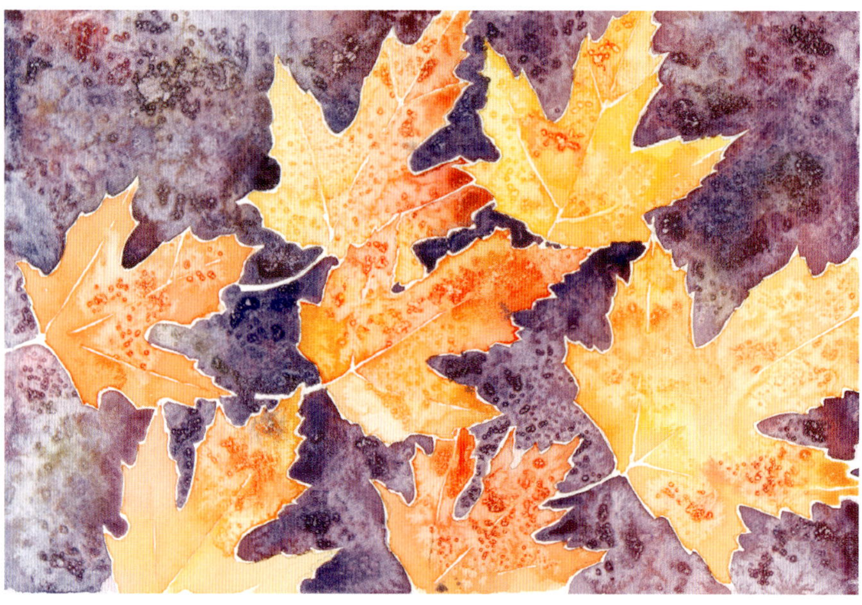

Applying Color Depth

Be intentional about the use of colors to communicate depth. For this watercolor painting, I chose to paint the leaves with warm colors and the background with cool colors. The choice of colors suggests that the leaves are closer than the background.

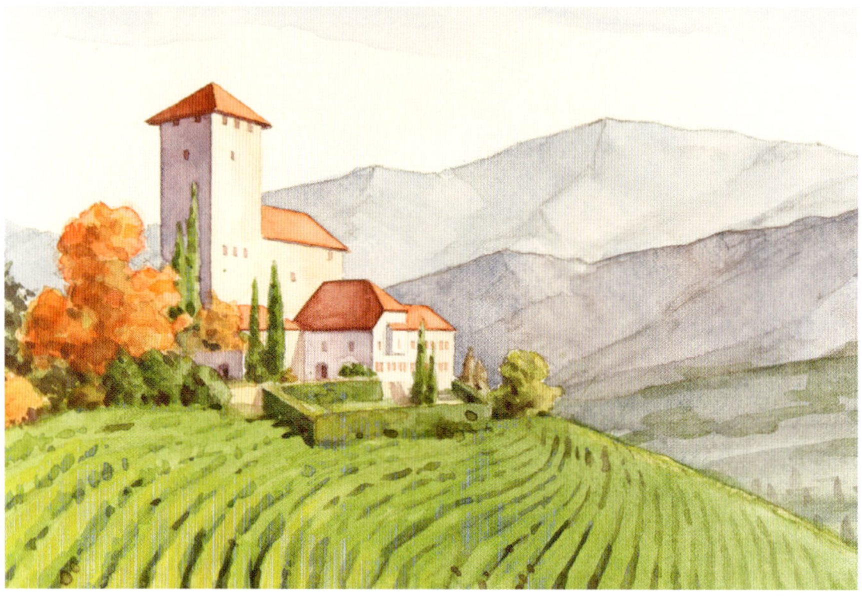

Utilizing Linear Perspective, Atmospheric Perspective and Color Together

Depth in art can best be expressed by purposely combining linear and atmospheric perspective along with intentional use of warm and cool colors. Can you identify where linear perspective, atmospheric perspective and the use of color have been used to emphasize depth in this painting?

Everyday Subjects

Everyday subjects are all around us just waiting to be sketched. While everything visual employs the principles of linear perspective, some subjects are noticeably more affected by perspective than others.

Obvious Perspective Study Subjects
The principles of linear perspective are more obvious in subjects that are basic, angular and geometric in form.

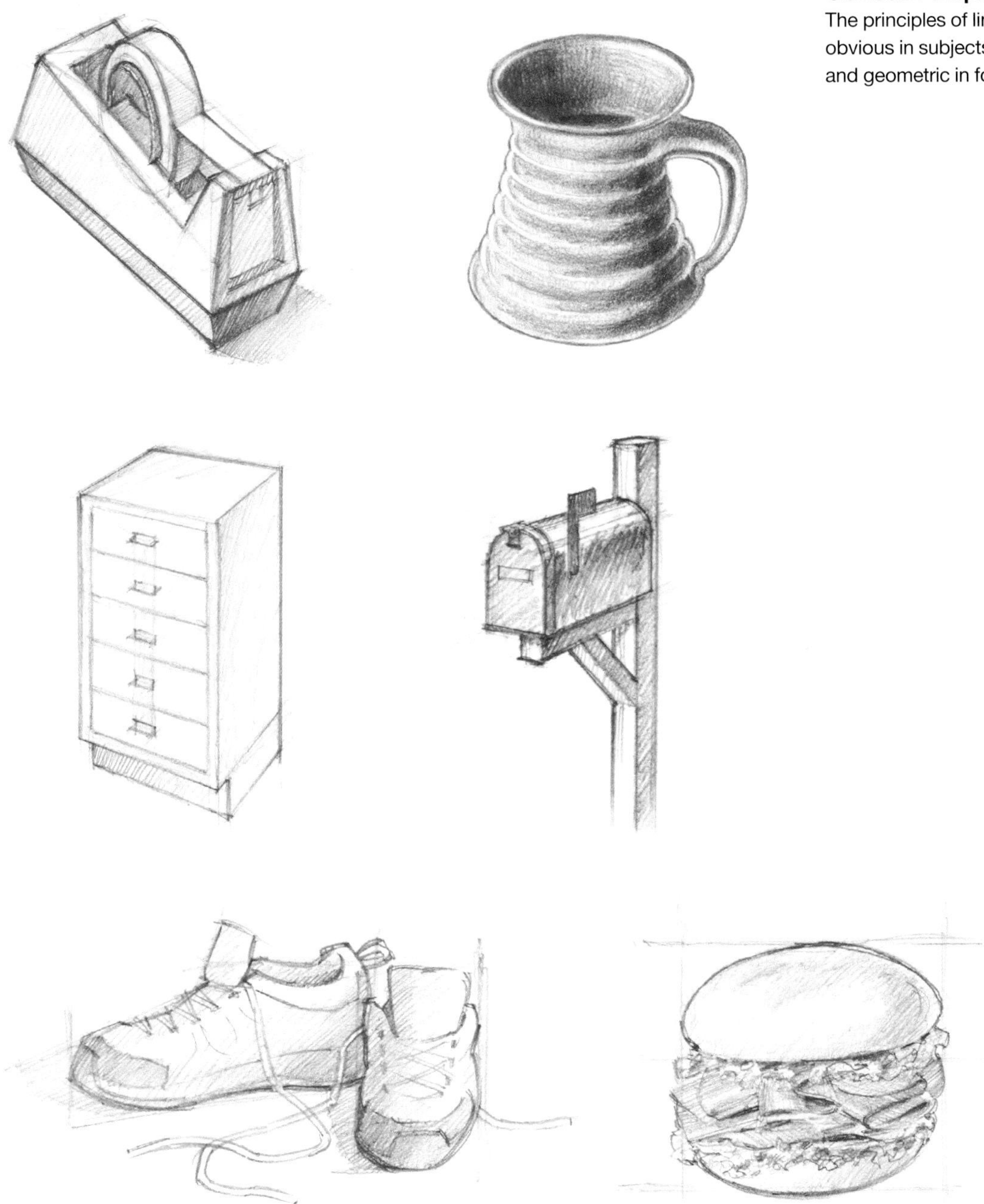

Less Obvious Perspective Study Subjects
The application of the principles of linear perspective may be less obvious in subjects that are irregular in form, but they are still present. Sketching shoes involves the principles of foreshortening while sketching a sandwich involves the principles of circles in perspective. As with any subject, the elevation (height that it is viewed from) is also taken into account.

Lamp

To keep the features symmetrical, a subject such as this lamp requires placing a vertical line through the center of the drawing. The ellipses are flatter at the top and rounder at the base.

Materials

Paper
medium-texture drawing paper

Pencils
2B

Other
kneaded eraser

Optional
drawing board; masking tape; ruler; triangle; T-square

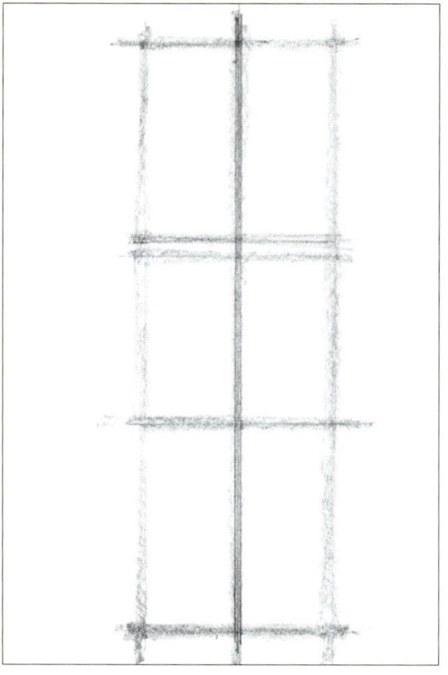

1 Sketch the Centerline and Block in the Features

Sketch a centerline vertically and block in the basic features with horizontal and vertical lines. The vertical lines are to be evenly spaced from the centerline to ensure symmetry.

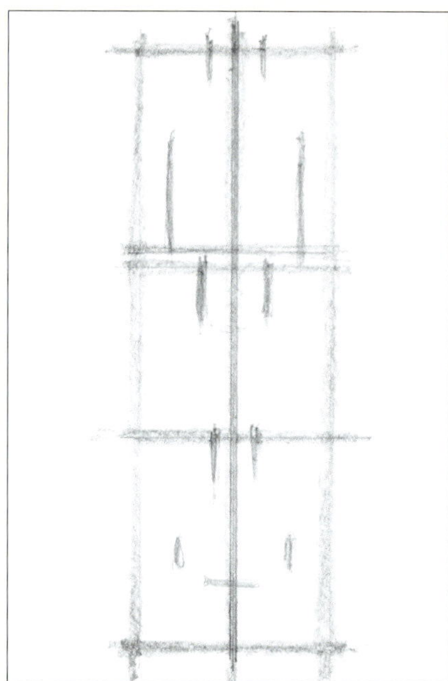

2 Block in More Features

Continue to add symmetrical lines to block in the features.

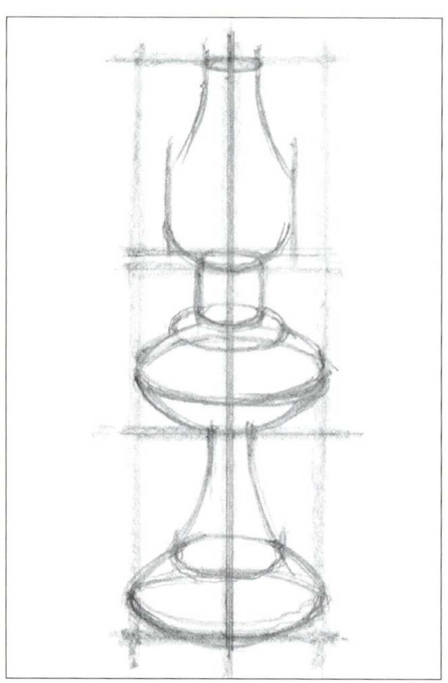

3 Develop the Form

Add ellipses and round the features to develop the form.

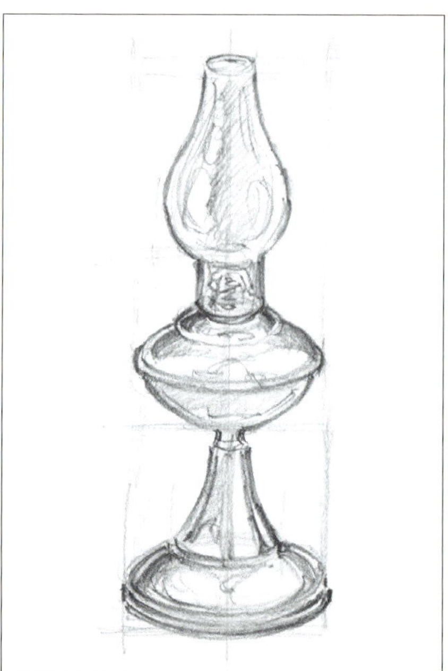

4 Add Details and Values

Erase any unwanted lines and add remaining structural details. Add values, leaving places for highlights to give the lamp the appearance of glass and polished metal.

Chair

The drawing of this chair starts with the box-shaped base. The attached back curves at the top and the legs narrow at the bottom.

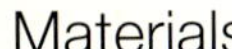

Materials

Paper
medium-texture drawing paper

Pencils
2B

Other
kneaded eraser

Optional
drawing board; masking tape; ruler; triangle; T-square

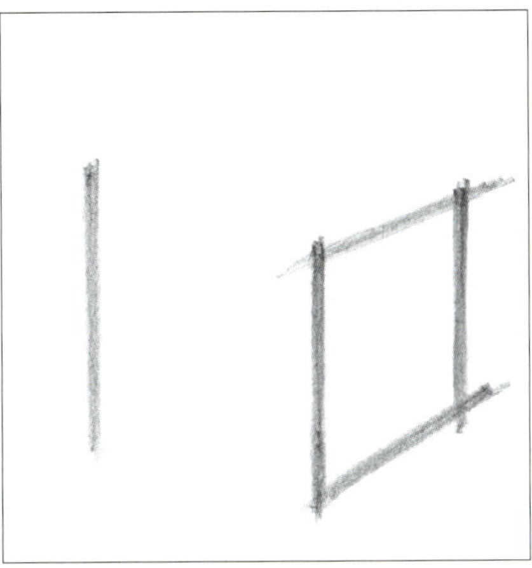

1 Sketch the Side and Left Corner of the Base

Sketch vertical lines for the front corner and the right back corners and orthogonal lines at the top and bottom to form the right side of the base. Add a vertical line to the left as the left front corner of the base.

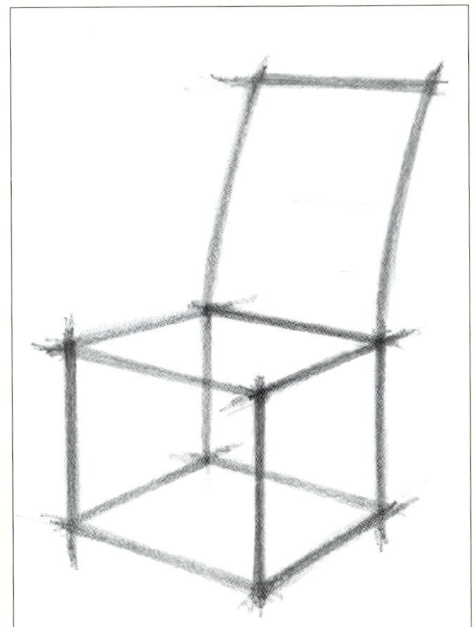

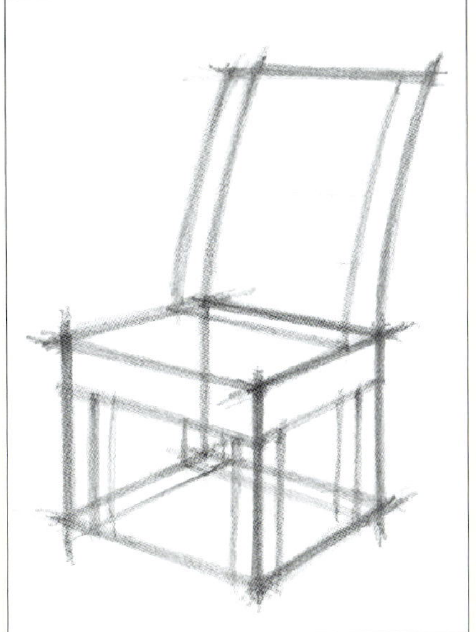

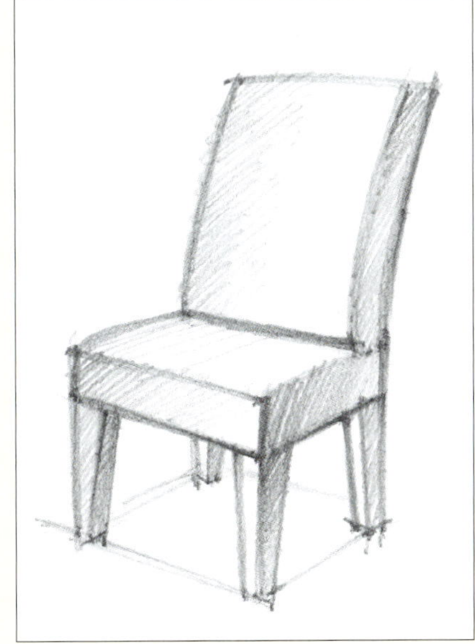

2 Form the Base and Back

Add orthogonal lines to form the base. Sketch slightly curved lines up from the base and add an orthogonal line at the top for the back of the chair.

3 Develop the Form

Add depth to the legs and back to develop the form of the chair.

4 Add Details and Values

Taper the legs. Erase unwanted lines and add the values.

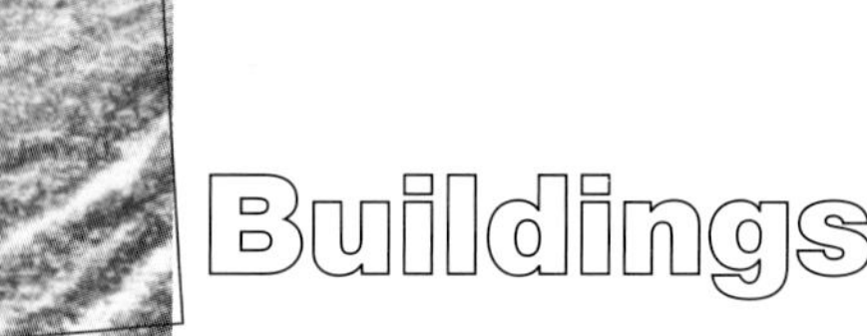

Buildings

From towering skyscrapers to detailed architectural components, buildings offer an endless amount of subject matter for drawing perspective.

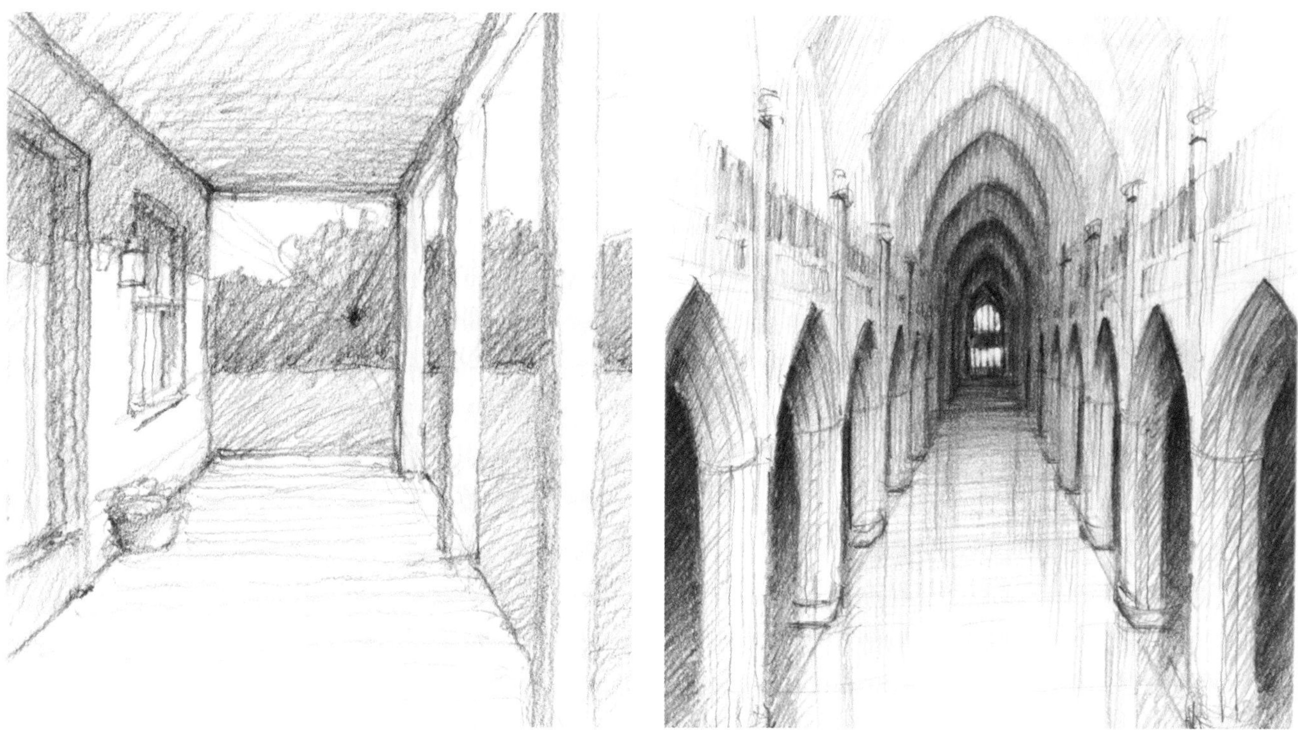

One-Point Perspective is not Always Simple

Though a one-point perspective drawing may seem simple, it doesn't have to be. Both the house porch and the cathedral interior were sketched as one-point perspective subjects, but the cathedral interior was a much more complex subject than the porch.

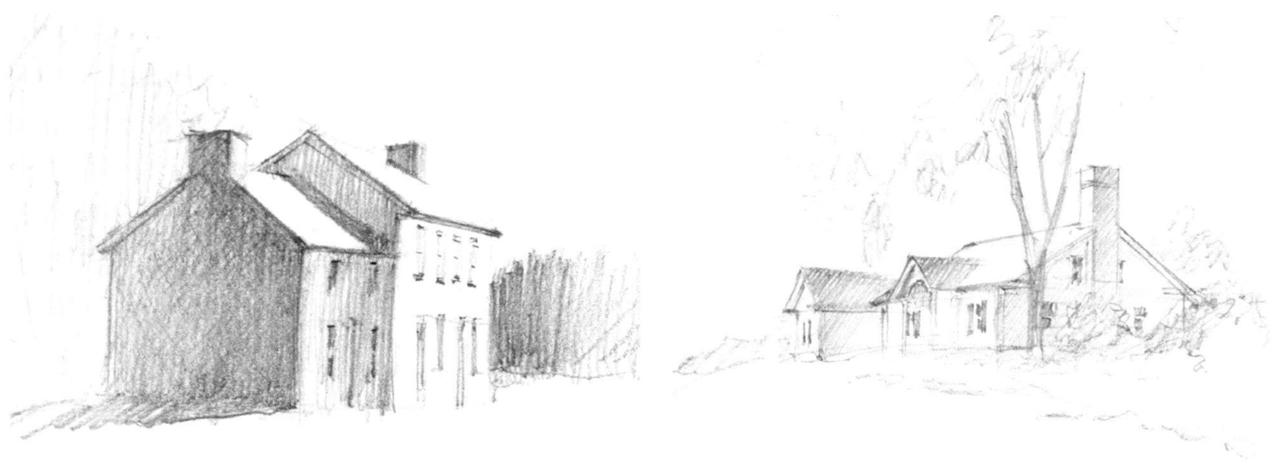

Two-Point Perspective Houses

These two-point perspective house sketches were done in my studio from photos that I had previously taken.

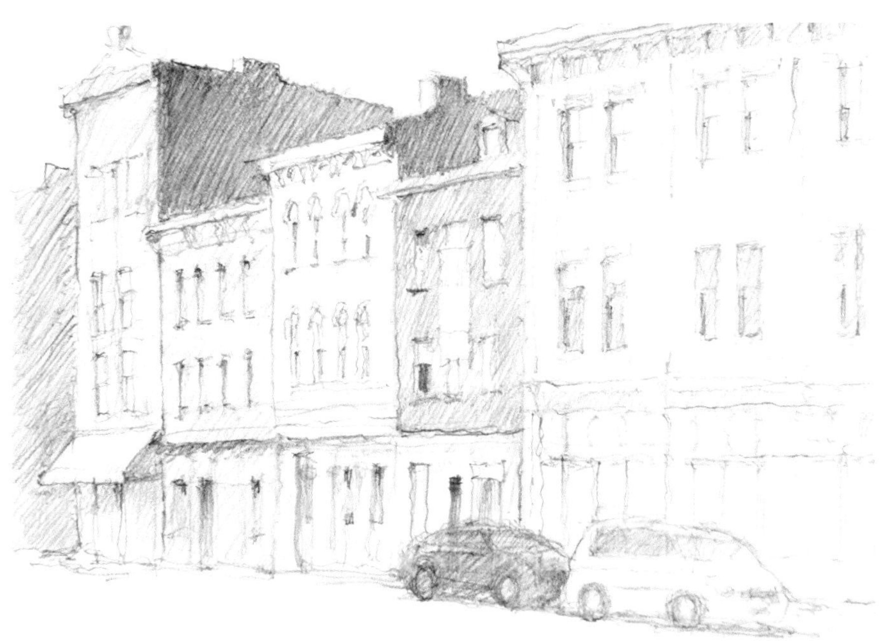

One-Point Perspective Street Scene
This one-point perspective drawing was completed outdoors without the use of a straightedge. The many orthogonal lines were established by following the first demonstration in chapter 2, which did not require plotting out the vanishing point.

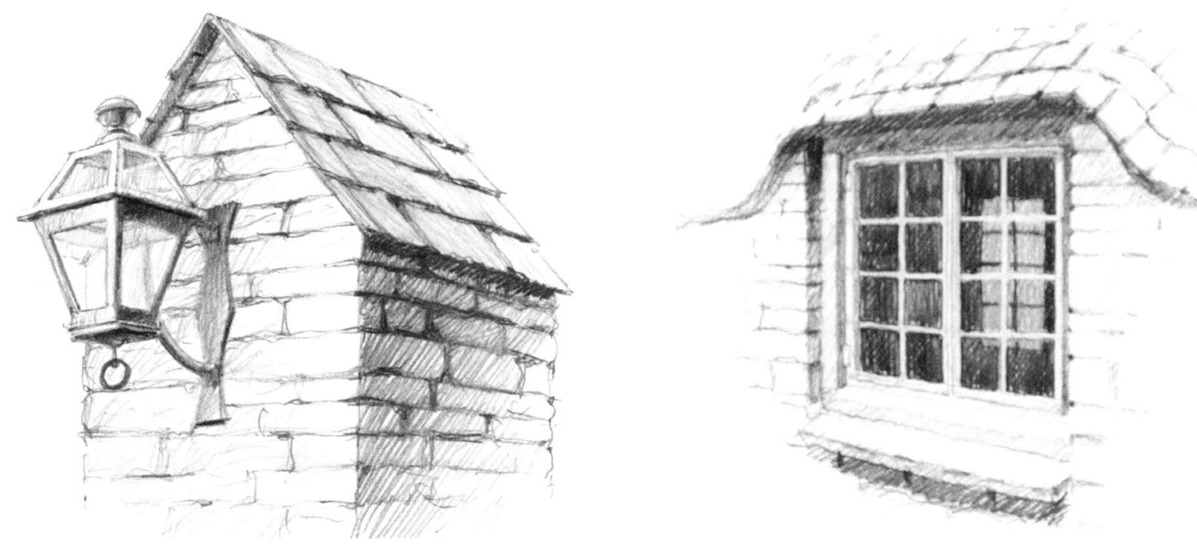

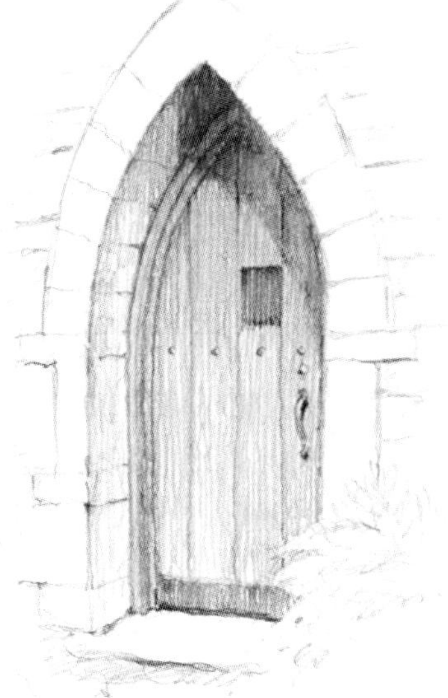

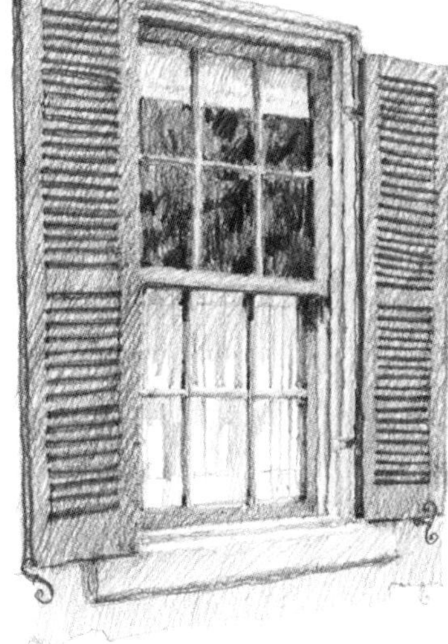

Making the Most of Details
Architectural features can add character to more involved subjects or make for complete drawings themselves. Though they may be detailed, these features are drawn using the same basic linear perspective principles as mentioned earlier in the book. Regarding windows, if they have a top and bottom sash, the bottom sash will be inset more than the top sash.

Rustic Barn

Creating this rustic barn is as easy as sketching a basic box with a roof and a few structural details including the tin roof and wooden boards. This barn has an inclined plane that leads up to the wide-open door. The drawing can be simplified by deleting this feature.

Materials

Paper
medium-texture drawing paper

Pencils
2B

Other
kneaded eraser

Optional
drawing board; masking tape; triangle; T-square

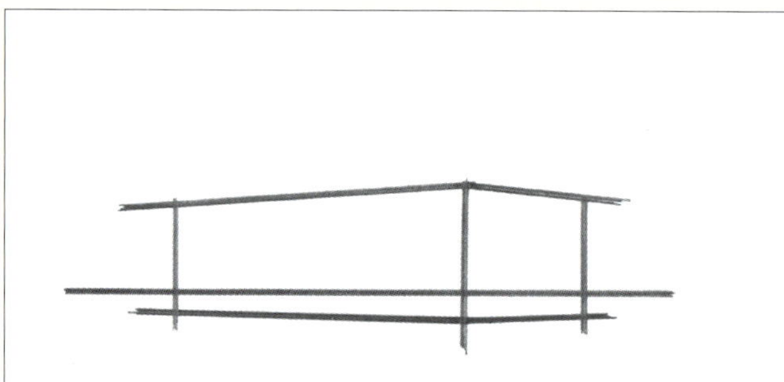

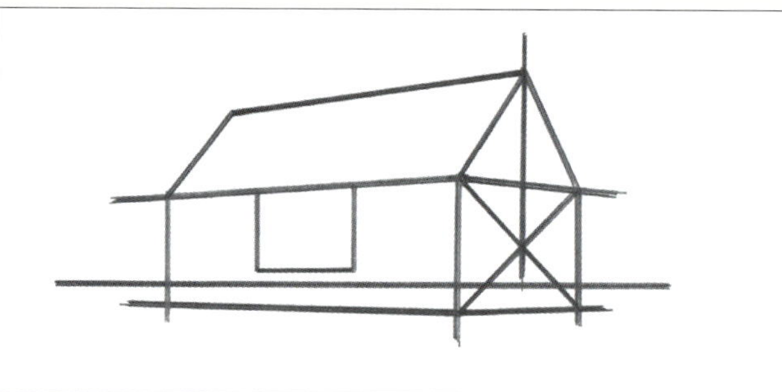

1 Sketch the Box Form

Sketch a horizontal line for the horizon, then add the vertical lines for the corners and orthogonal lines to form the box.

2 Add the Roof and a Door

On the right side of the box, sketch an X by connecting the four corners. From the centerpoint, sketch a vertical line upward as the centerline. Sketch the roof peak from the centerline, then the roof ridge along with the left edge of the roof. On the left front side of the box, sketch the door, which is above the baseline.

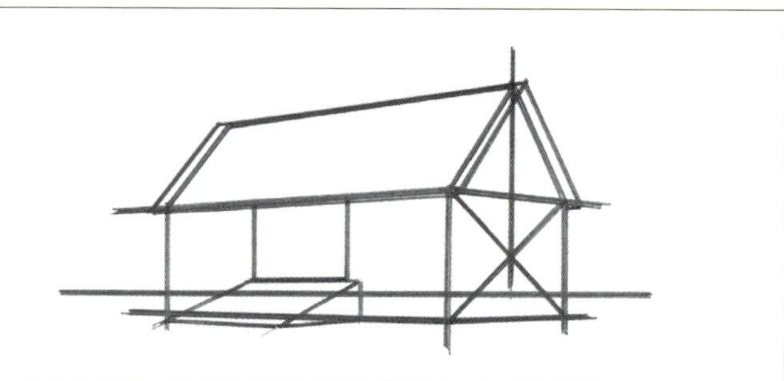

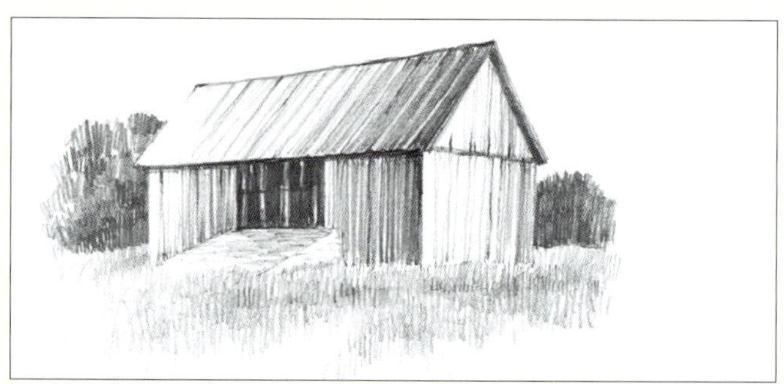

3 Develop the Form

Add overhangs to the ends of the roof. Sketch the inclined plane as the ramp beneath the door.

4 Add Details and Values

Add lines for the tin roof and the wood sideboards. Sketch the outlines of the trees in the background. Erase unwanted lines and add values with the light source coming from the right.

Lighthouse

This drawing is a simple box with a roof combined with the cylindrical form of the tower. The horizon is clearly visible where the water and sky meet beyond the structure.

Materials

Paper
medium-texture drawing paper

Pencils
2B

Other
kneaded eraser

Optional
drawing board; masking tape; ruler; triangle; T-square

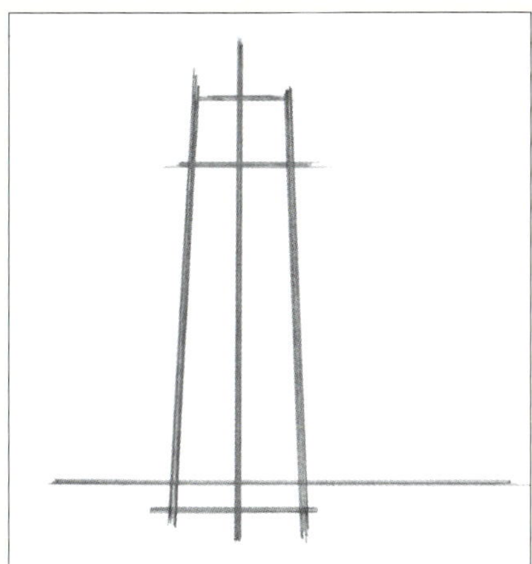

1 Block in the Tower

Block in the basic portions and form of the tower by first sketching the vertical centerline, then adding the sides, which narrow slightly at the top. Add horizontal lines for the base, top and upper platform. Add a horizontal line for the horizon.

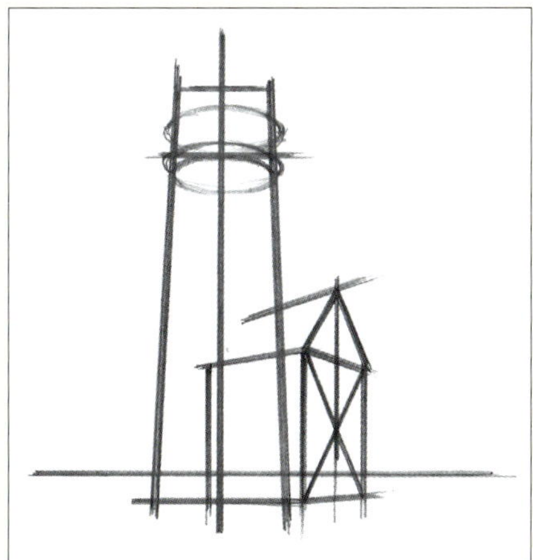

2 Sketch the House Structure and Ellipses

Add the house portion of the lighthouse, which is joined to the tower. This form is a box with a roof. The previous barn demonstration can be followed for creating this part of the structure. Add some ellipses to the tower.

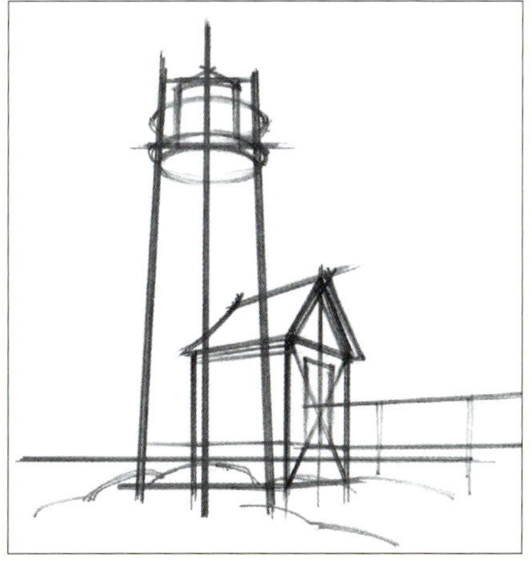

3 Add Details

Add details including overhangs, a walkway and foreground rocks. Sketch the left edge of the house roof to curve around the form of the tower.

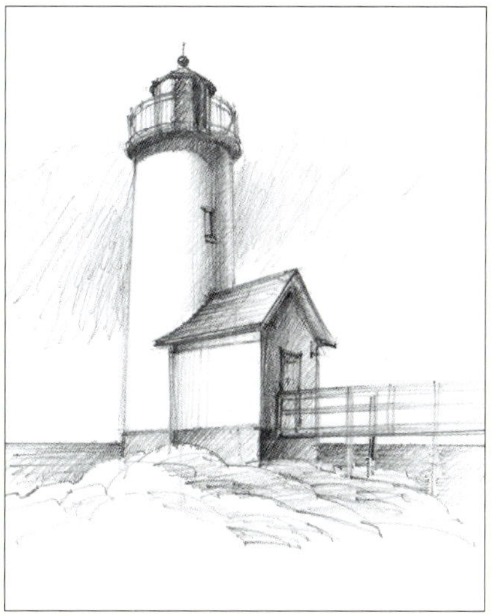

4 Add More Details and Values

Erase any unwanted lines. Add structural details throughout, including a railing and a cap to the tower. Add values with the light source coming from the left causing the left sides of the forms to be lighter than the right sides.

Airplanes & Cars

Square, angular and sleek aircraft and automobiles are drawn beginning with box forms that are chiseled and rounded to create smooth, flowing contours. Ellipses are prevalent in the forms of the wheels and headlights.

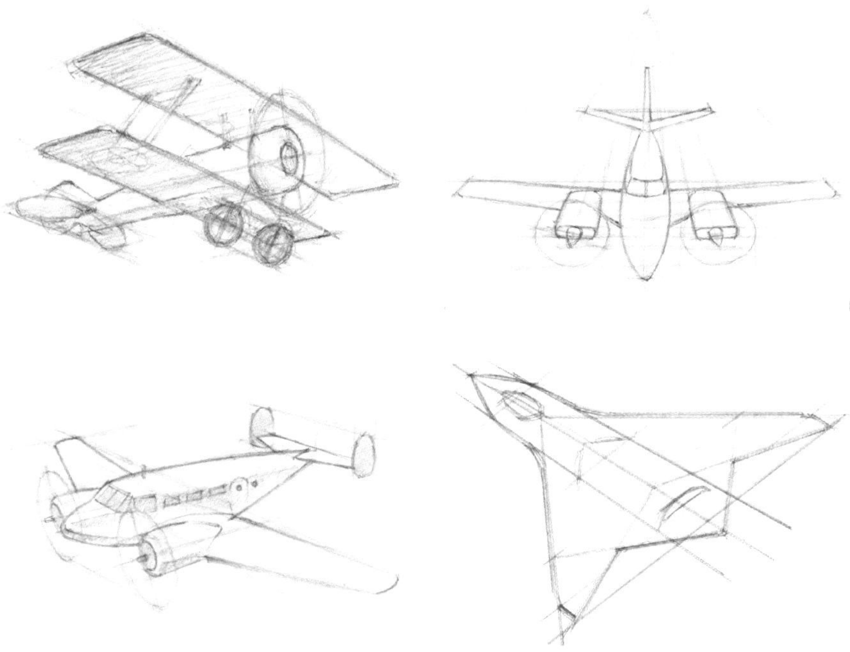

Aircraft
Symmetry is a characteristic of aircraft. A centerline is sometimes helpful to align the features of the aircraft from side to side.

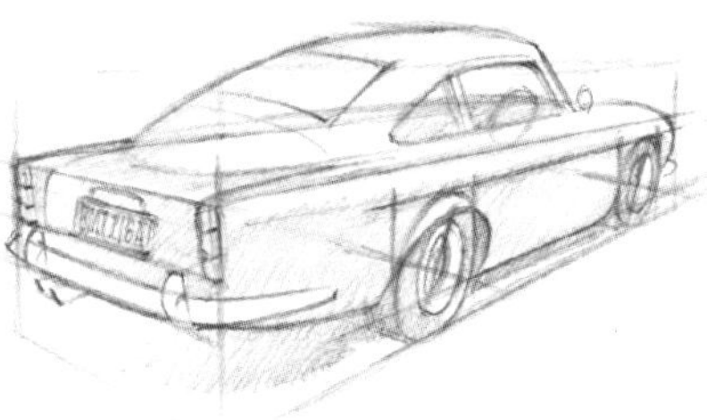

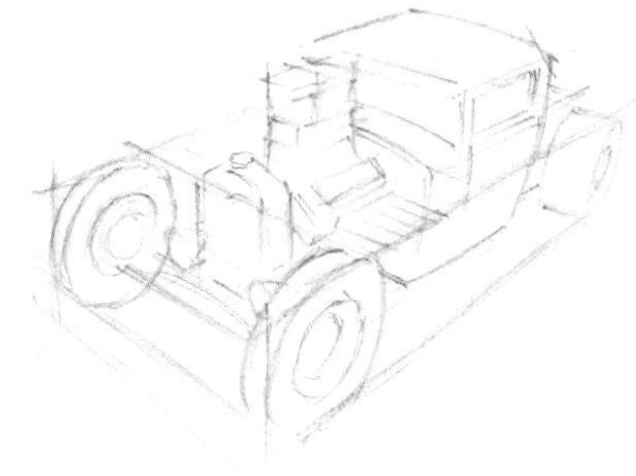

Automobiles
Ellipses are present on vehicles in the forms of tires, steering wheels and headlights. Capturing the correct elliptical shape will enhance the appearance of the drawing.

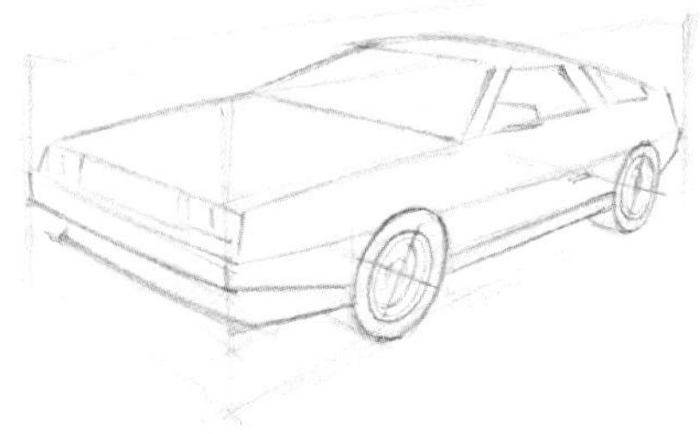

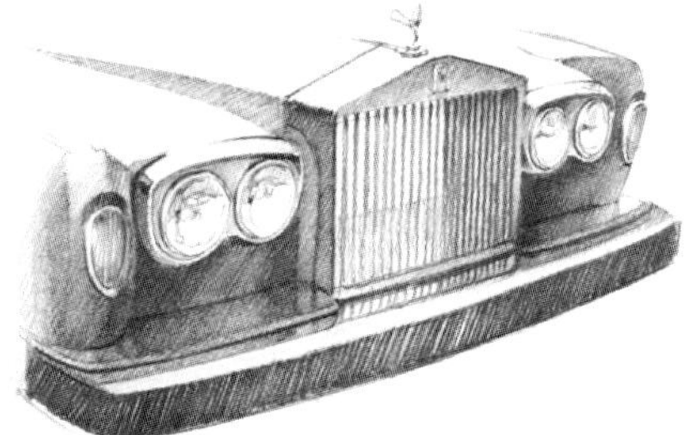

Concept Car

Design your own concept car by following the simple steps for this demonstration.

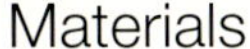

Materials

Paper
medium-texture drawing paper

Pencils
2B

Other
kneaded eraser

Optional
drawing board; masking tape; ruler; triangle; T-square

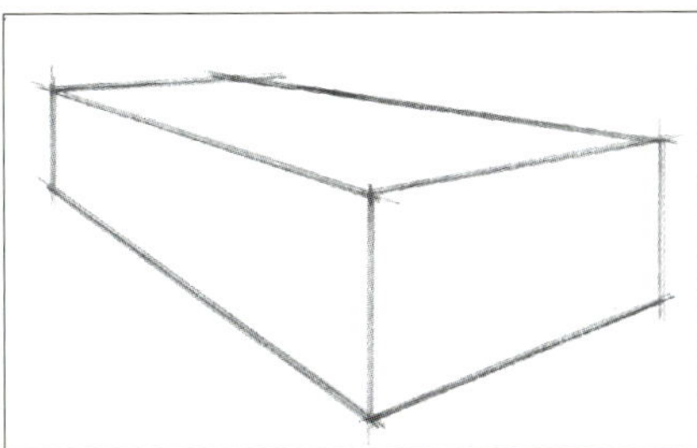

1 Sketch a Box Form

Sketch a box to represent the lower portion of the car.

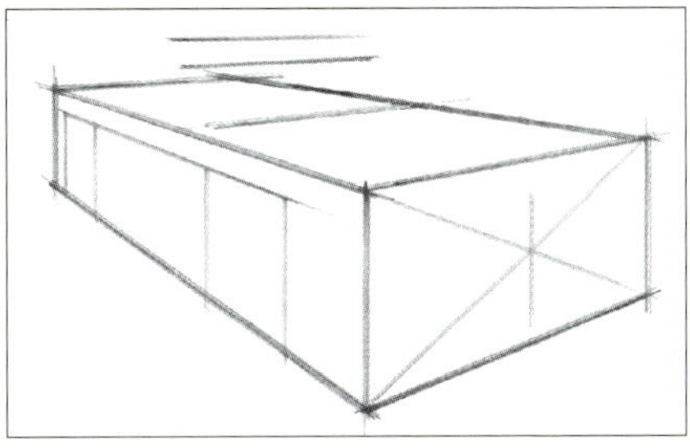

2 Add Lines for the Top and Block in the Wheels

Sketch orthogonal lines for the top and windshield. Sketch squares for the placement of the wheels. Determine the centerpoint and centerline of the front by connecting the four corners of the front rectangle.

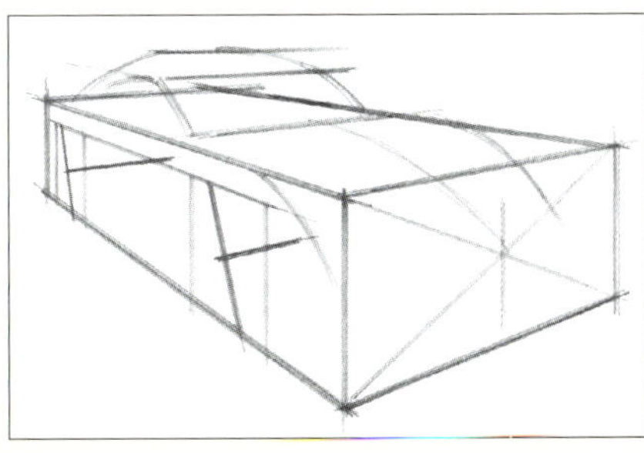

3 Add the Upper Form, Wheels and the Centerline

Add the upper glass area of the car. Sketch in the minor and major axes of the wheels. Begin sculpting the hood and front fenders.

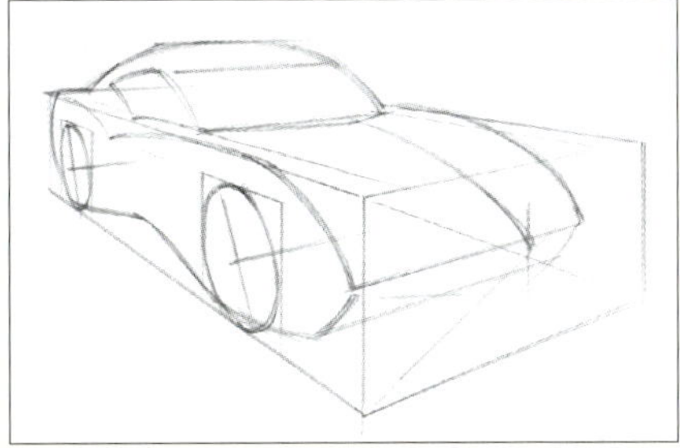

4 Define the Shape

Add circular forms for the wheels and sketch curved lines to form the body within the box shapes. More orthogonal lines may be added or changed throughout the development of the sketch to define the unique shape of the automobile. Erase unwanted lines throughout the process.

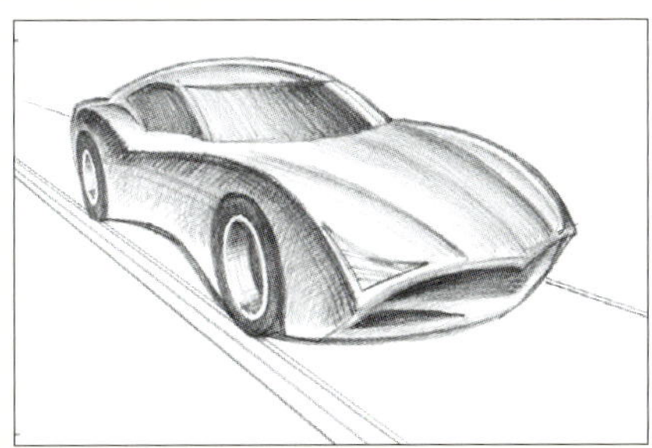

5 Add Details and Values

Refine the form and add details and values. Orthogonal lines can be added to the background to emphasize depth.

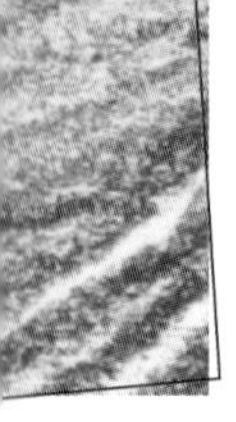

Twists, Turns & Hills

Contour subjects such as hills and slopes are fun to capture in perspective. These forms utilize vanishing points to create contours. When the vanishing points rest above or below the horizon, they give an up or down appearance to the hills and slopes.

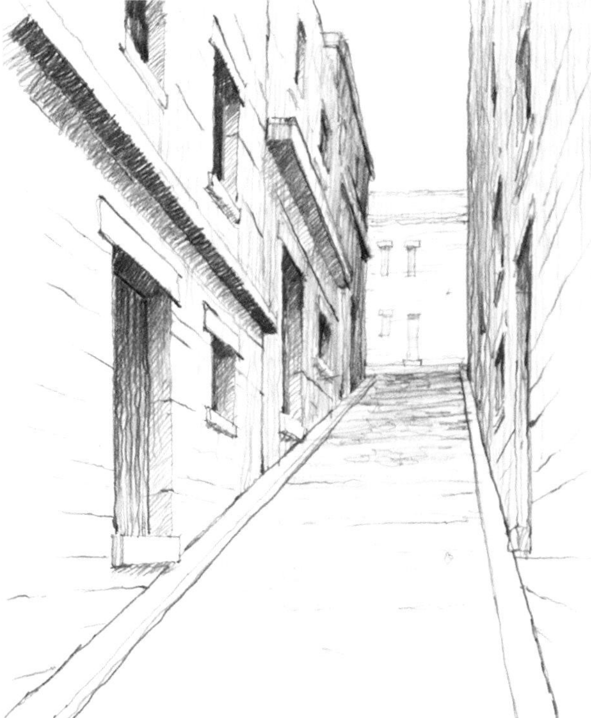

Sketching an Uphill Alley

For this sketch, the orthogonal lines of the buildings are directed to a vanishing point at the lower right of the drawing. The orthogonal lines of the alley, which is an incline, are directed to a vanishing point directly above the vanishing point of the buildings.

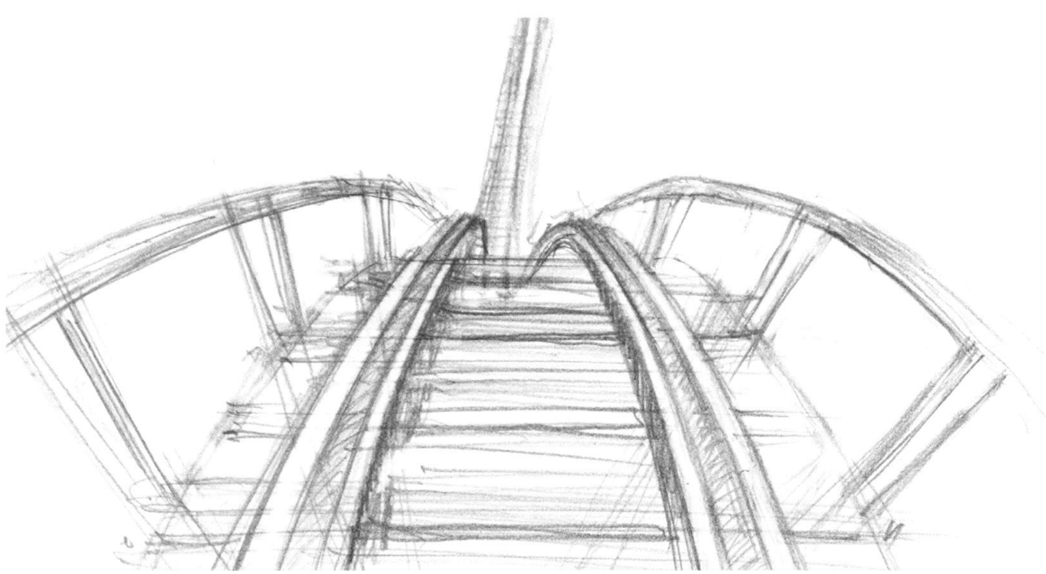

Using Curved Orthogonal Lines

Curved orthogonal lines of this track merge at a vanishing point that is also obscured by the track.

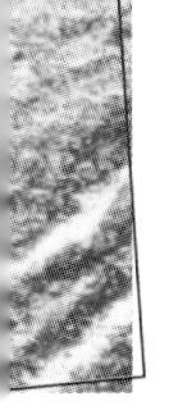

People

Though they may not be as obvious as they are with angular subjects, the principles of perspective also apply to people. The placement of the horizon correlates with the scene and where the people are in that scene.

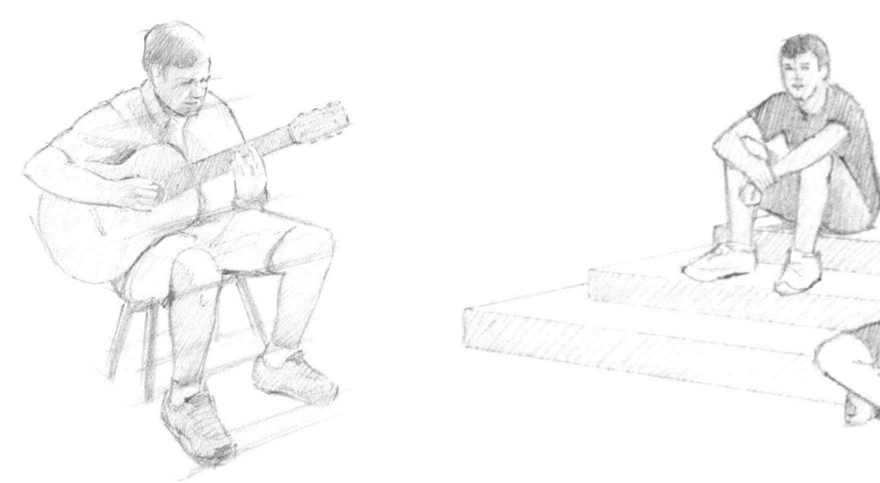

Putting People in Proper Perspective

People are bound to the same principles of perspective as other subjects. When drawing people the orthogonal lines visible with their surroundings are applicable and share the same perspective. Notice that the lines of the chair and steps in these drawings align with the knees, shoulders and other features. These lines are helpful when drawing people in perspective.

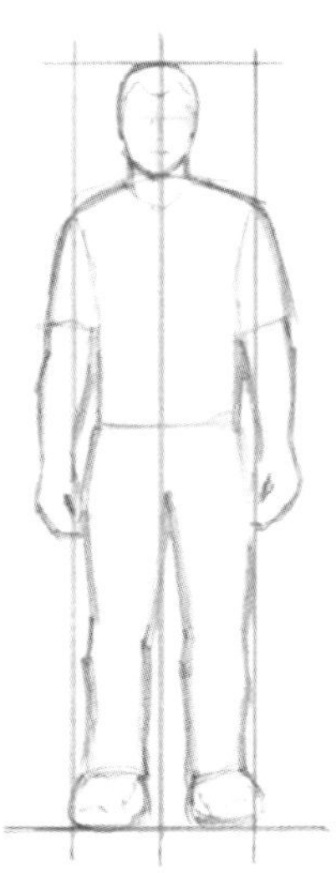

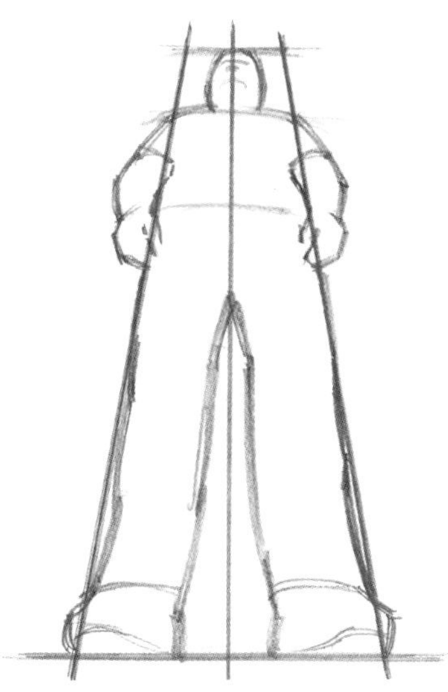

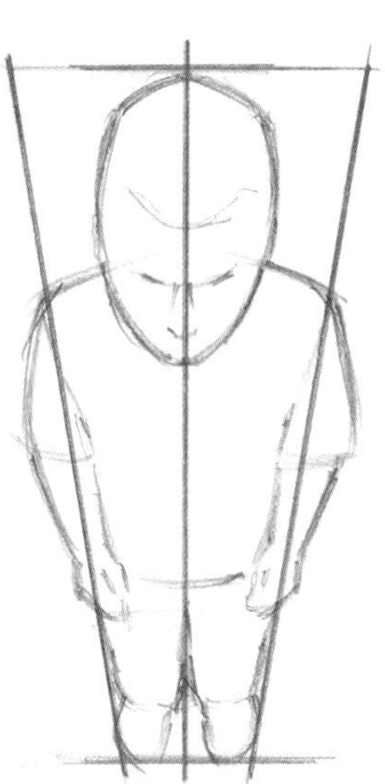

Looking Across, up and Down

When looking across at a person, perspective may not be noticeable. A person can be drawn in one-point perspective when the vantage point is changed to be looking up or down.

4 Let's Draw **Perspective**

The demonstrations for this chapter were designed to include all of the principles and techniques of perspective covered in previous chapters. Each demonstration begins by developing a structural sketch, which is traced or transferred onto drawing paper. The drawings are then completed through the application of values.

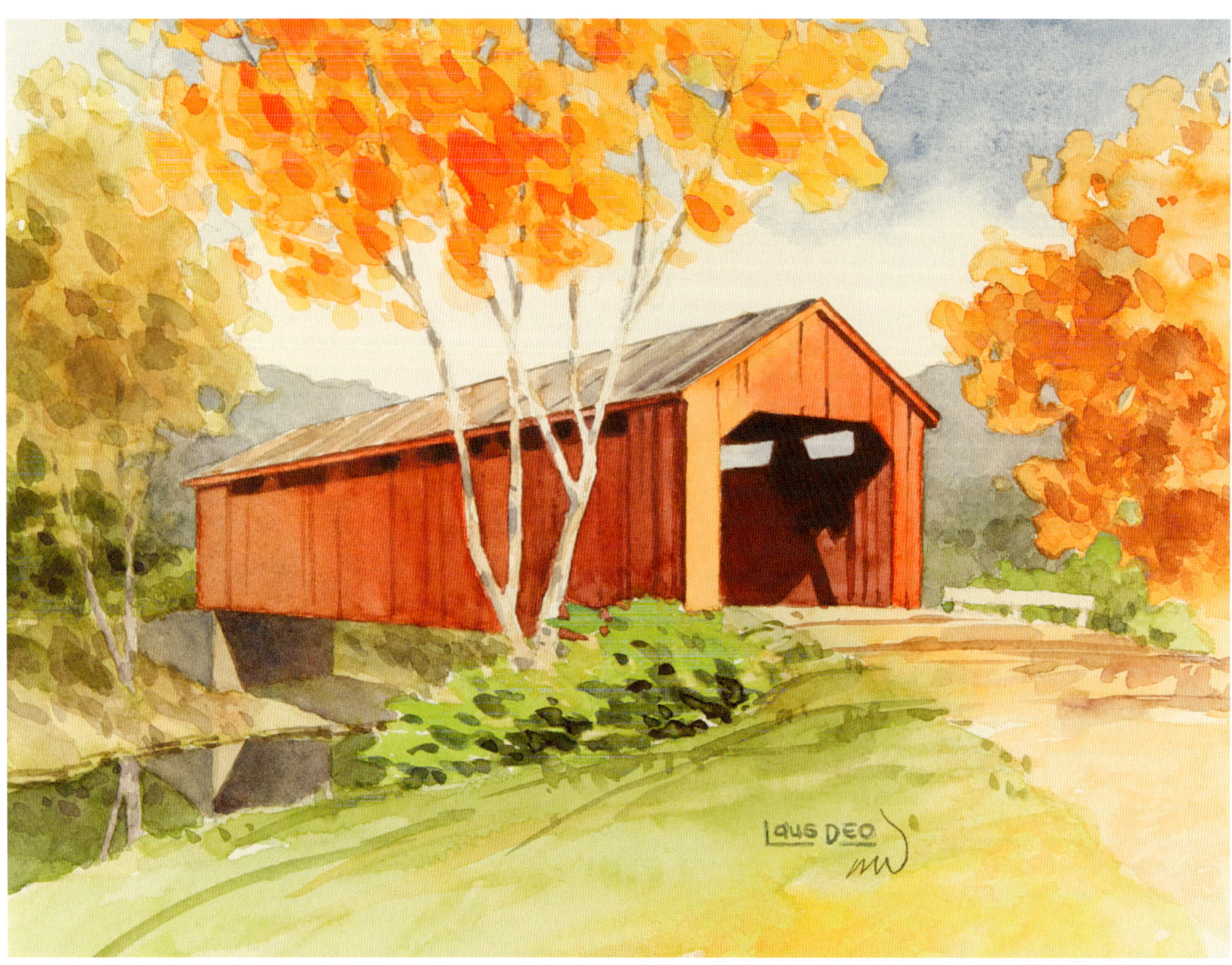

Covered Bridge
Watercolor on watercolor paper
8" × 10" (20cm × 25cm)

External Boxes

This demonstration involves sketching squares with lines that recede to a single vanishing point. The finished drawing of the box forms will appear in front of a dark background. The forward surfaces of the box forms will remain white. The sides will become darker as they recede into the distance, with the background being the darkest value of the drawing. The depth in this piece is implied through linear perspective and the use of values.

Materials

Paper
8" × 8" (20cm × 20cm) medium-texture drawing paper; 8" × 8" (20cm × 20cm) medium-texture sketch paper

Pencils
2B and 6B

Other
kneaded eraser; lightbox or transfer paper; ruler; triangle; T-square

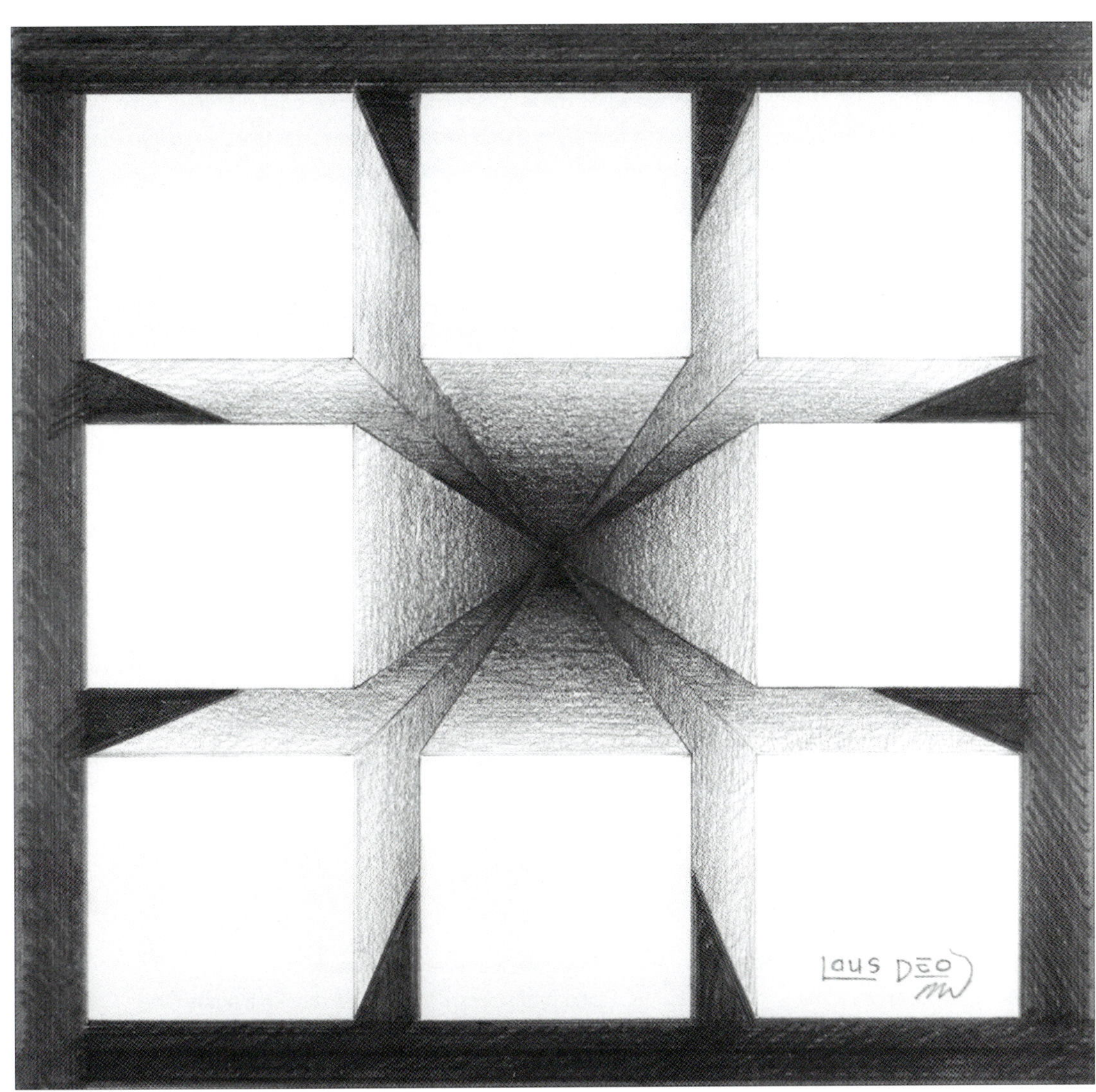

External Boxes
Graphite pencil on drawing paper
8" × 8"
(20cm × 20cm)

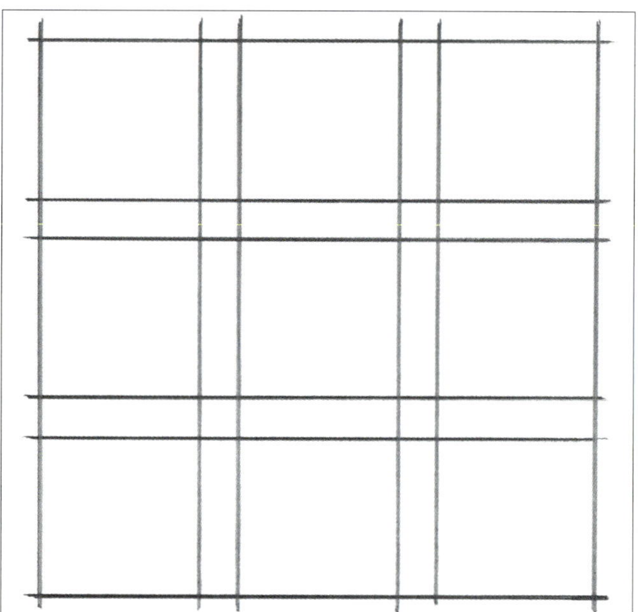

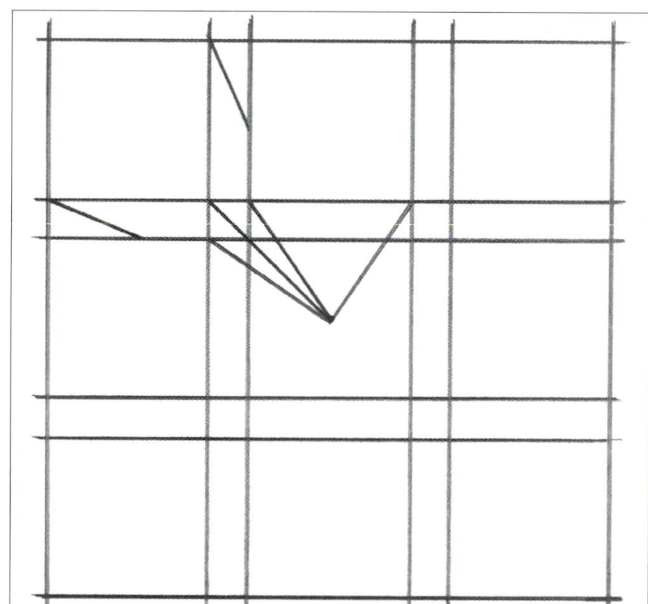

1 Sketch the Squares

On a piece of sketch paper, use a 2B pencil to form a large square that is 8"× 8" (20cm × 20cm). Sketch smaller squares inside the large square using a ruler to mark off the lines. The measurements should be the same from both top to bottom and left to right: ½", 2", ½", 2", ½", 2" (1.3cm, 5cm, 1.3cm, 5cm, 1.3cm, 5cm). Draw the lines using a T-square and triangle to ensure they are straight and accurate.

2 Add the Vanishing Point and Orthogonal Lines

Place a dot at the center of the paper for the vanishing point. Begin adding orthogonal lines from the corners of the squares to the vanishing point. Avoid sketching the lines over the squares except for the central squares, which will be omitted for the final drawing. Also, avoid sketching the orthogonal lines that will be hidden in the final drawing. Adding these would make the sketch more confusing.

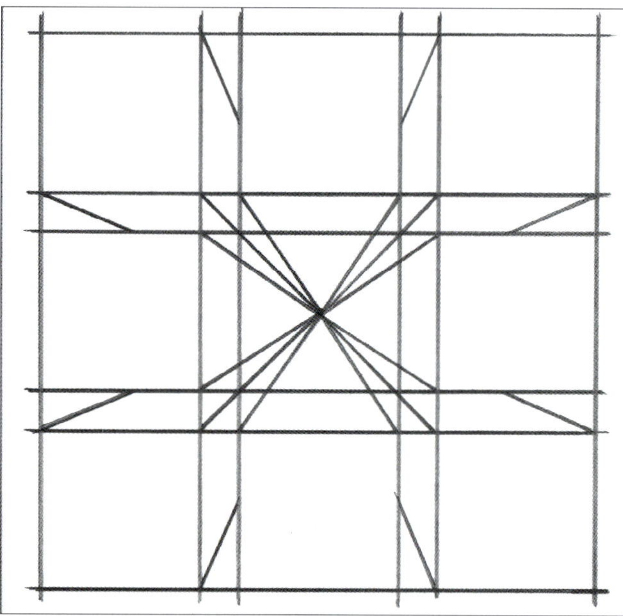

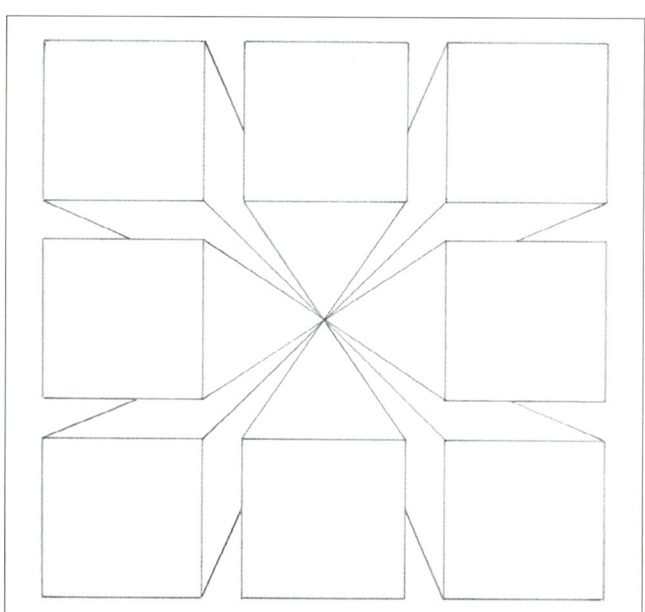

3 Add More Orthogonal Lines

Continue adding the lines that converge at the vanishing point.

4 Trace or Transfer the Image

Use a 2B pencil to lightly trace or transfer the structural sketch onto a sheet of 8"× 8" (20cm × 20cm) drawing paper. Leave out any unwanted lines.

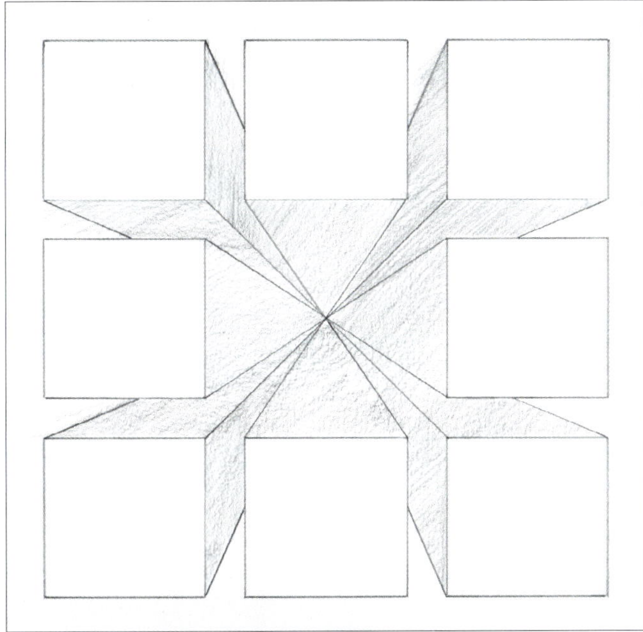

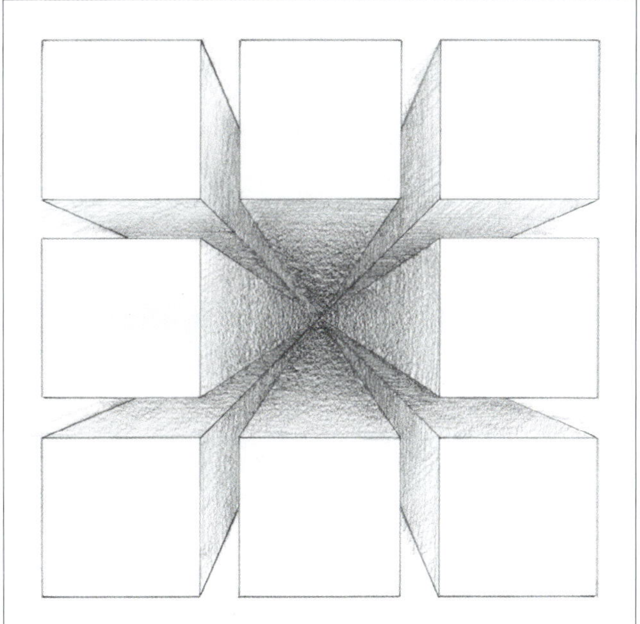

5 Add the Light Values

Add the lighter values with a 2B pencil. The forward surface of the forms should remain the white of the paper.

Add the Middle Values

Add the middle values. Gradually darken them as they recede into the distance.

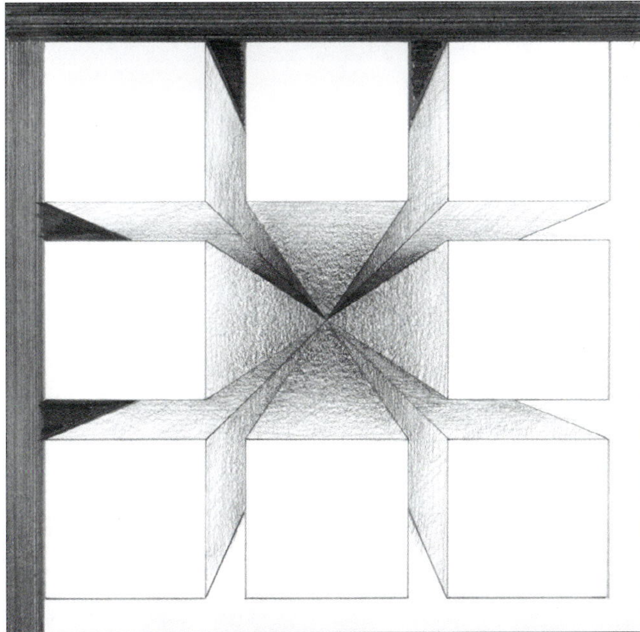

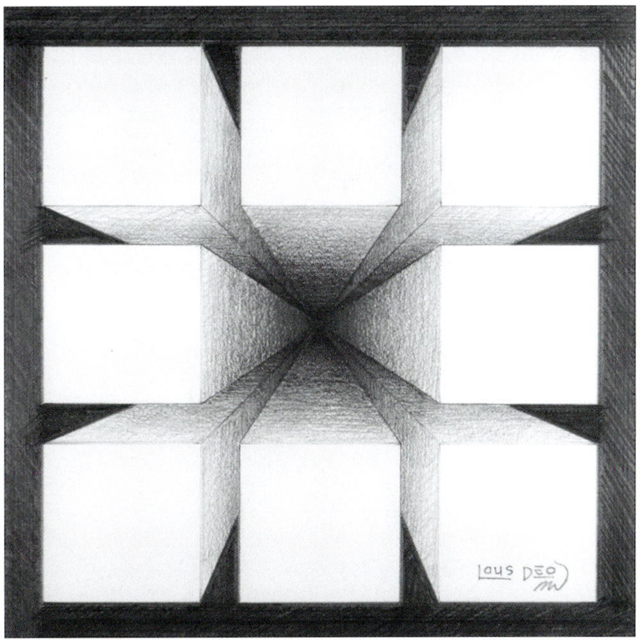

7 Add the Dark Values

Begin adding the dark values with a 6B pencil. The outer perimeter can be darkened. Use a T-square to make a series of straight lines.

8 Add More Darks

Continue adding darks and details with 2B and 6B pencils. If needed, lighten any areas with a kneaded eraser. Sign the front and write the date on the back of the drawing.

Internal Boxes

Both the Internal Boxes and External Boxes demonstrations share similar grid patterns for the structural sketch, and both use one-point perspective and values to express depth. The main difference is that this exercise views internal forms rather than external forms.

Materials

Paper
8" × 8" (20cm × 20cm) medium-texture drawing paper; 8" × 8" (20cm × 20cm) medium-texture sketch paper

Pencils
2B and 4B

Other
kneaded eraser; lightbox or transfer paper; ruler; triangle; T-square

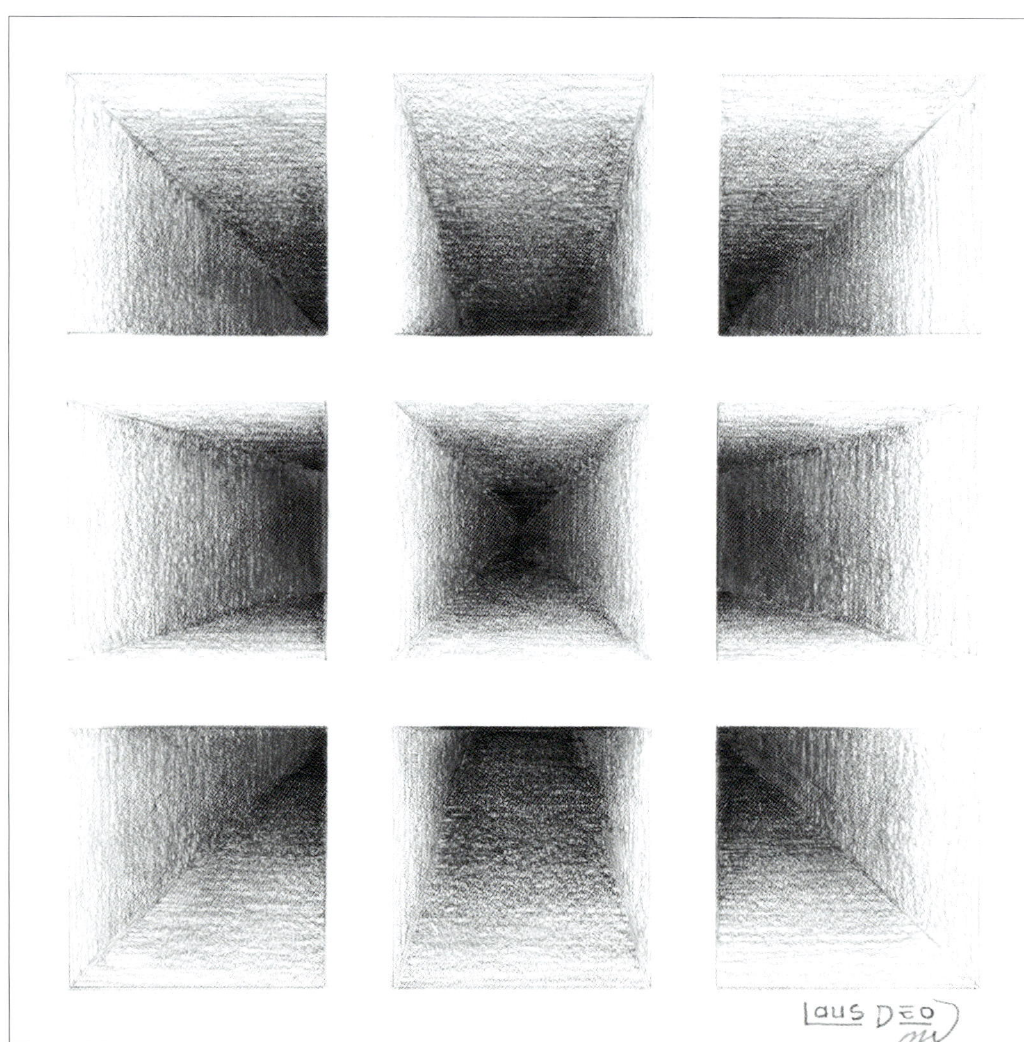

Internal Boxes
Graphite pencil on drawing paper
8" × 8"
(20cm × 20cm)

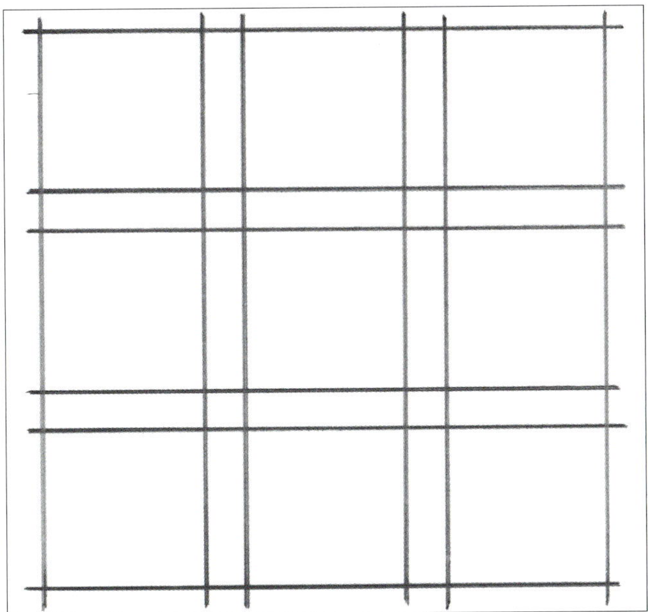

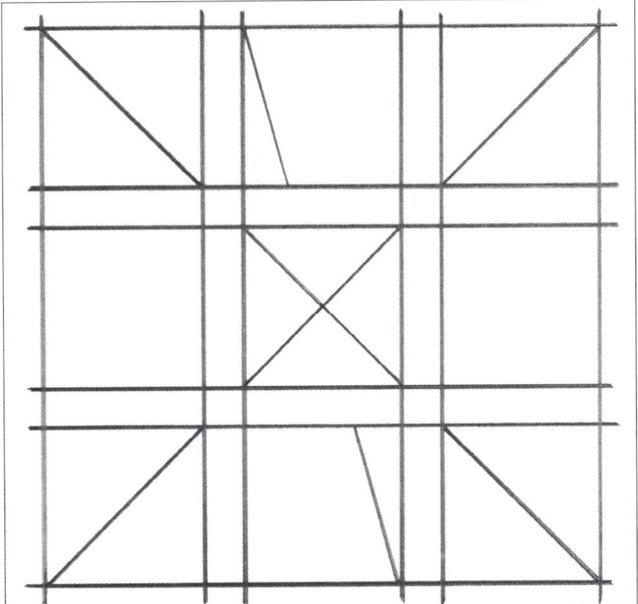

1 **Sketch the Squares**
On a piece of sketch paper, use a 2B pencil to form a large square that is 8"× 8" (20cm × 20cm). Sketch smaller squares inside the large square using a ruler to mark off the lines. The measurements should be the same from both top to bottom and left to right: ½", 2", ½", 2", ½", 2" (1.3cm, 5cm, 1.3cm, 5cm, 1.3cm, 5cm). Draw the lines using a T-square and triangle to ensure they are straight and accurate.

2 **Add the Vanishing Point and Orthogonal Lines**
Place a dot at the center of the paper for the vanishing point. Begin adding orthogonal lines from the corners of the squares to the vanishing point. Avoid sketching the lines over the forward surface that is to remain white.

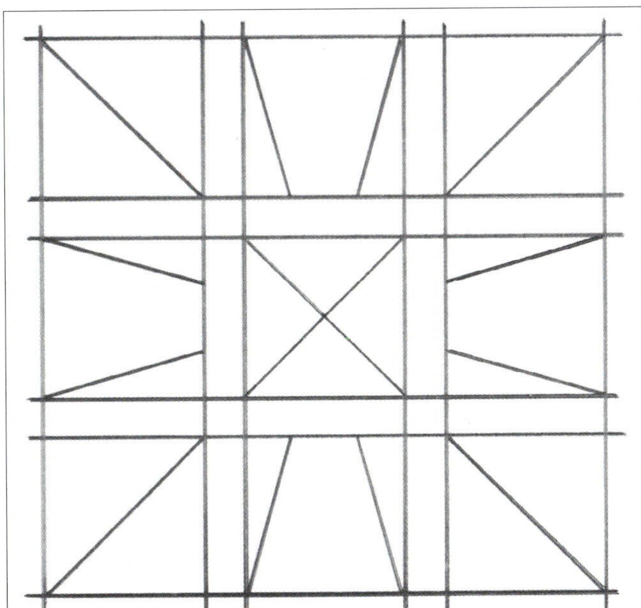

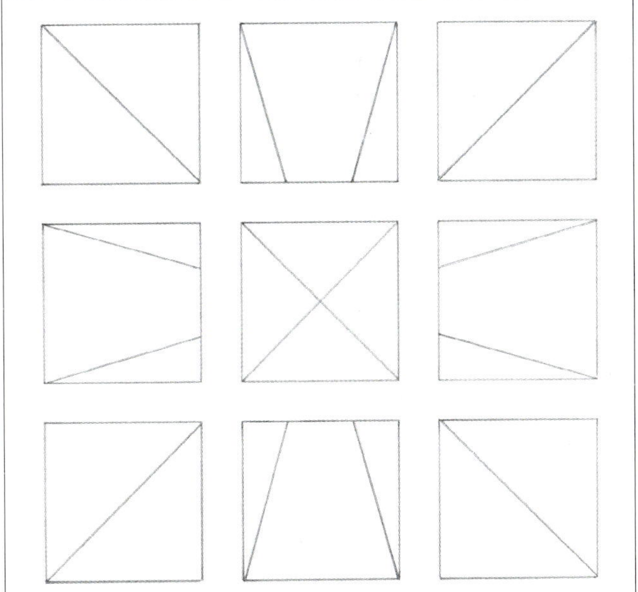

3 **Add More Orthogonal Lines**
Continue adding lines that converge at the vanishing point.

4 **Trace or Transfer the Image**
Use a 2B pencil to lightly trace or transfer the structural sketch onto a sheet of 8"× 8" (20cm × 20cm) drawing paper. Leave out any unwanted lines.

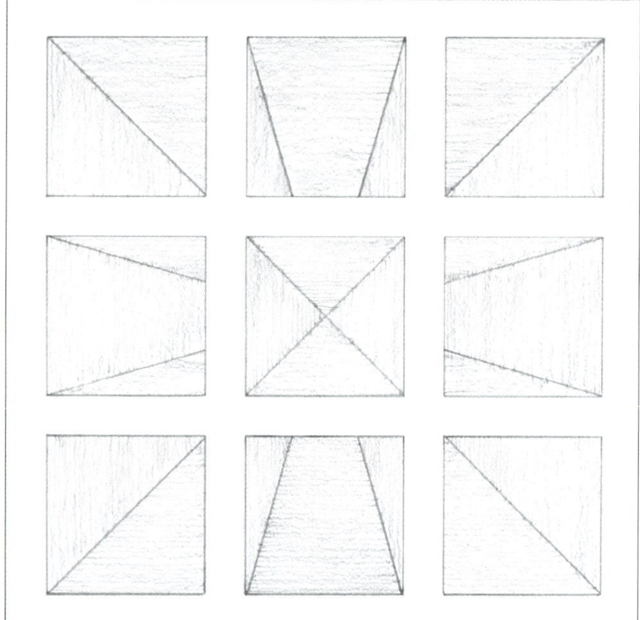

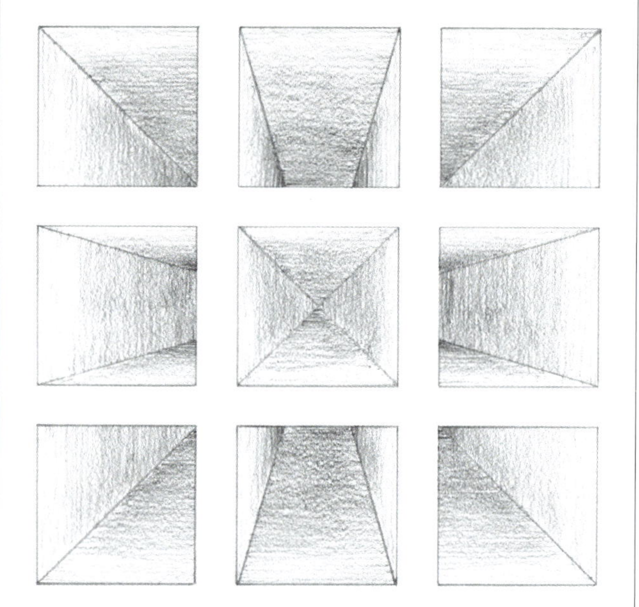

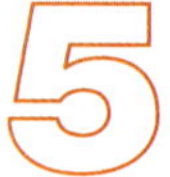

Add the Light Values

Add the lighter values with a 2B pencil. Make the values darker as the internal forms recede.

Add the Middle Values

Add the middle values. Continue to darken the tunnel like forms as they recede into the distance.

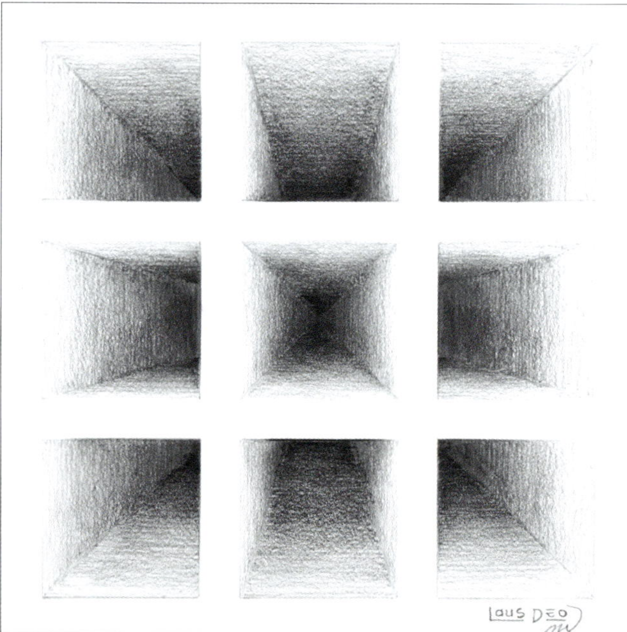

7 Add the Dark Values

Add more darks and details with 2B and 4B pencils. Lighten any areas with a kneaded eraser if needed. Sign the front and write the date on the back of the drawing.

Don't Forget to Sign Your Work!

Because your artwork is a unique expression of yourself, sign and date each drawing. This will give you a sense of accomplishment and also help you to track the progression of your artistic skills.

Roller Coaster

Capture the thrill of your favorite wooden roller coaster with this demonstration. Whereas railroad tracks usually rest flat on a ground plane, roller coaster tracks go up and down, giving the receding orthogonal lines a curved appearance.

This scene uses three vanishing points. The first is the convergence of the downhill slope track. The second is formed by continuing the lines of the railing posts below the track. The third vanishing point is formed by the convergence of the distant rail ties as the track curves up and around. The light source comes from the upper left, which affects only the roller coaster, not the background.

Tilting the drawing will add a sense of drama to the scene. You may find it easier to draw the foreground track straight upright on the paper, then tilt the image when you're farther along in the process.

Materials

Paper
5¾" × 7½" (15cm × 19cm) medium-texture drawing paper; 9" × 12" (23cm × 30cm) medium-texture sketch paper

Pencils
2B and 6B

Other
kneaded eraser; lightbox or transfer paper; ruler; triangle; T-square

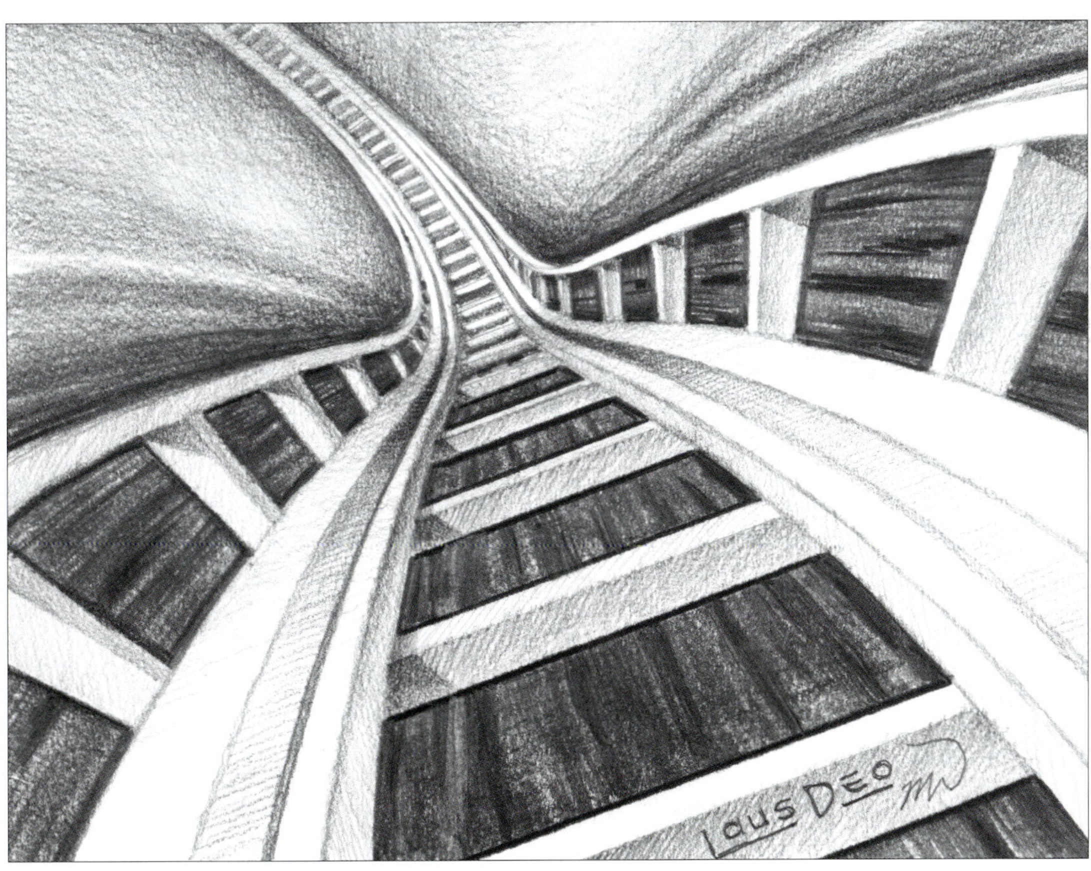

Roller Coaster Thrills
Graphite pencil on drawing paper
5¾" × 7½" (15cm × 19cm)

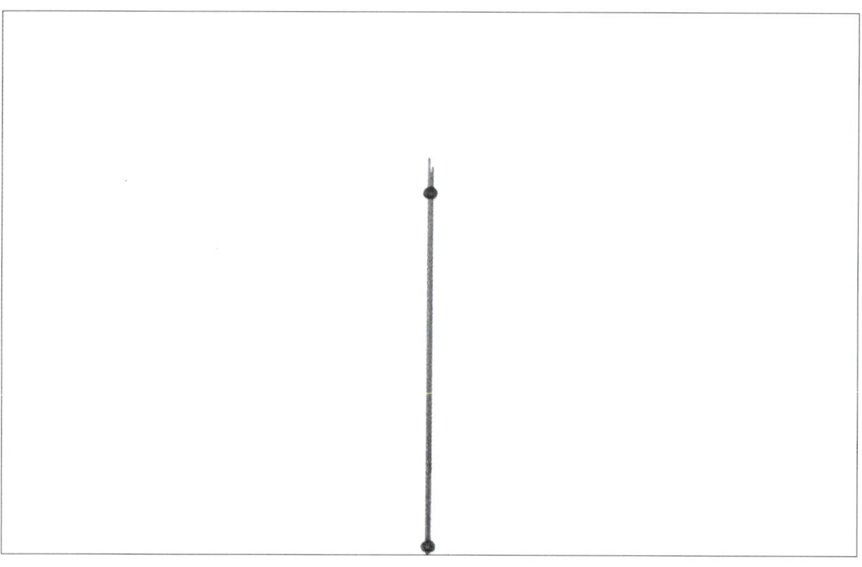

1 Sketch the First Two Vanishing Points

Use a 2B pencil to place the first vanishing point for the foreground track and railing slightly above the center on a piece of sketch paper. Sketch a vertical line down from the vanishing point to the bottom of the paper and add the second vanishing point. This vanishing point will be used to construct the railing.

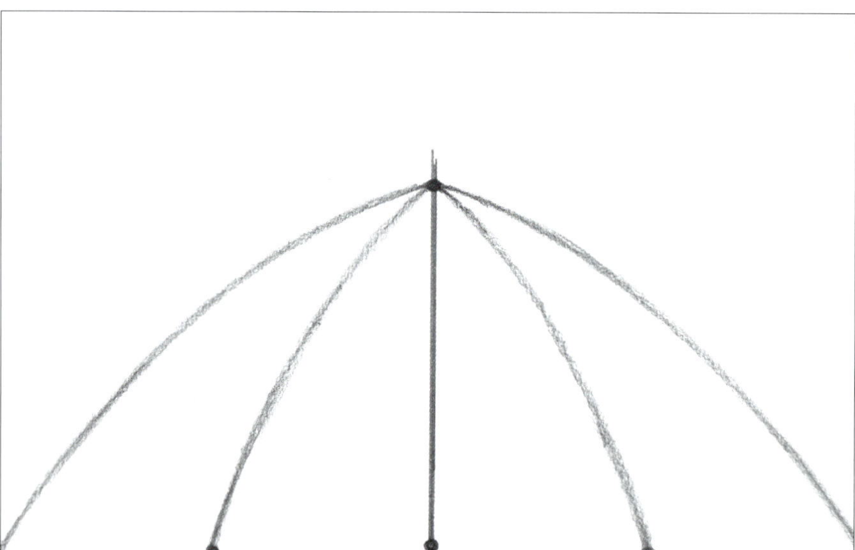

2 Add Two Line Points and Orthogonal Lines

Add two points at the bottom edge of the paper to place the receding track lines. Center one point between the left edge of the paper and the lower vanishing point. Center the other point between the right edge of the paper and the lower vanishing point.

Sketch curved orthogonal lines from these points to the center vanishing point along with curved orthogonal lines from the lower corners of the paper.

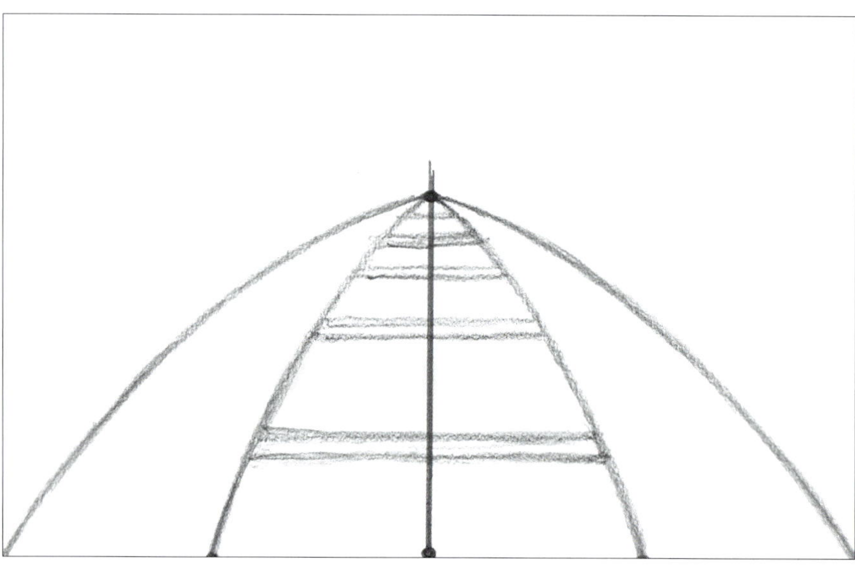

3 Add Lines for the Ties

Add horizontal lines for the tops of the ties. The distance between the sets of lines should diminish as they get closer to the center vanishing point.

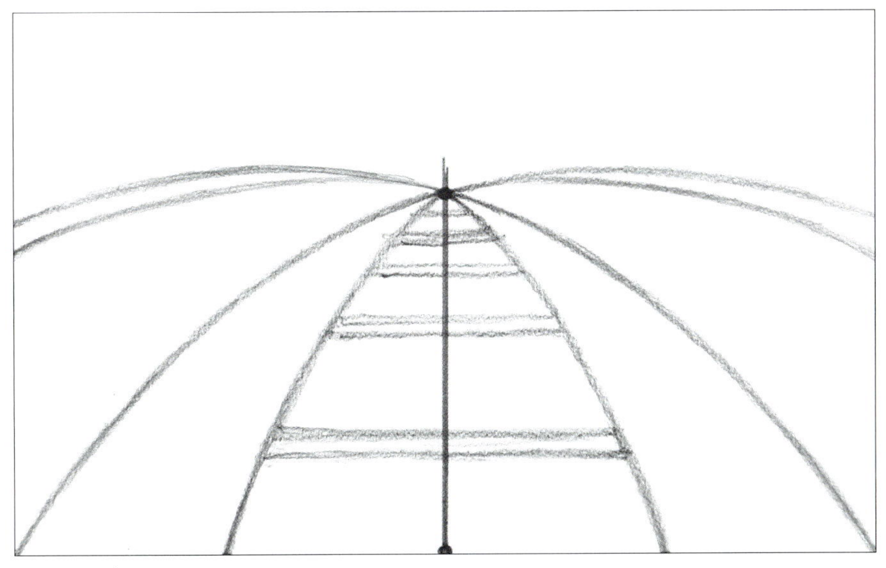

4 Add Side Railings

Add railings on the sides of the track. Sketch two curved orthogonal lines on the left and two curved orthogonal lines on the right that connect the sides of the paper to the center vanishing point. As you progress through this sketch, keep the foreground track and railing symmetrical.

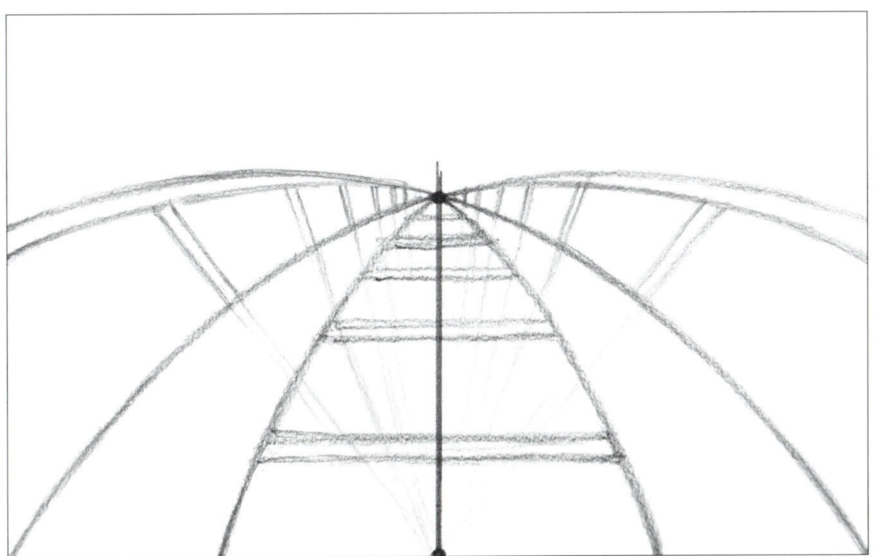

5 Add Side Railing Posts

Add orthogonal lines for the side railing posts that converge at the lower vanishing point. The lines should be placed in sets of two; the distance between each set diminishes as they get closer to the center vanishing point.

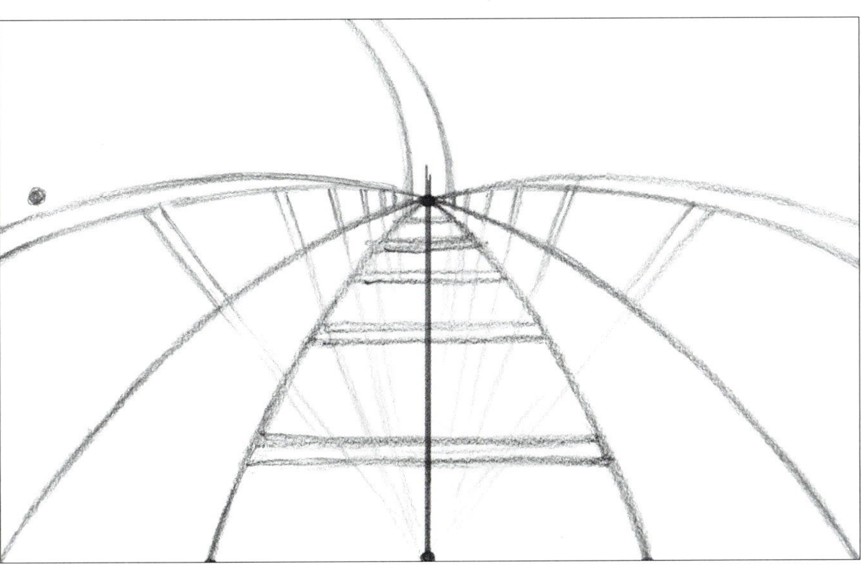

6 Add the Distant Track and Vanishing Point

Sketch two curved lines for the distant tracks that get closer as they go farther up. Place a vanishing point at the far left. This will be used when sketching the distant track ties.

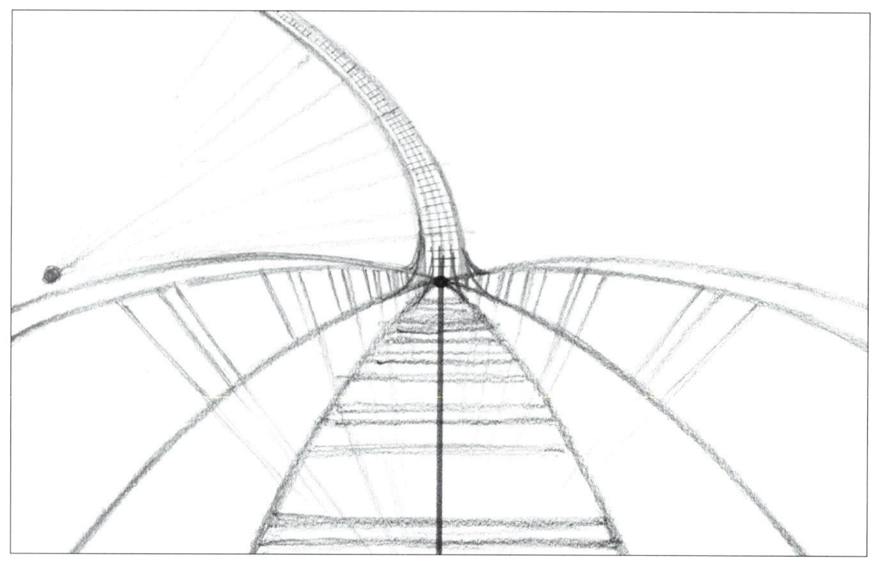

7 Add the Track and Track Ties, Connect the Tracks

Add orthogonal lines that converge at the far left vanishing point for the distant track ties. Add lines to add depth to the foreground track ties and the railing posts. Add curved lines to connect the foreground track and railing to the distant track and railing.

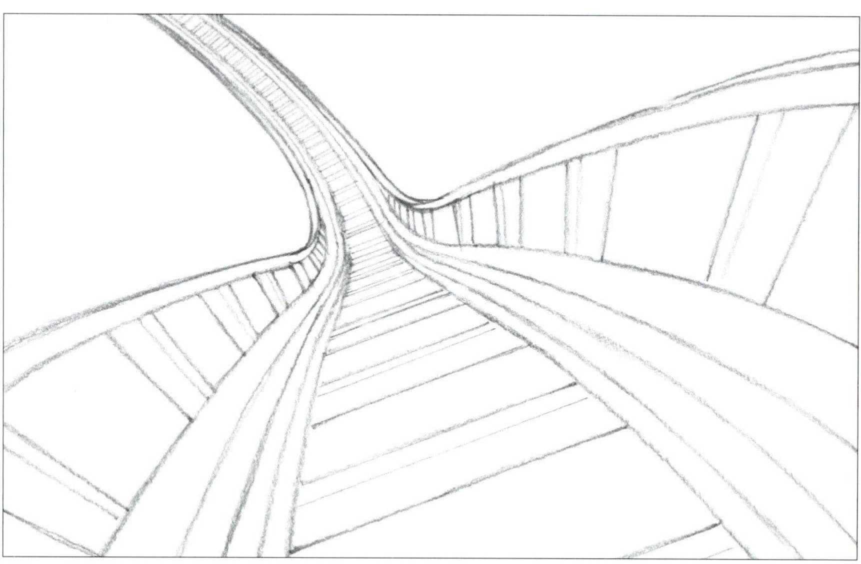

8 Trace or Transfer the Image

Use a 2B pencil to lightly trace or transfer the structural sketch onto a sheet of drawing paper. Leave out any unwanted lines. Add extra track lines. The image can be cropped and tilted to enhance the appearance.

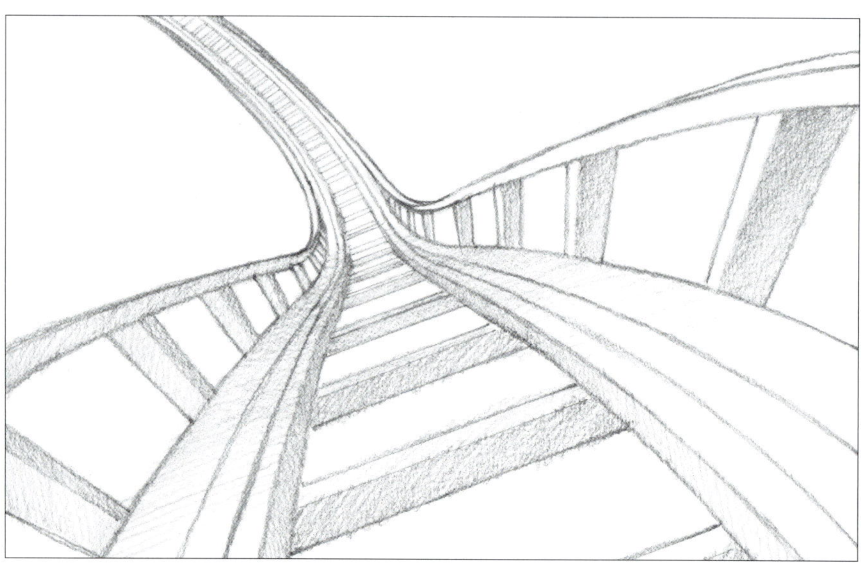

9 Add Values

Add the light and middle values of the track and railing using a 2B pencil.

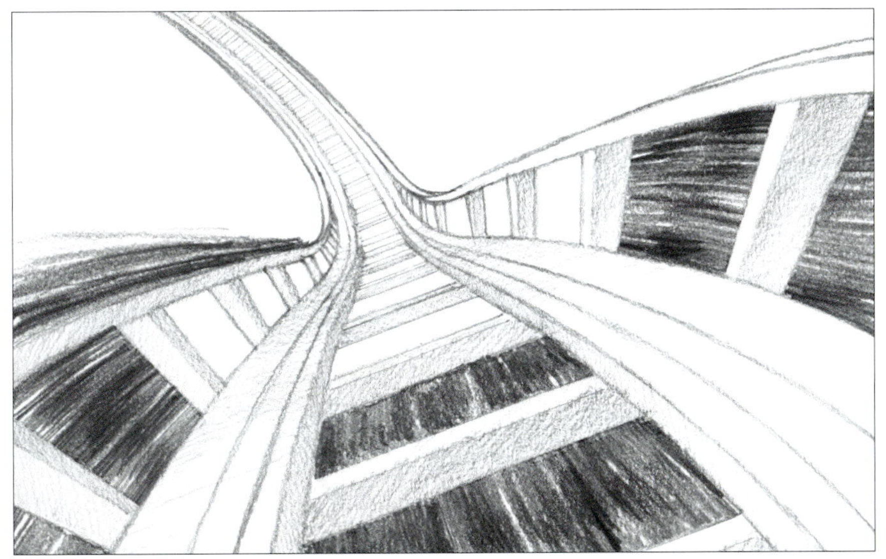

10 Add Value to the Background

Start adding values to the background, still using the 2B pencil. Direct the pencil strokes around the track and railing to the central vanishing point to give a sense of motion.

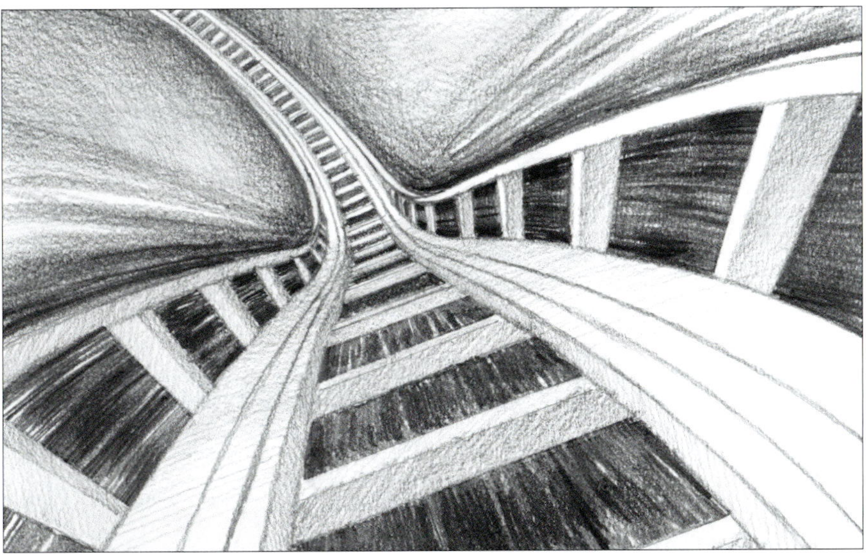

11 Continue Adding Background Values

Continue adding values to the background. The background behind and around the distant track should have less contrast than the background behind the foreground track and railing.

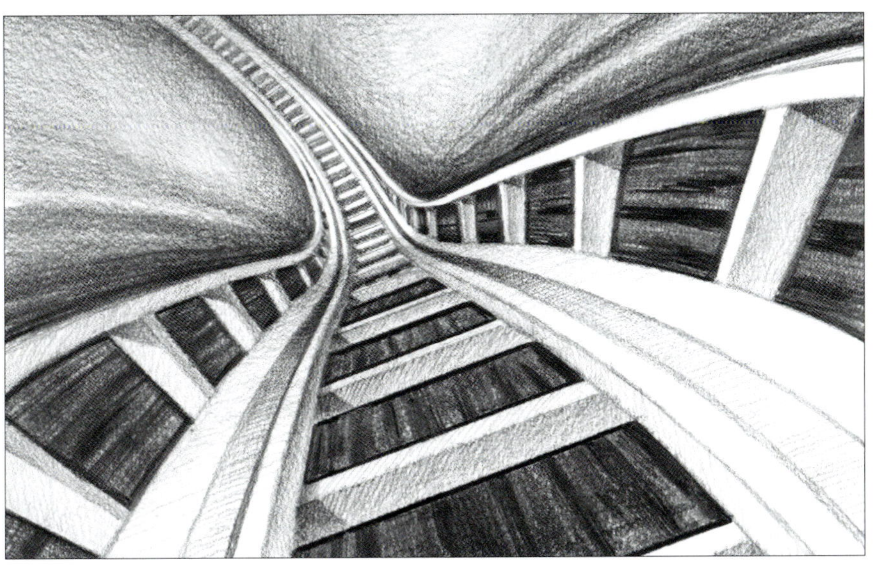

12 Add Details and Make Adjustments

Add details and darks with 2B and 6B pencils. Use a kneaded eraser to lighten any areas if needed. Sign the front and write the date on the back of the drawing.

Covered Bridge

Covered bridges can still be found in parts of the United States. Their nostalgic presence goes back to a time before motor cars, when life moved at a slower pace.

The light source in this scene comes from the upper right, causing the right side of the bridge to appear lighter than the left side. These highly contrasting values enhance the depth of the scene.

The reference photo used for this subject worked well for the structure, but the lighting and shadows needed improvement. Rather than taking new reference photos to study lighting and shadows, we formed a cardboard box similar in shape to the covered bridge and observed the effects of light and shadow. The study from the model was used along with the reference photo for this demonstration.

Consider using a value scale for this demonstration as well as the others. A value scale is a cardboard strip displaying a range of values. It is used to compare values in order to make the best use of lights and darks.

Materials

Paper
19" × 24" (48cm × 61cm) medium-texture drawing paper; 19" × 24" (48cm × 61cm) medium-texture sketch paper

Pencils
2B and 6B

Other
kneaded eraser; lightbox or transfer paper; ruler; triangle

Optional
value scale

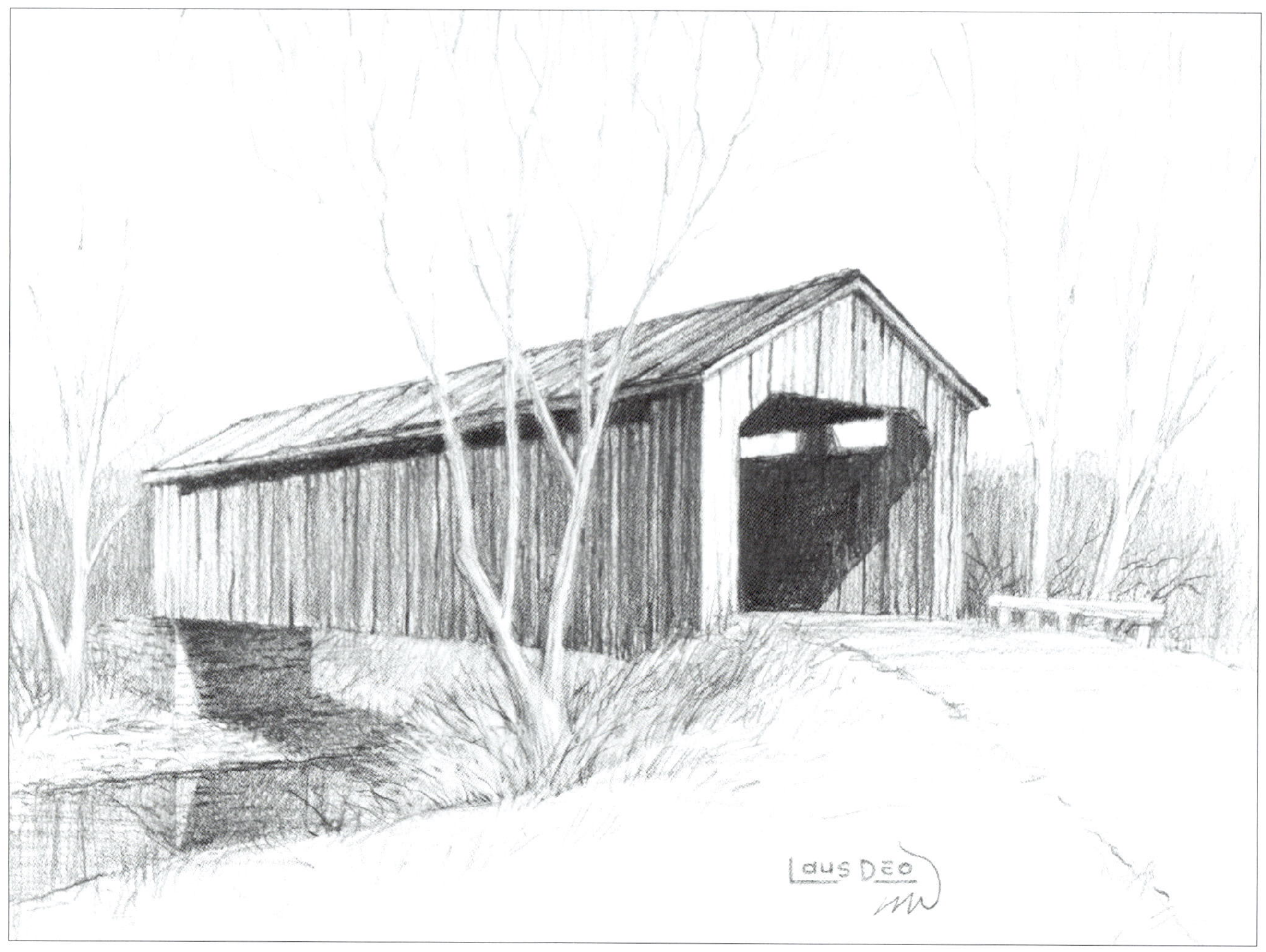

Covered Bridge
Graphite pencil on drawing paper
8" × 10" (20cm × 25cm)

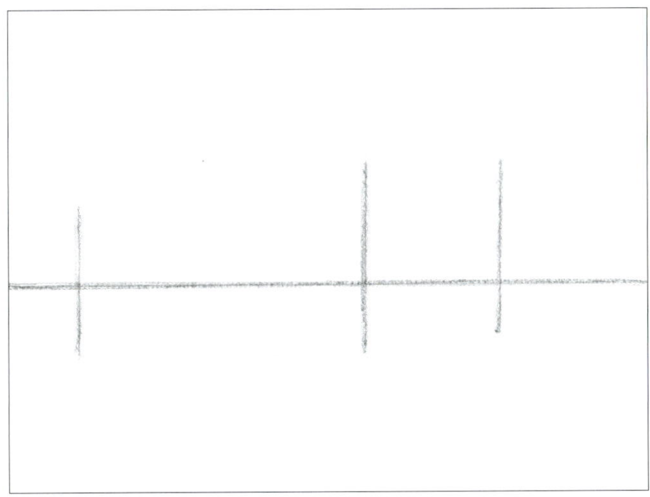

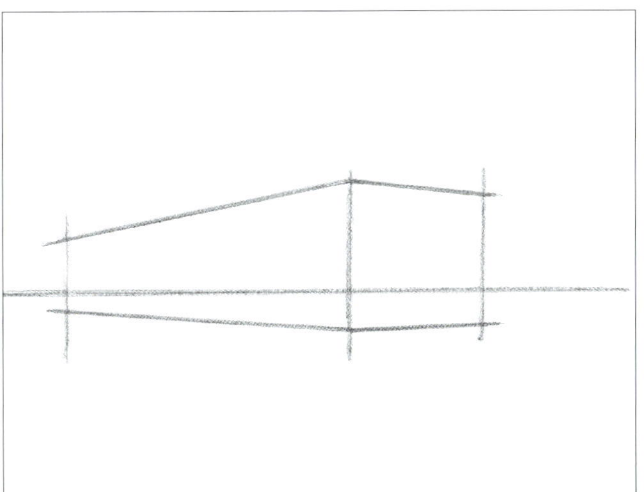

1 Sketch the Horizon, Front, Left and Right Corners

Use a 2B pencil to place a horizon line just below the center on a piece of sketch paper. Sketch a vertical line 8¾" (22cm) from the left edge of the paper as the front corner. Sketch a vertical line at the far left of the left corner (4⅜" [11cm] left of the front corner) and a vertical line on the right (2" [5cm] to the right of the front corner) as the right corner. (Although vanishing points were used to create the structural sketch, they were cropped out in order to show the images as large as possible.)

2 Sketch the Box Form

Sketch orthogonal lines from the front corner to the vanishing points on the horizon to form the sides of the box. The left vanishing point is 8¼" (22cm) left of the front corner. The right vanishing point is 15¼" (39cm) right of the front corner. The upper orthogonal lines meet the front corner 1¾" (4cm) above the horizon. The lower orthogonal lines meet the front corner ⅝" (16mm) below the horizon.

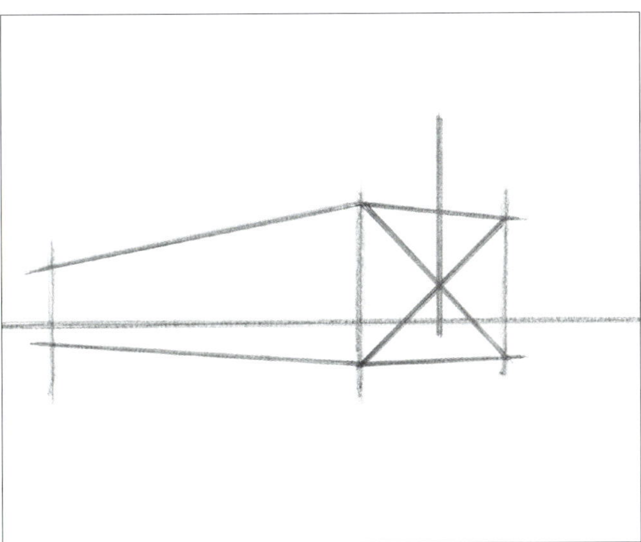

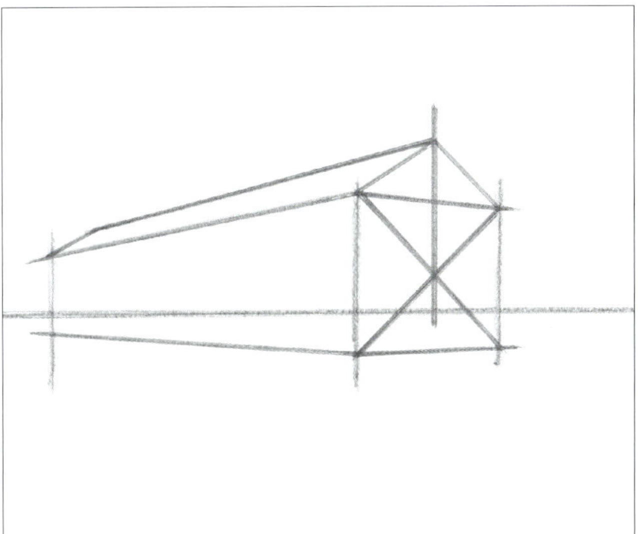

3 Establish the Centerline for the Right Side

Sketch an X on the right side of the box by connecting the opposing corners. Sketch a vertical line through and up from the center of the X as the centerline.

4 Add the Roof

Sketch lines connecting the centerline with the top right corners of the box to form the front roof peak. Sketch an orthogonal line from the front roof peak to the left vanishing point to form the roof ridge. To complete the roof, add a diagonal line connecting the roof peak to the top left corner of the box.

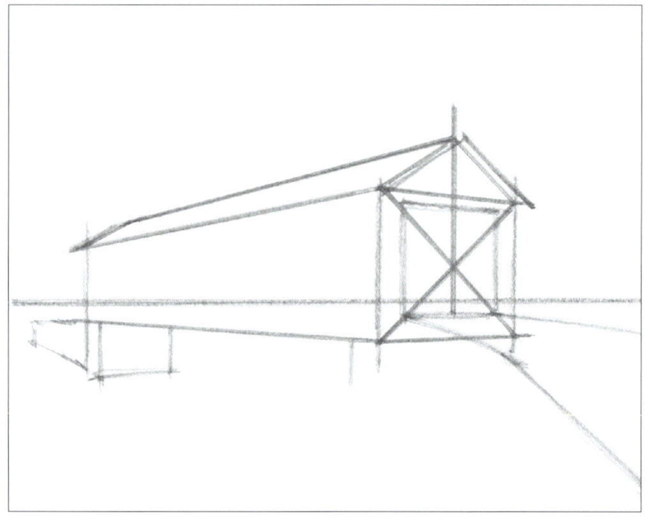

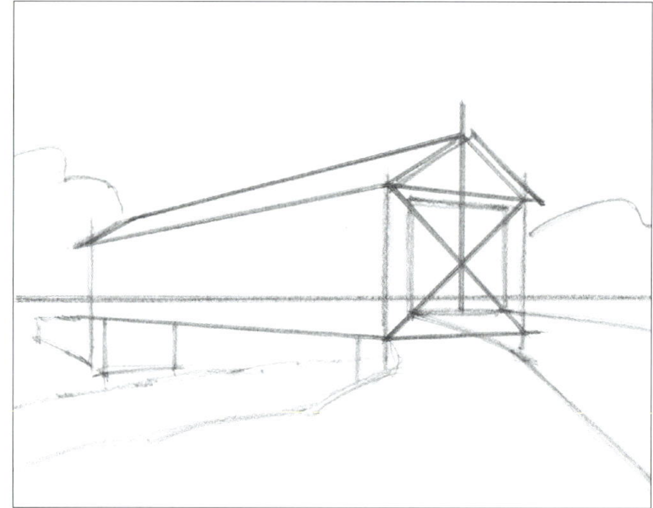

5 Develop the Form of the Bridge

Sketch the opening on the right side of the bridge. Add the road coming out off the right side of the bridge. Leave some space under the road as the lower structure. Extend the edges of the roof and add the stone foundation to both ends of the bridge.

6 Sketch the Scene Around the Bridge

Sketch the turf in front of the bridge. Then sketch the creek under the bridge. Block in the forms of the distant trees.

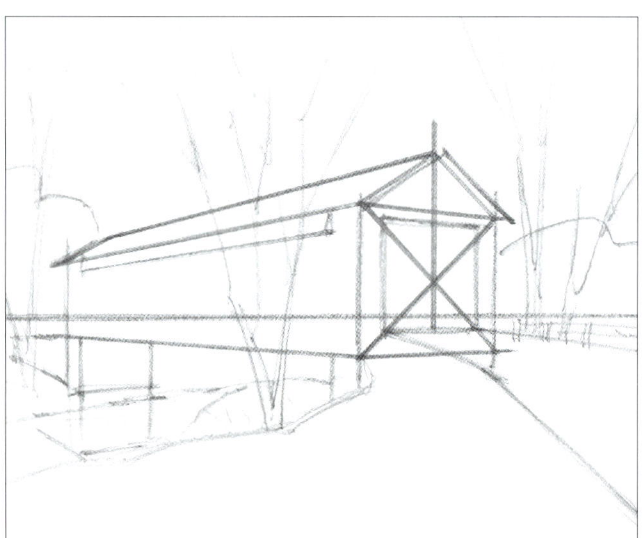

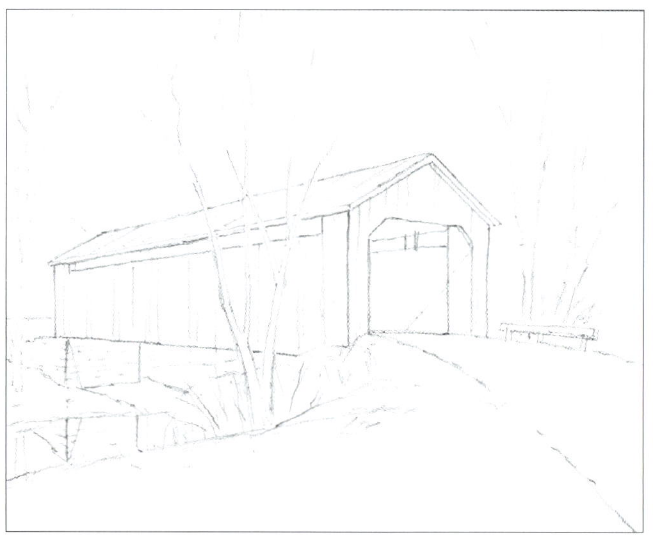

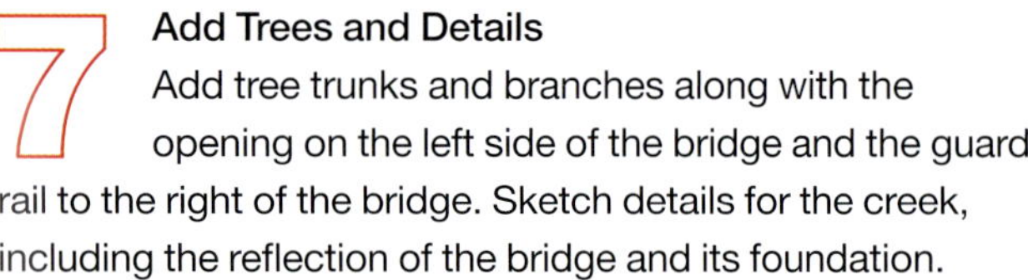

7 Add Trees and Details

Add tree trunks and branches along with the opening on the left side of the bridge and the guard rail to the right of the bridge. Sketch details for the creek, including the reflection of the bridge and its foundation.

8 Trace or Transfer the Image and Continue Adding Details

Use a 2B pencil to lightly trace or transfer the structural sketch onto a sheet of drawing paper. Leave out any unwanted lines. Add more structural details to the overall scene.

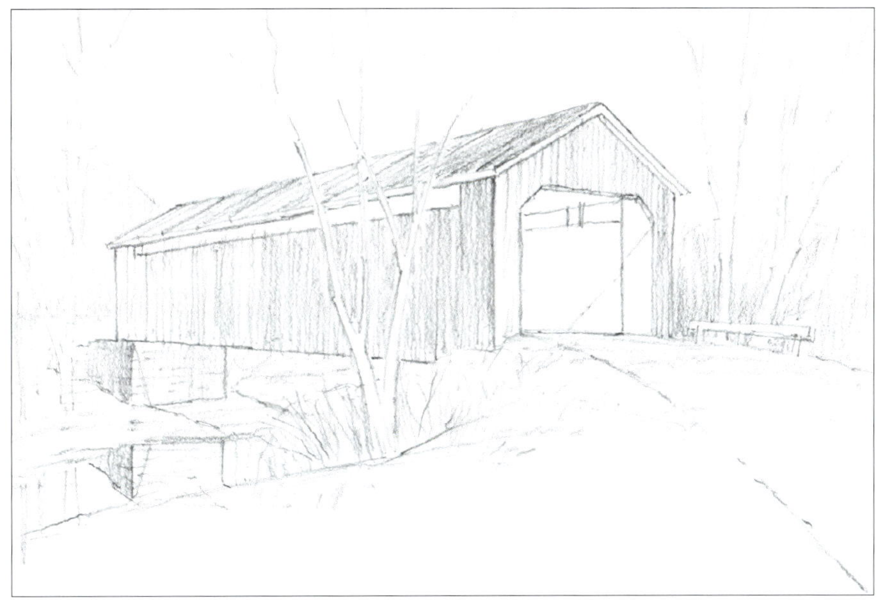

9 Add the Light and Middle Values

Add the light and middle values to the scene using a 2B pencil. Some of the tree trunks and branches should be left white to contrast against their background.

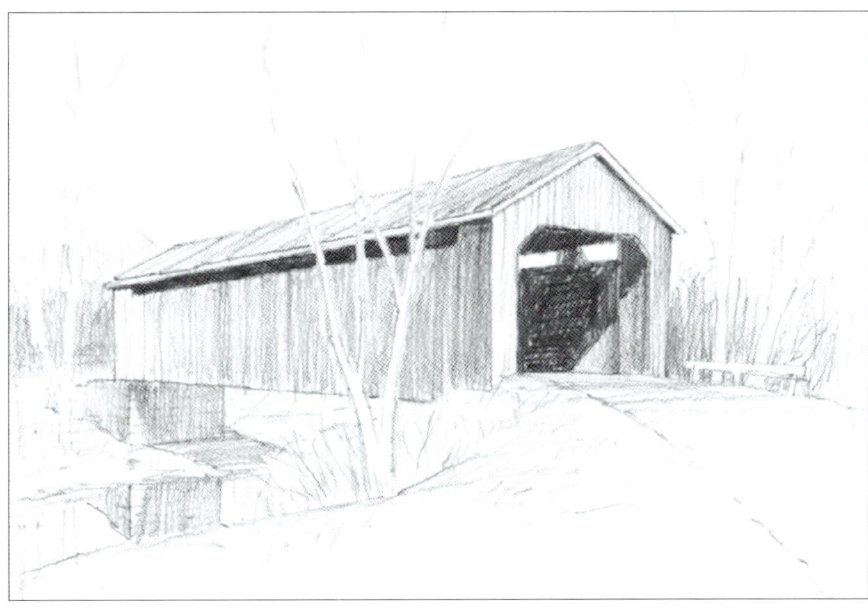

10 Darken the Values

Darken the values by building up the pencil strokes. You may wish to use a value scale for this part of the process.

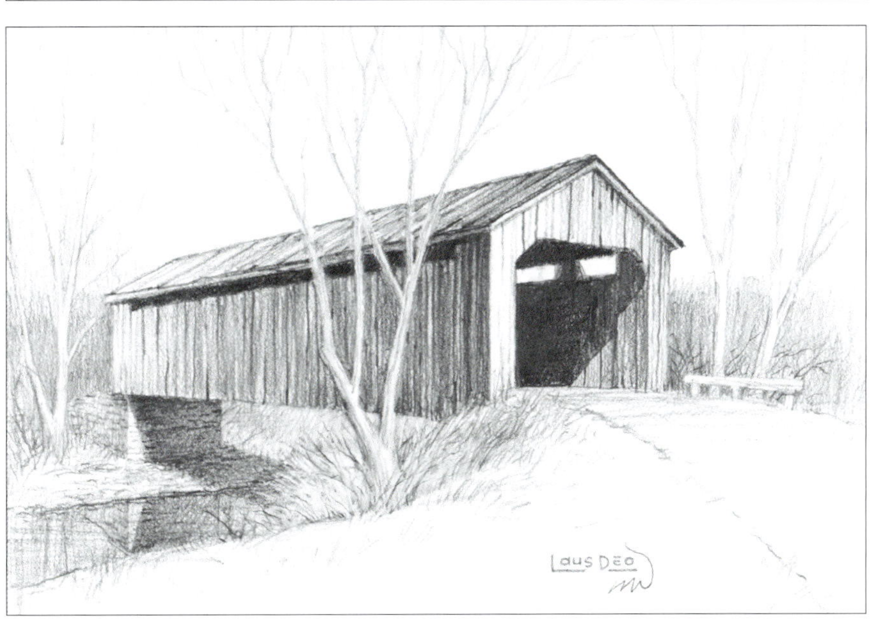

11 Continue Adding Dark Values and Details

With 2B and 6B pencils, continue adding darks and details. Make adjustments as needed by lightening some areas with a kneaded eraser. Sign the front of your drawing and write the date on the back.

A painted version of this subject appears on the first page of this chapter. It utilizes both linear and atmospheric perspectives together with color to suggest depth.

Reflections on a Spoon

This demonstration uses a large spoon to study the perspective of an image distorted by a convex reflecting surface. Straight lines will appear curved because of the round, outward form of the spoon. The finished drawing is cut out and mounted on dark gray construction paper. As an alternative to using construction paper, the background can be shaded in graphite, but this process may be tedious because of the large surface area.

Materials

Paper
12" × 9" (30cm × 23cm) 80-lb. (170gsm) dark gray construction paper; 12" × 9" (30cm × 23cm) medium-texture drawing paper; 12" × 9" (30cm × 23cm) medium-texture sketch paper

Pencils
2B and 6B

Other
craft knife; double-sided tape; heavy cardboard sheet; kneaded eraser; large highly reflective spoon; lightbox or transfer paper; straightedge

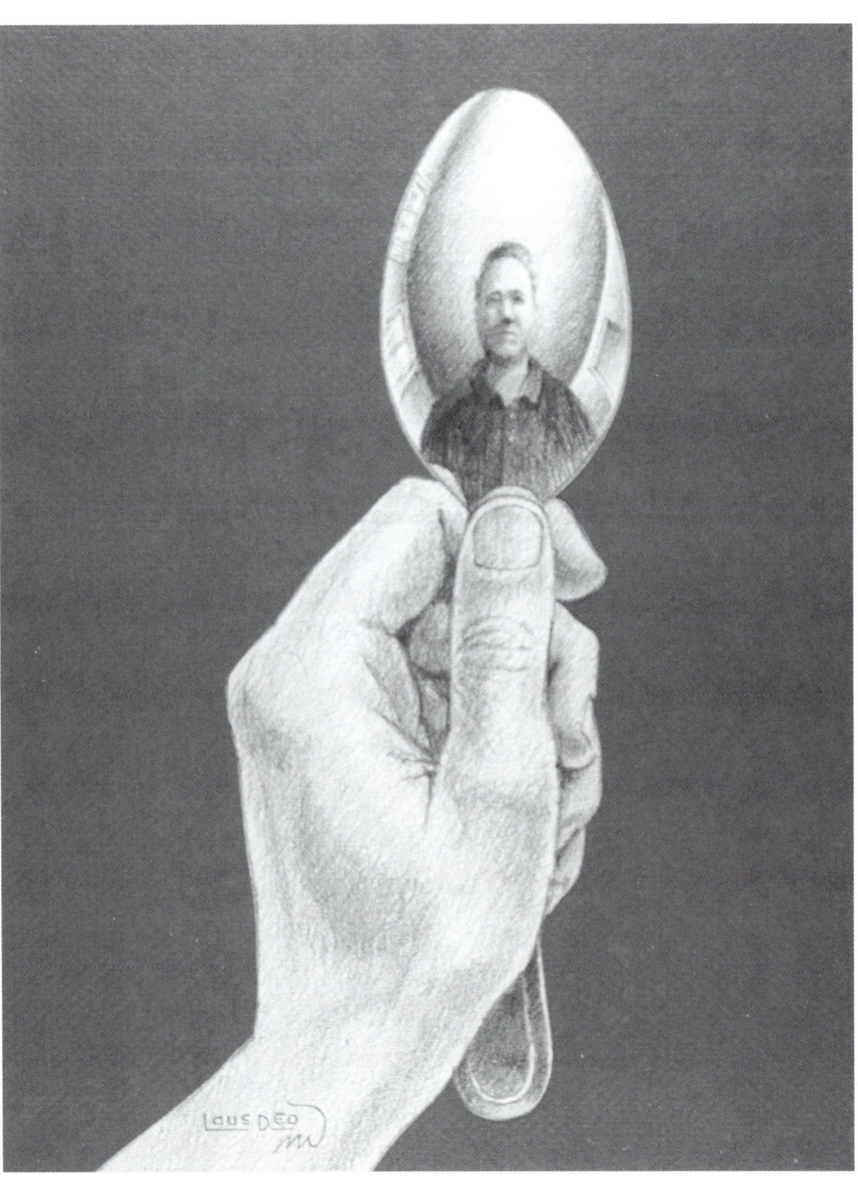

Spoon Reflections
Graphite pencil on drawing paper with construction paper
12" × 9" (30cm × 23cm)

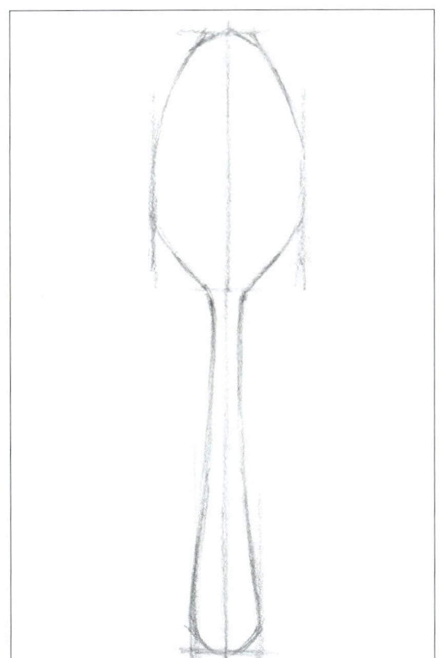

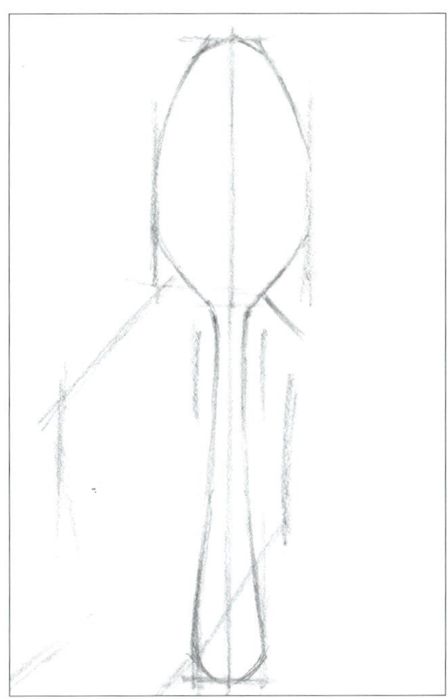

1 Sketch the Form
Using a 2B pencil, block in the outer form of the spoon on a piece of sketch paper. Sketch a vertical line from top to bottom to keep the shape symmetrical. This is the beginning of the structural sketch.

2 Develop the Spoon Shape
Continue sketching to develop the outer shape of the spoon. The paper can be folded along the vertical line, and the side images compared or traced to ensure symmetry. Include the handle that will be hidden from view. This will allow for the proper placement of the spoon handle.

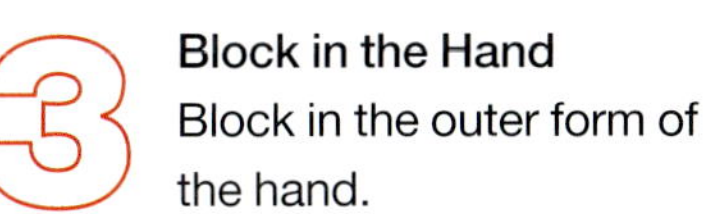

3 Block in the Hand
Block in the outer form of the hand.

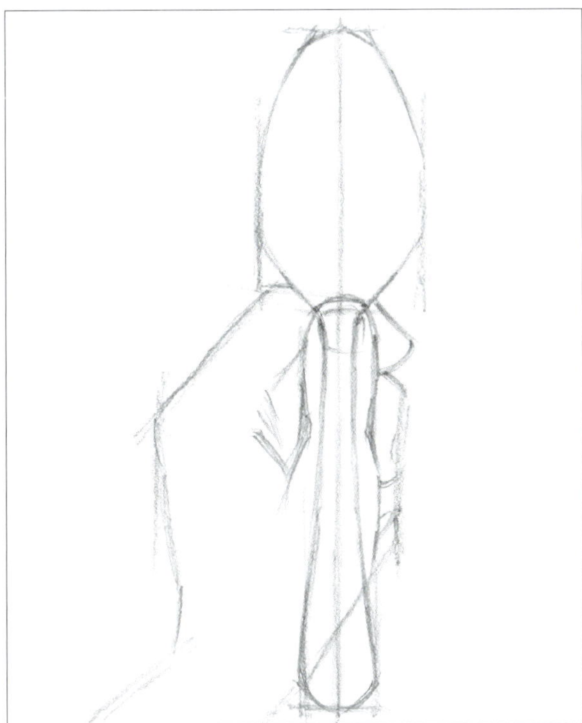

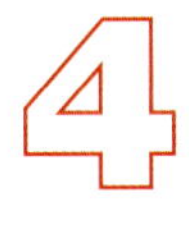

4 Sketch the Fingers and Refine the Hand
Sketch in the fingers and refine the form of the hand.

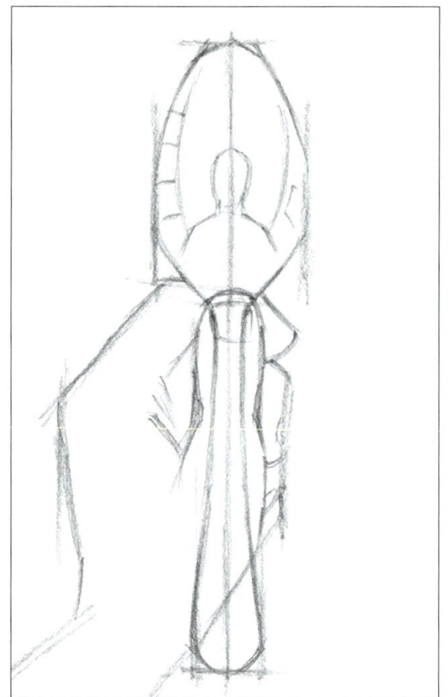

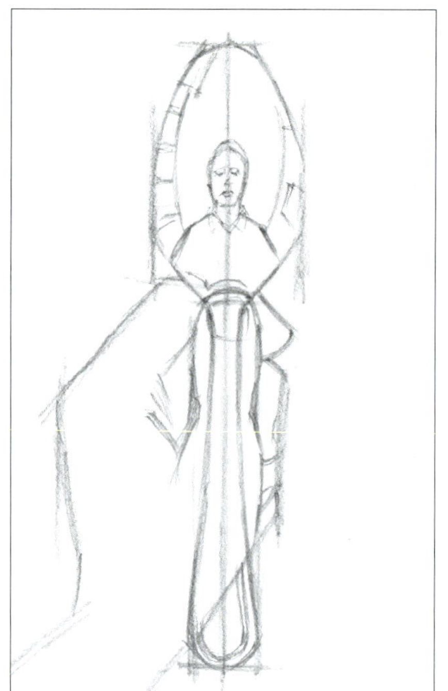

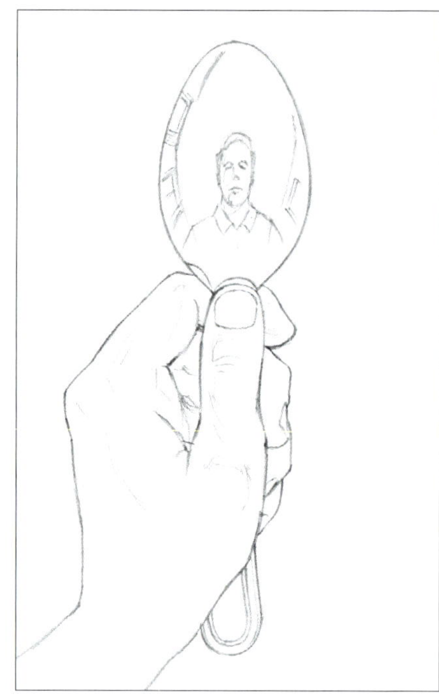

5 Add Reflections

Hold the spoon with the convex side toward you and sketch the most basic forms reflected on the spoon surface. Study the reflection. If you are indoors sitting at a table, you should be able to see the ceiling and corners of the room along with the windows and, of course, yourself.

6 Develop the Spoon Handle and Reflections

Add details to develop the reflections and the base of the spoon handle.

7 Trace or Transfer the Image

Using a 2B pencil, lightly trace or transfer the structural sketch onto a sheet of drawing paper. Leave out any unwanted lines. Add details and shadow lines.

8 Add the Light Values

Add light values to the spoon and the hand with a 2B pencil. When observing the spoon, look for the light areas and dark areas and place them accordingly.

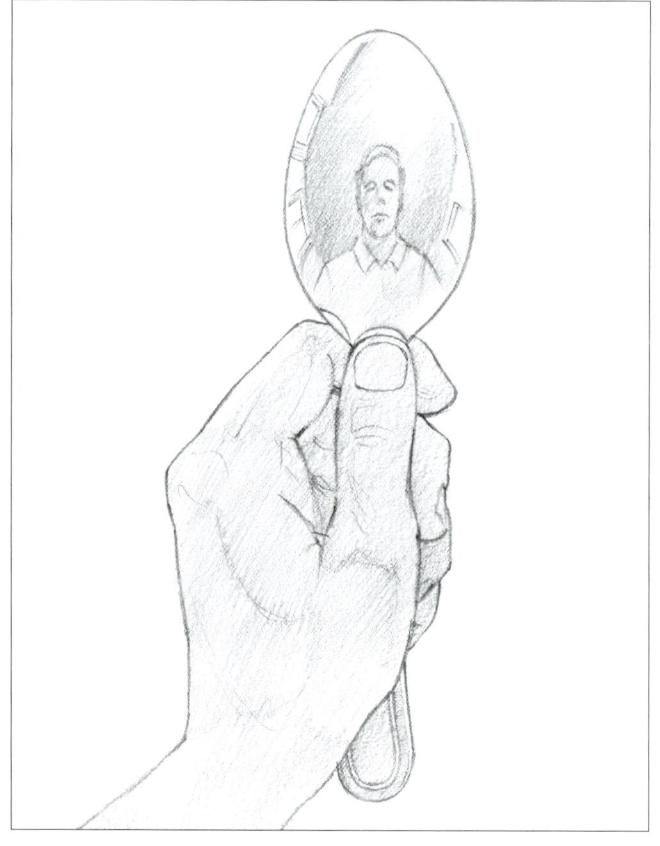

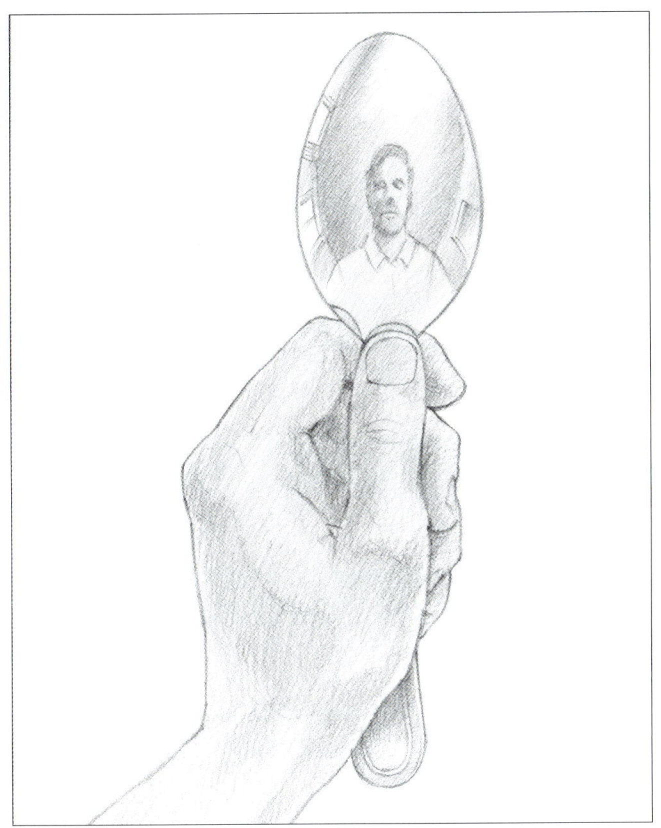

9 Add the Middle Values

Darken the pencil lines to add the middle values.

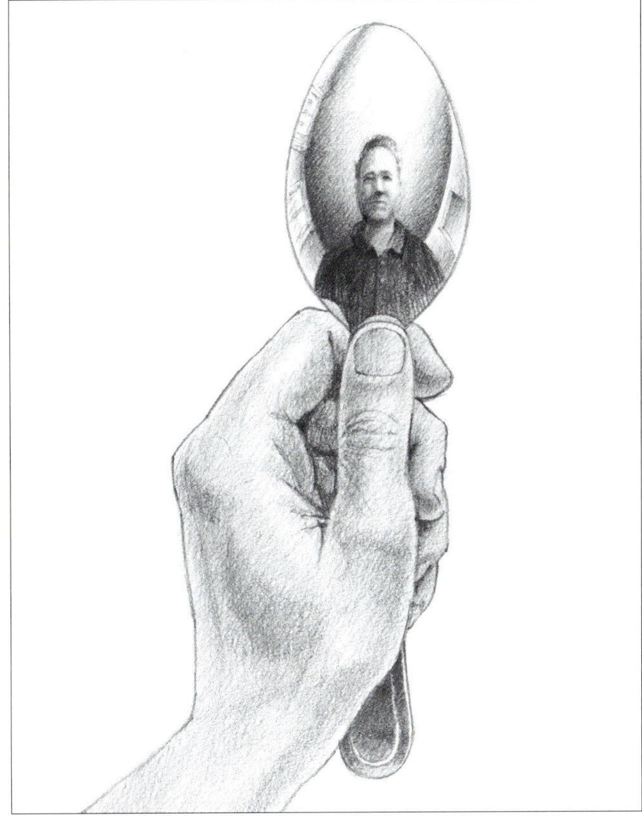

10 Add Dark Values and Details

Continue developing the drawing by adding dark values and details. The darkest darks can be added with a 6B pencil. Lighten any areas with a kneaded eraser as needed. Take into consideration that the drawing will probably look lighter after it is placed on the gray background.

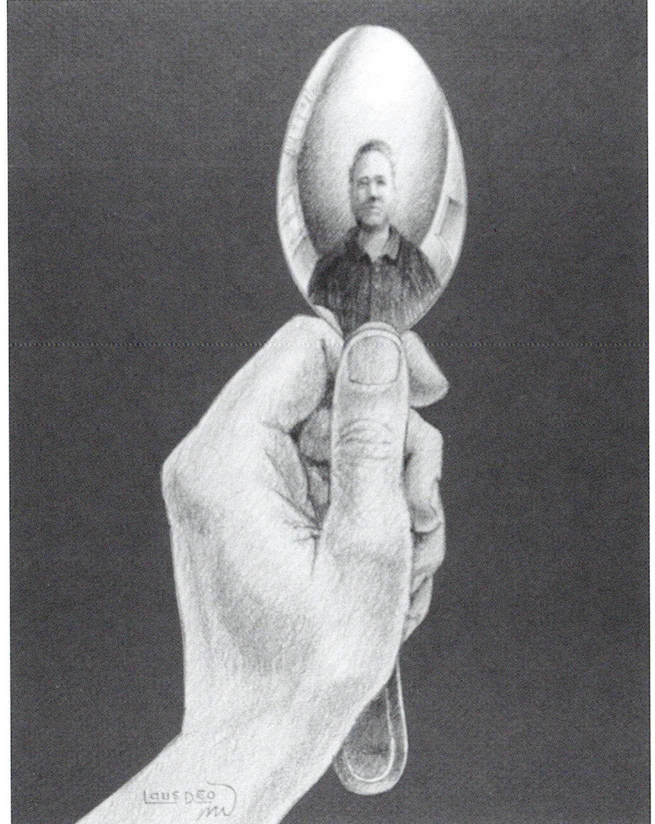

11 Cut and Mount

Place the drawing on top of a piece of heavy cardboard and use a craft knife to carefully cut out the image. Apply double-sided tape to the back of the image and adhere it to a piece of dark gray construction paper. Sign the front and write the date on the back of the drawing.

Bullet Train

Though this scene has a vanishing point at the left near the tail end of the train, there is also a vanishing point on the right, which influences the form of the front of the train. The front is developed by first sketching a box shape, then chiseling away at it to create the round form. The light source comes from the upper right, causing the left side of the train to be in shadow. All of the foreground and background lines are directed to the left vanishing point to enhance the scene with a sense of motion. The scene should also to be tilted during the drawing stage to add even more tension.

Materials

Paper
8" × 10" (20cm × 25cm) medium-texture drawing paper; 8" × 10" (20cm × 25cm) medium-texture sketch paper

Pencils
2B and 6B

Other
kneaded eraser; lightbox or transfer paper; ruler; triangle

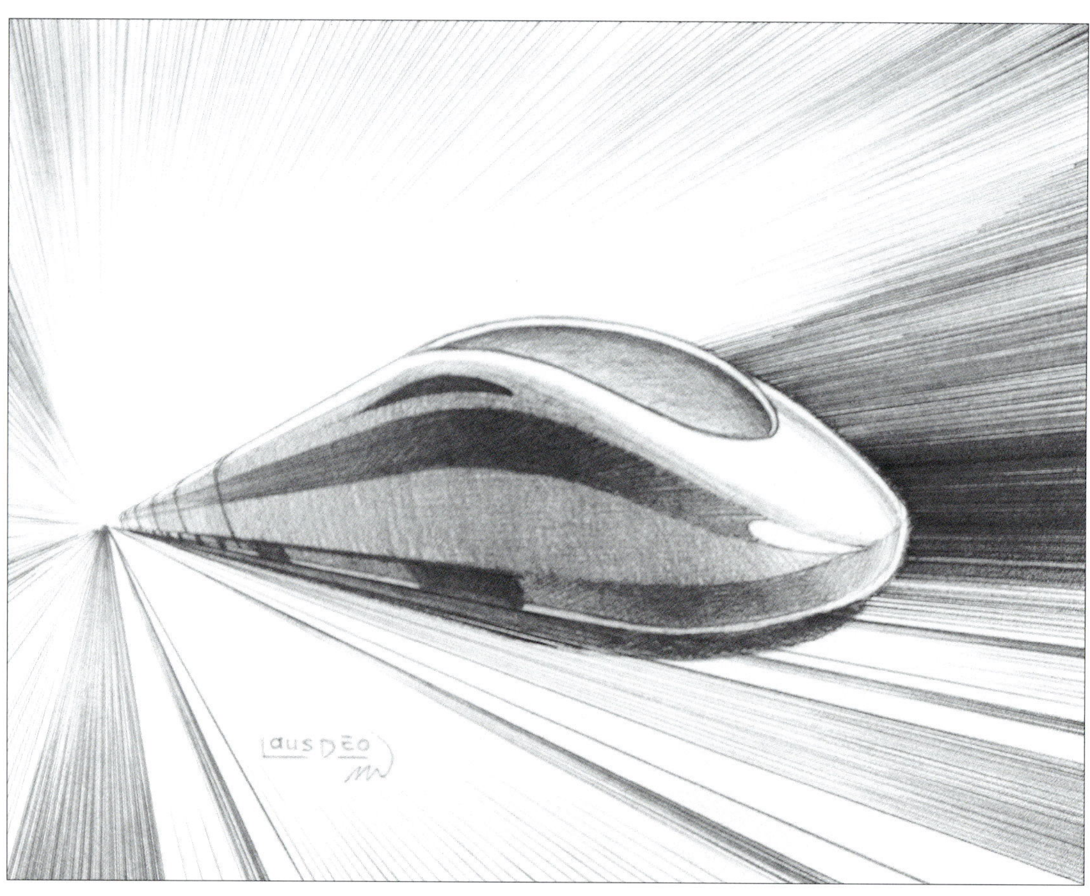

Bullet Train
Graphite pencil on drawing paper
8" × 10" (20cm × 25cm)

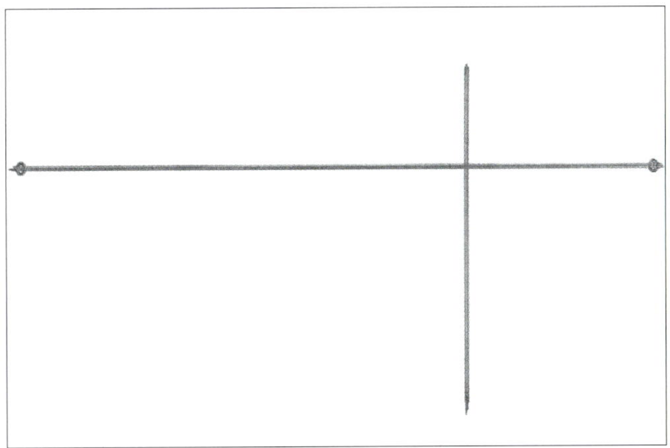

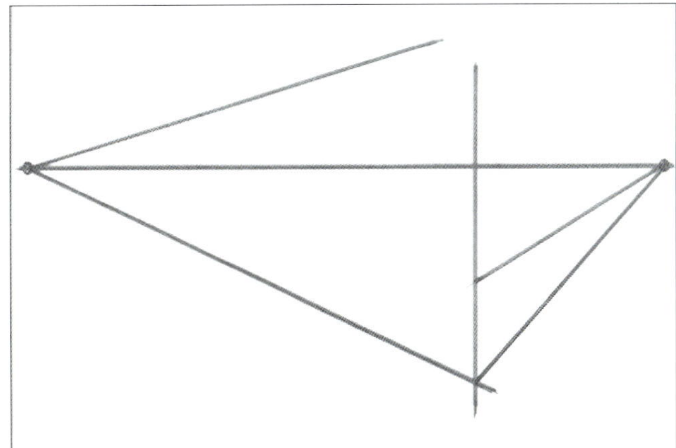

1 Sketch the Horizon, Vanishing Points and Forward Corner

Using a piece of sketch paper and a 2B pencil, place a horizon line 4½" (11cm) up from the lower edge of the paper. Place two dots on the horizon ¼" (6mm) in from the sides, 9½" (24cm) apart from each other as the left and right vanishing points. Sketch a vertical line 3⅜" (9cm) left of the right edge of the paper as the forward corner of the train.

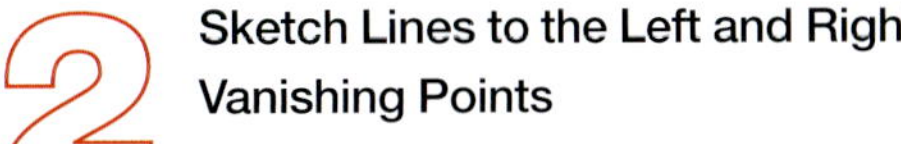

2 Sketch Lines to the Left and Right Vanishing Points

Sketch an orthogonal line that intersects the forward corner line 2" (5cm) above the horizon to the left vanishing point. Sketch an orthogonal line that intersects the forward corner line 3¼" (8cm) below the horizon to the left vanishing point. The forward lines represent the outermost dimensions of the train. The track lines will be added later.

Sketch an orthogonal line from the intersection of the forward corner line and the lowest orthogonal line to the right vanishing point. Sketch another orthogonal line that intersects the forward corner line 1¾" (4.4cm) below the horizon to the right vanishing point.

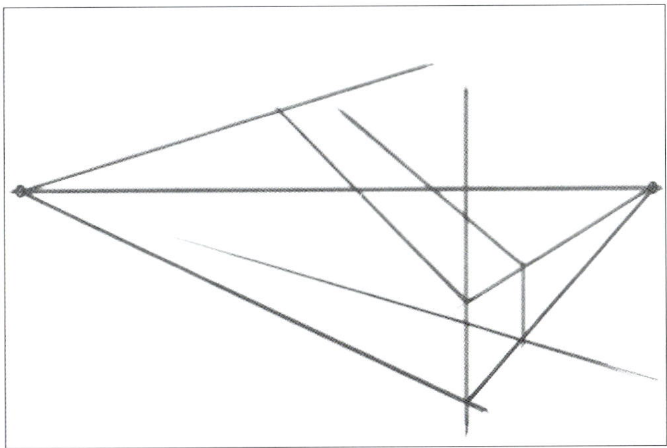

3 Add the Right Corner and Diagonal Lines

Sketch a vertical line ⅞" (22mm) to the right of the forward corner line as the right corner line. Sketch a diagonal line upward from the intersection of the forward corner and the upper right vanishing point orthogonal line. Sketch another diagonal line upward from the intersection of the right corner and the upper right vanishing point orthogonal line. Sketch an orthogonal line from the left vanishing point through the intersection of the right corner and the lower right orthogonal line. Obsolete lines may be erased at any point.

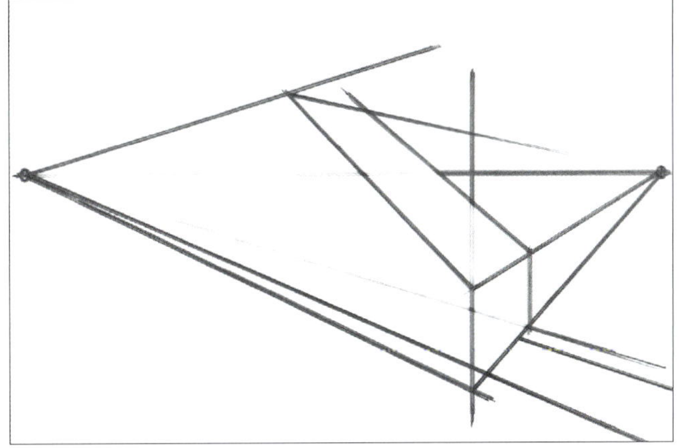

4 Add the Top Line and Track Lines

Sketch an orthogonal line that goes to the right vanishing point from the intersection of the top orthogonal line and the forward diagonal line. Sketch two orthogonal lines that go to the left vanishing point as two track lines between the previous two orthogonal lines. The lower track line is also the lowest edge of the train.

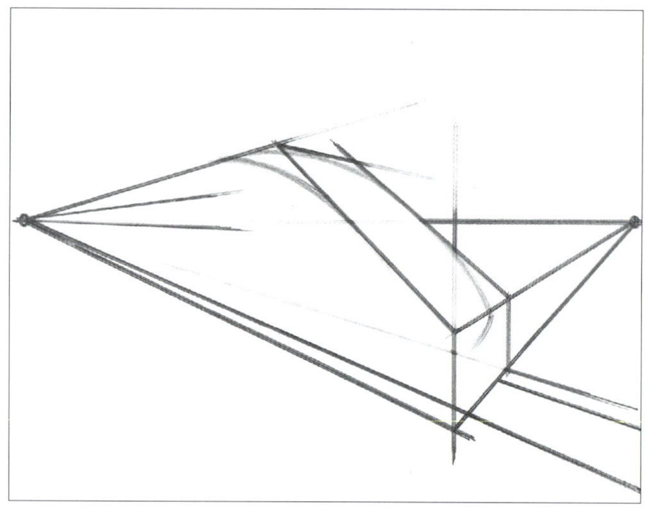

5 Develop Form

Sketch curved lines for the forward section of the train, chiseling away at the box form. Add orthogonal lines down the length of the train.

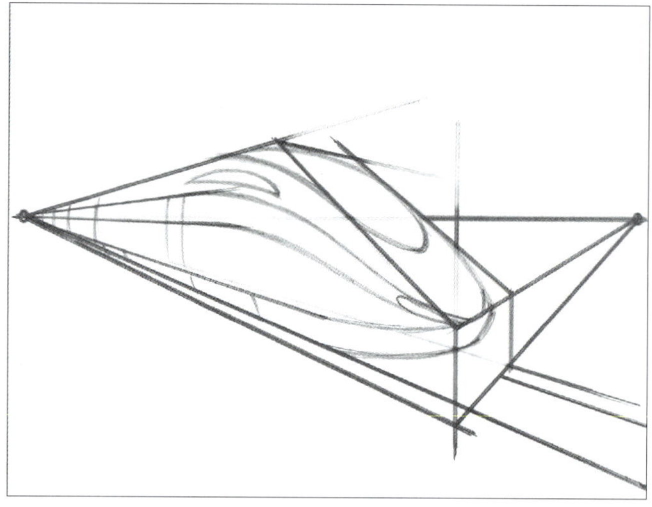

6 Continue Developing the Form

Continue adding lines to develop the form of the train including the teardrop shapes of the side window, windshield and headlight.

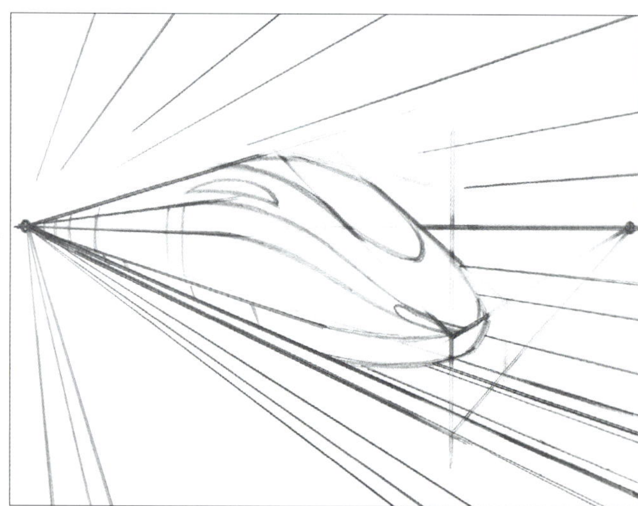

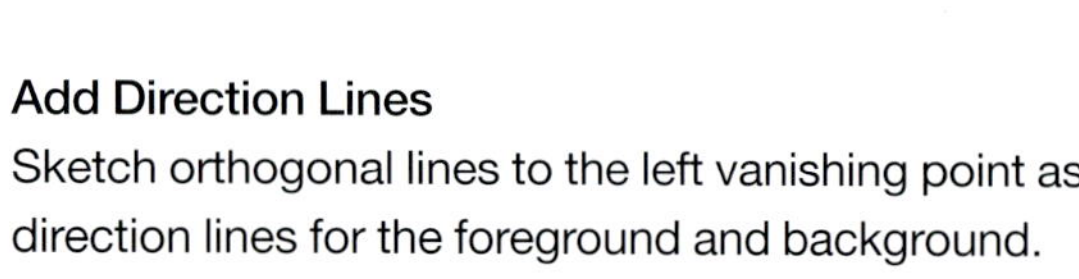

7 Add Direction Lines

Sketch orthogonal lines to the left vanishing point as direction lines for the foreground and background.

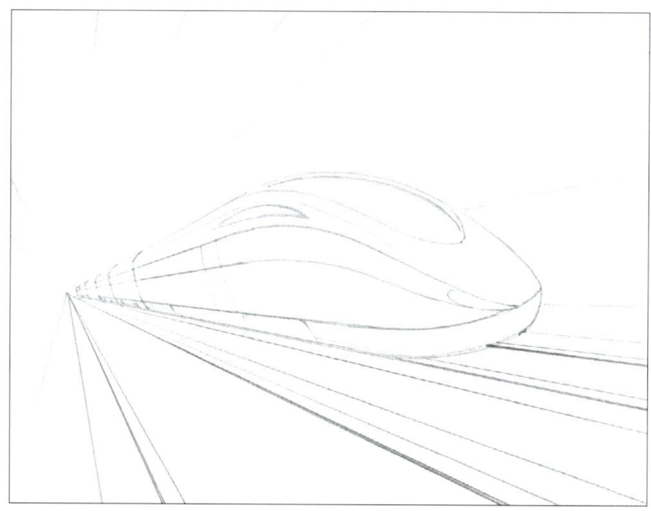

8 Trace or Transfer the Image

With the image tilted, trace or transfer the sketch onto drawing paper using a 2B pencil. Omit any unwanted lines during this process.

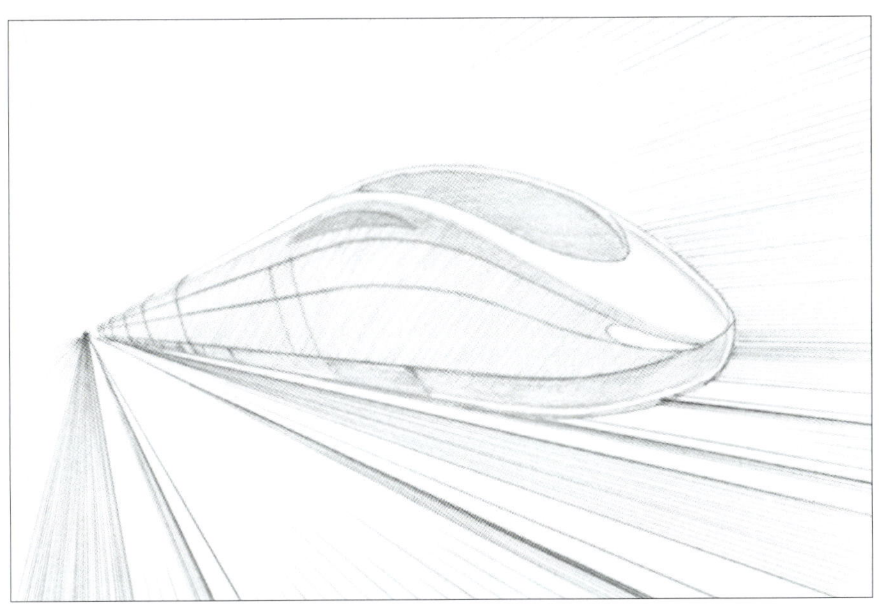

9 Add the Light and Middle Values

Add the light and middle values to the scene using a 2B pencil. The pencil lines can be drawn with a triangle placed at the left vanishing point.

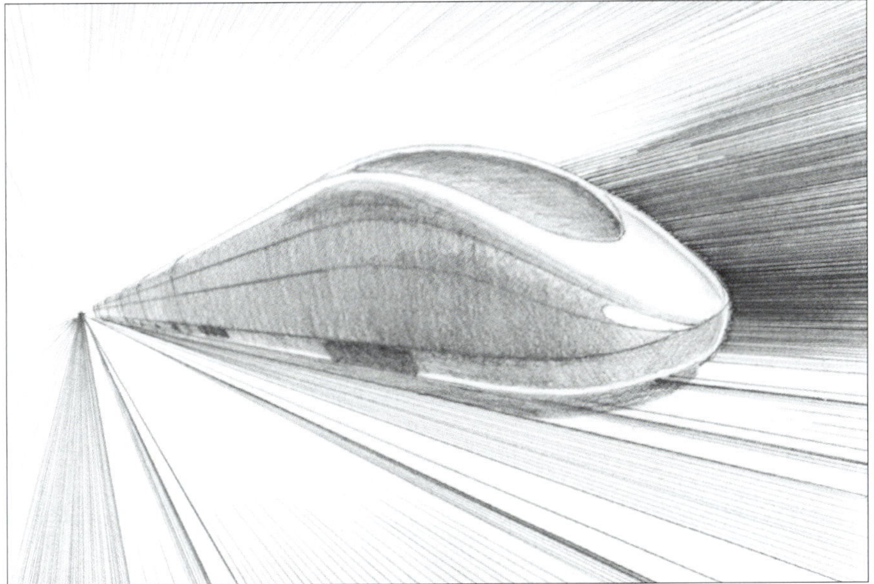

10 Add the Dark Values

Build up the pencil strokes to add in dark values.

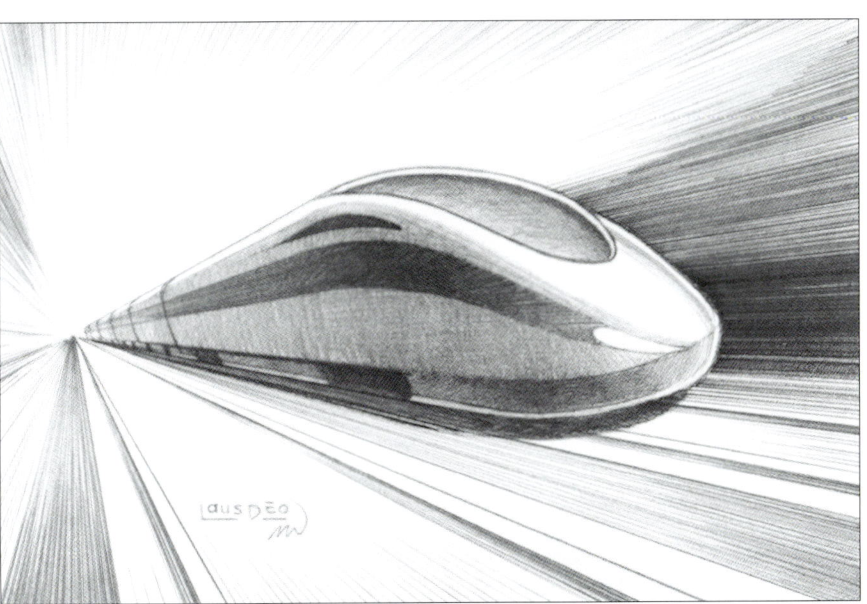

11 Continue Adding Darks and Details

Continue adding darks and details with 2B and 6B pencils. A kneaded eraser can be used to lighten and adjust as needed. Sign the front and write the date on the back of the drawing.

DEMONSTRATION

Stone Cottage

The development of this cottage drawing starts as a box with a roof, which then has a forward box and roof added. Plotting out the vanishing points is possible; however, you may choose to estimate their placement along with the angles of the orthogonal lines of the building instead. The light source is from the upper left making the left side of the cottage lighter than the right side.

Materials

Paper
19" × 24" (48cm × 61cm) medium-texture drawing paper; 19" × 24" (48cm × 61cm) medium-texture sketch paper

Pencils
2B and 6B

Other
kneaded eraser; lightbox or transfer paper; ruler; triangle

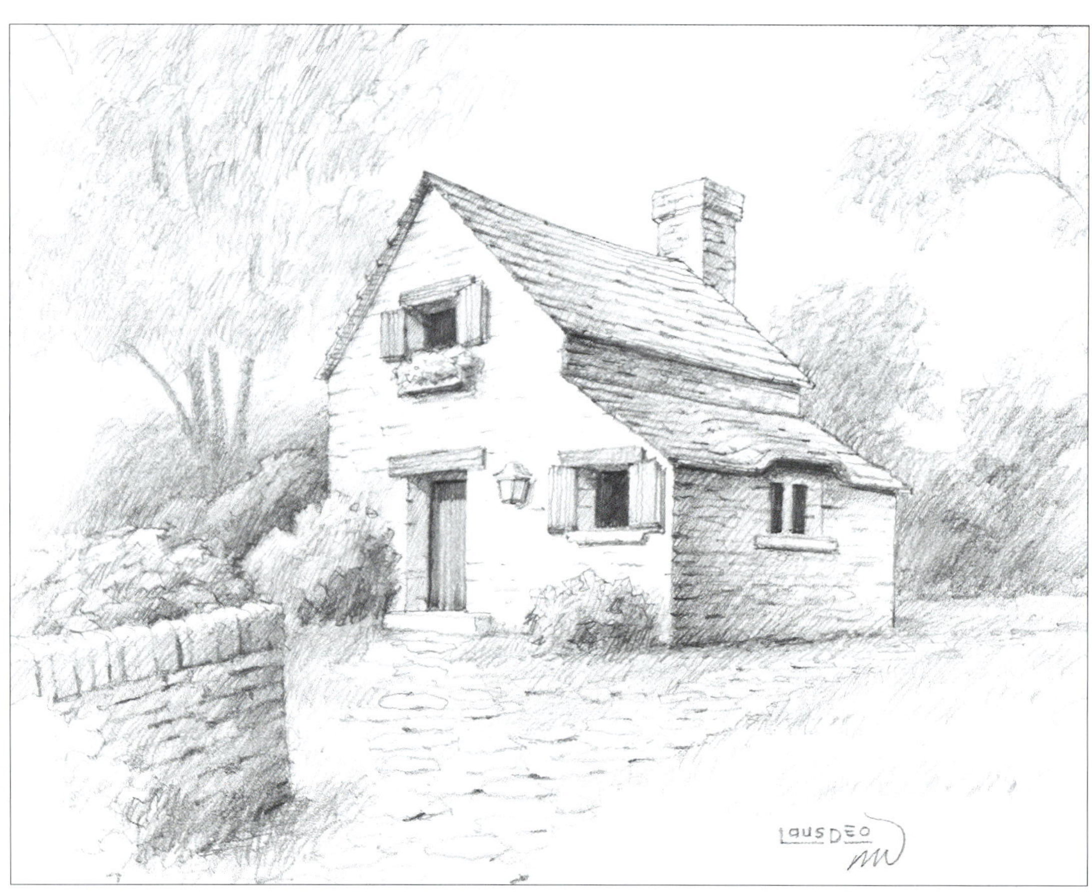

Stone Cottage
Graphite pencil on drawing paper
8" × 10" (20cm × 25cm)

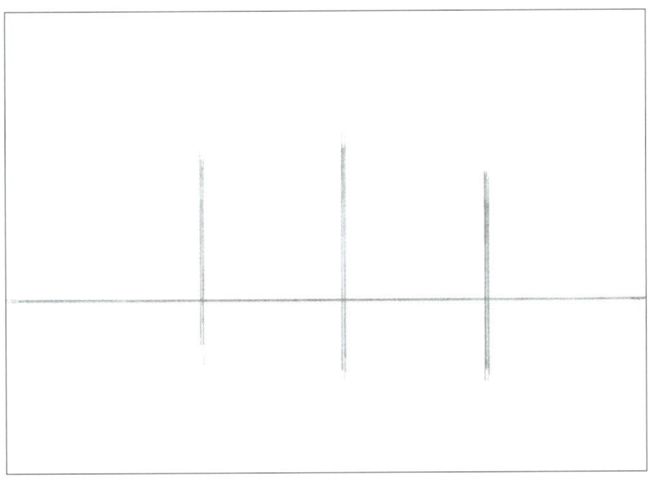

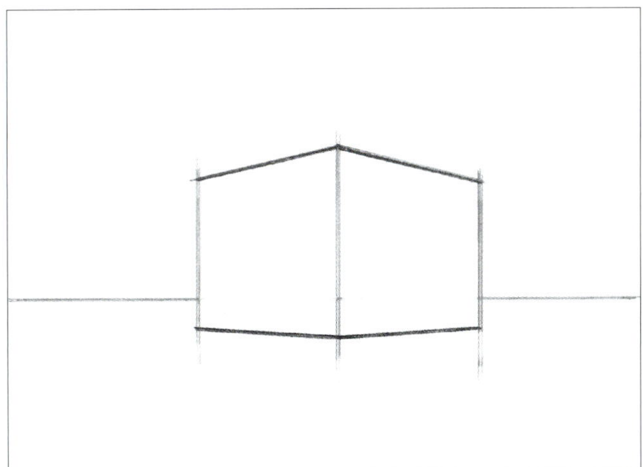

1 **Sketch the Horizon and Corners of the Central Box**
On a piece of sketch paper, use a 2B pencil to place a horizon line 3" (8cm) up from the lower edge of the paper. Sketch a vertical line at the center as the front corner of the central box form. Sketch another vertical line 2⅛" (5.4cm) left of center as the left corner, and another vertical line 2¼" (5.7cm) right of center as the right corner.

2 **Sketch the Central Box Form**
Sketch orthogonal lines from the front corner to the vanishing points on the horizon to form the sides of the central box. The left vanishing point is 10½" (27cm) left of the front corner. The right vanishing point is 9½" (24cm) right of the front corner. The upper orthogonal lines meet the front corner 2¼" (5.7cm) above the horizon. The lower orthogonal lines meet the front corner ½" (1.2cm) below the horizon. Throughout the process of the structural sketch, unwanted lines may be erased.

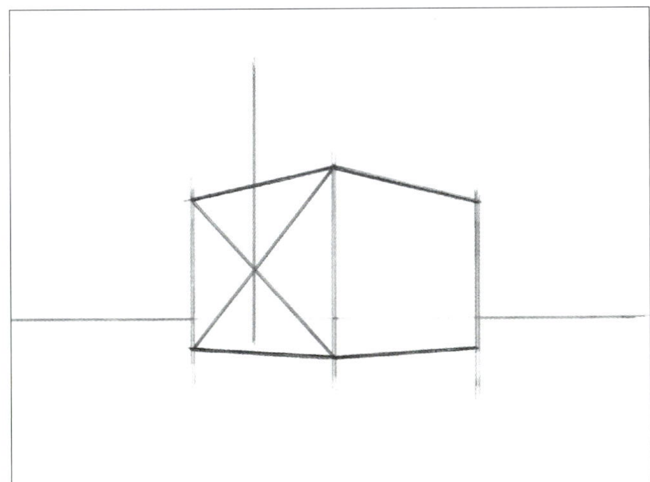

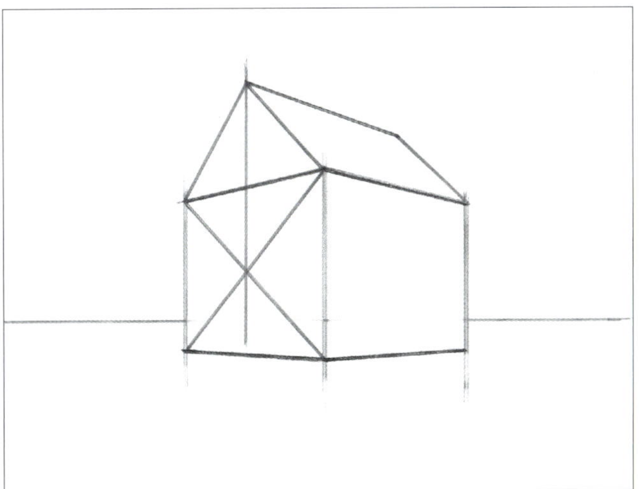

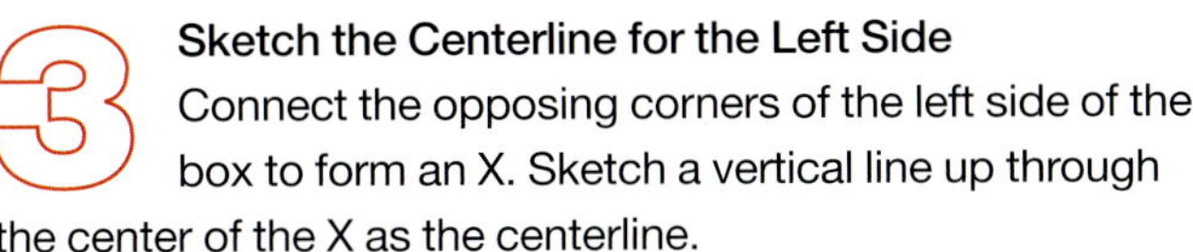

3 **Sketch the Centerline for the Left Side**
Connect the opposing corners of the left side of the box to form an X. Sketch a vertical line up through the center of the X as the centerline.

4 **Sketch the Roof**
Add lines that connect the centerline with the top left corners of the box to form the front roof peak. Add the roof ridge by sketching an orthogonal line from the front roof peak to the right vanishing point. Complete the roof by connecting a diagonal line from the top right corner of the box to the roof ridge.

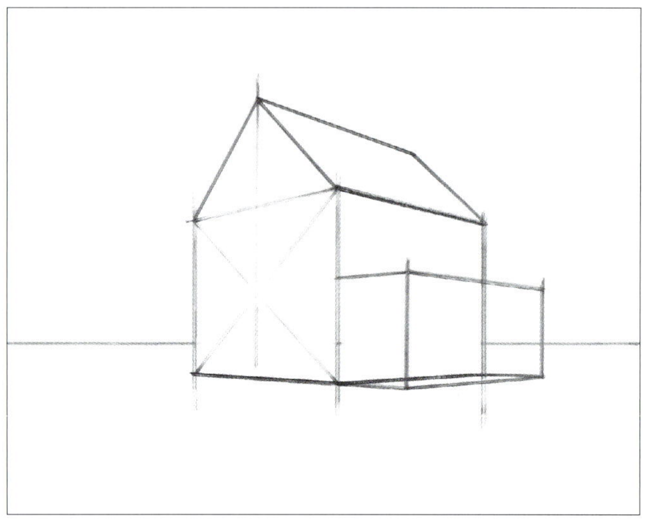

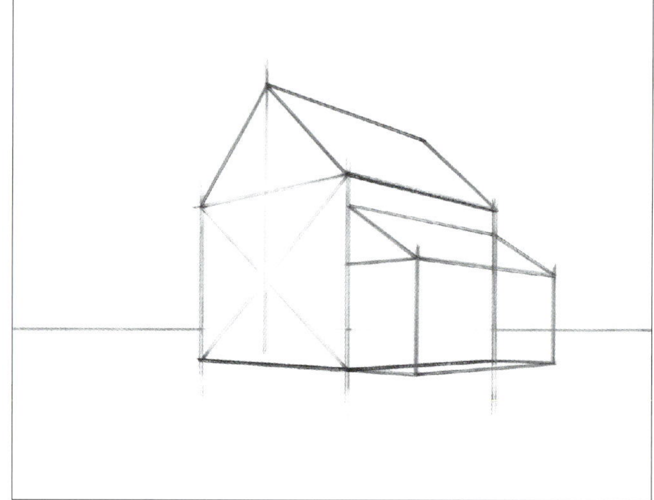

5 Sketch and Form the Front Box

Sketch a vertical line 1" (2.5cm) right of the central box front corner as the front corner of the front box. Continue the lower orthogonal line that is directed to the left vanishing point forward of the vertical line. Continue the lower orthogonal line around the corner to form the base of the front box.

Add a vertical line up from the intersection of the orthogonal lines on the right as the right corner of the front box. Add orthogonal lines—one to the left vanishing point, the other to the right vanishing point—from a point 1¾" (4.4cm) up from the base on the front corner of the front box.

6 Sketch the Front Box Roof

On the right side of the central box, add an orthogonal line directed to the right vanishing point as the top edge of the front box roof. Add diagonal lines from the intersections of the top roof edge and the corners of the central box down to the top corners of the front box to form the roof. The slope of the roof of the front box should be flatter than the slope of the central box roof.

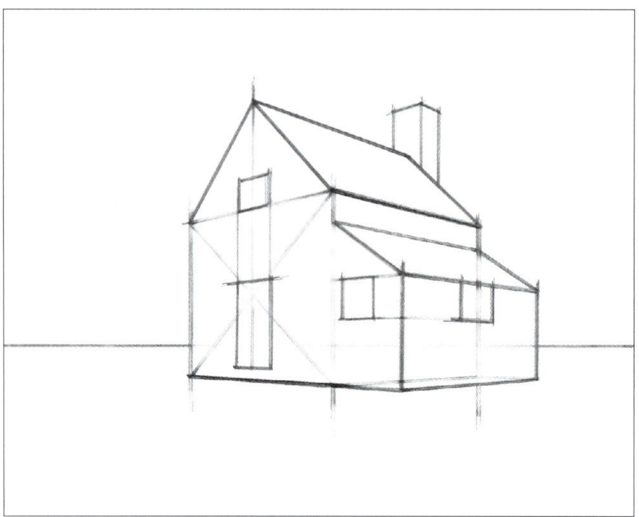

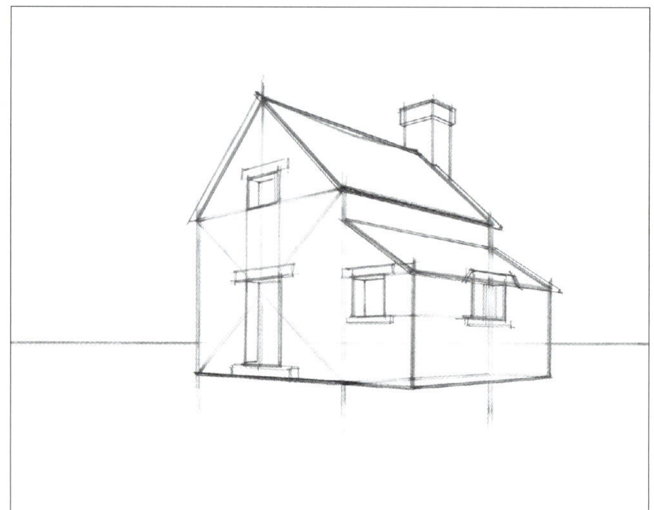

7 Add Windows and a Chimney

Sketch the rectangular forms of the windows with their lines being either vertical or orthogonal. The top of the window on the right should be high enough to cause a hump in the roof. Sketch the chimney as a tall box form.

8 Develop the Features

Add depth to the windows and doors, which are inverted box forms. Develop the form of the chimney and the hump of the roof. Extend the edges of the roof to form overhangs, and curve the roof ridge.

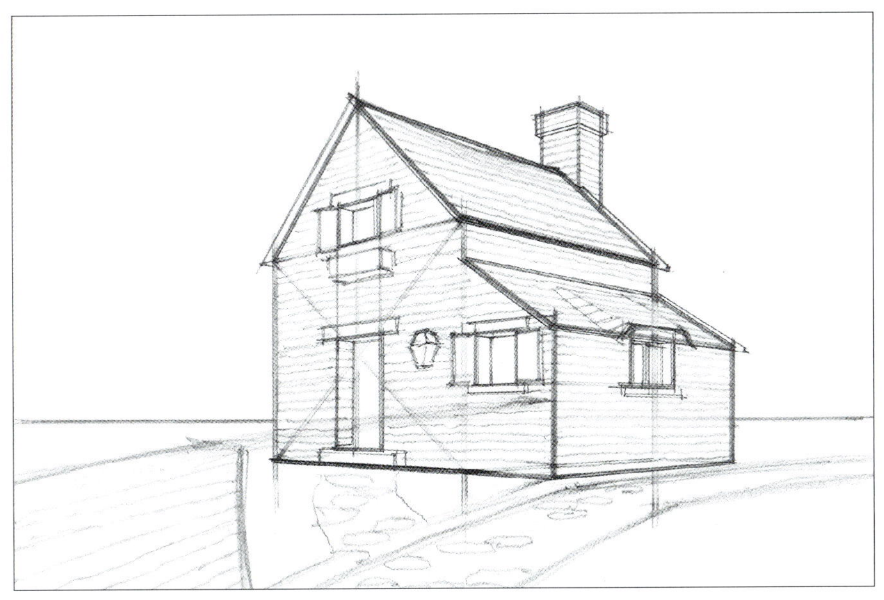

9 Add Building Details, Walls and Walkways

Add details to the building and to the windows and door. Add orthogonal lines for the placement of stone and roof slate. Sketch in the stone wall and walkways sloping down from the building. Add lines for the stonework and the slate roof.

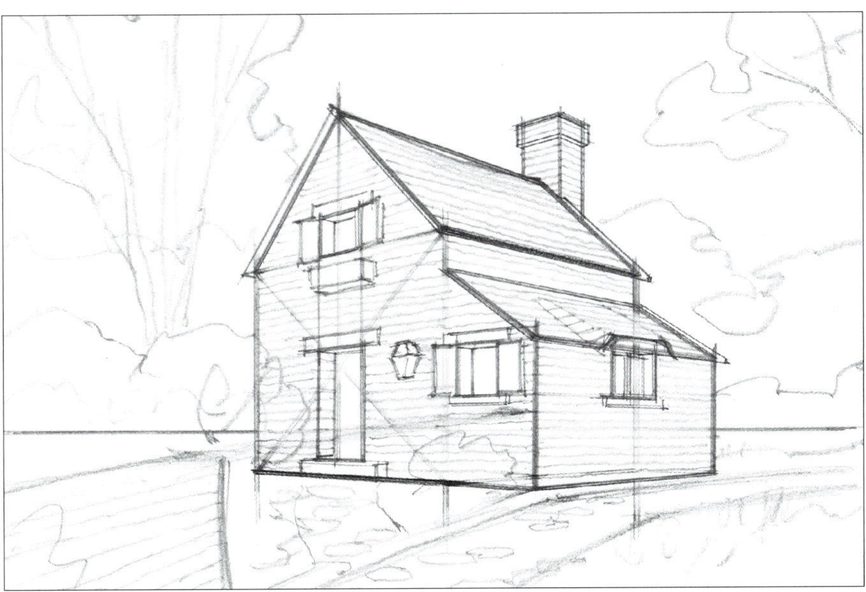

10 Add Landscaping

Sketch the forms of the trees, bushes and shrubs that are part of the scene.

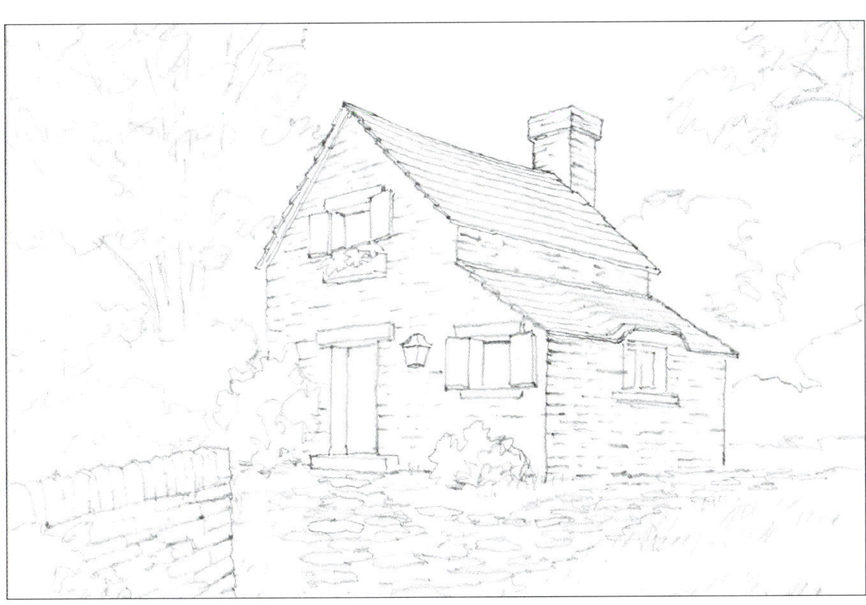

11 Trace or Transfer the Image

Leaving out unwanted lines, trace or transfer the image onto a sheet of drawing paper using a 2B pencil.

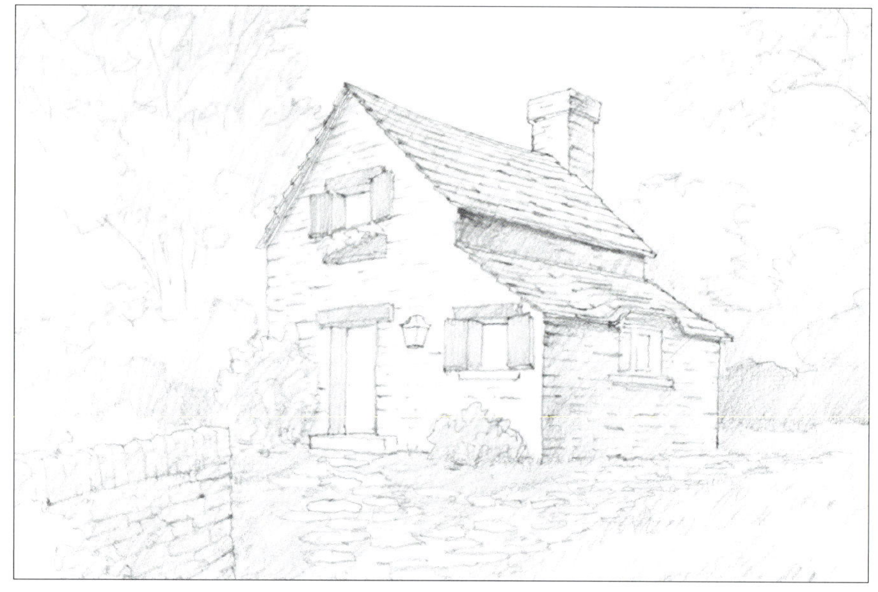

12 Add Light and Middle Values

Continue using the 2B pencil to add light and middle values to the scene.

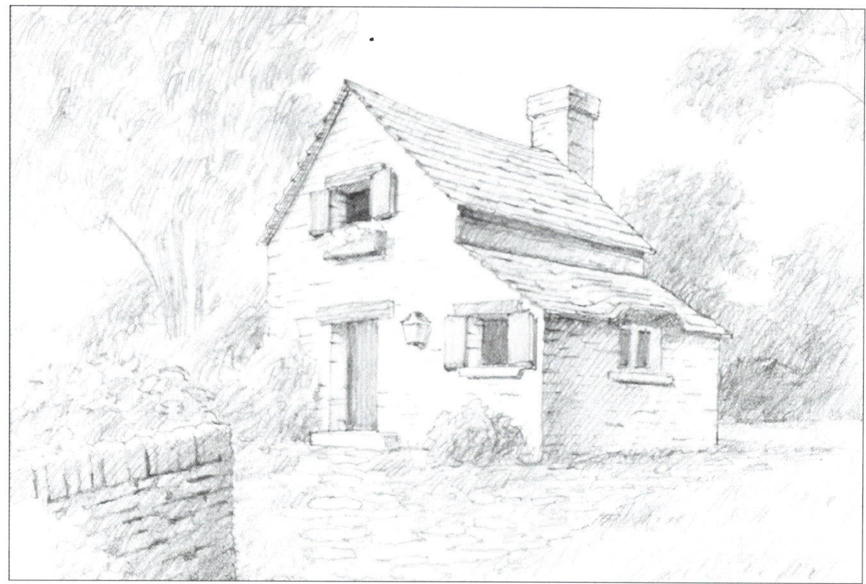

13 Add Dark Values

Make the values darker by building up the pencil strokes. Some dark values can be added to better gauge the range of values.

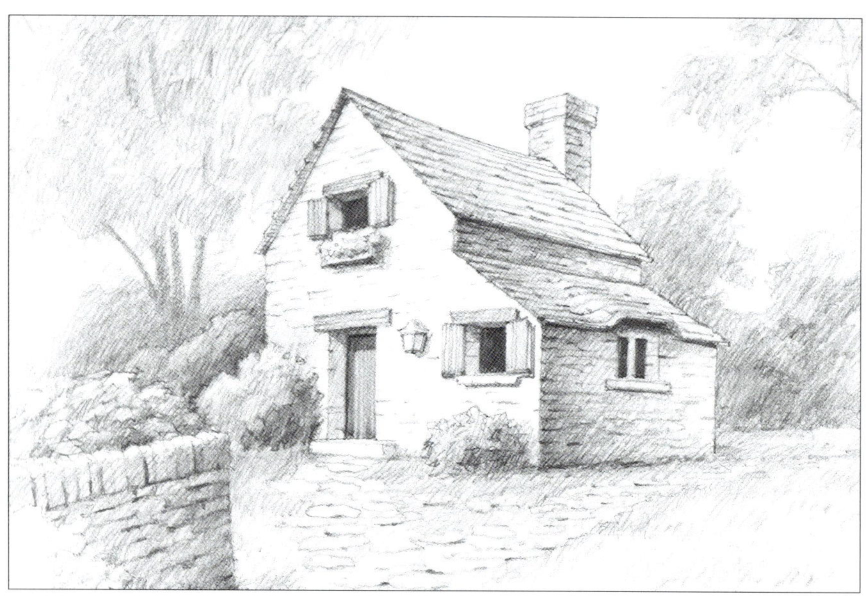

14 Continue Adding Darks and Details

Continue adding darks and details with 2B and 6B pencils. Make adjustments by lightening some areas with a kneaded eraser. Sign the front and write the date on the back of the drawing.

Medieval Castle

This castle scene was formatted vertically to accentuate the tower forms of the subject. Two-point perspective was used along with atmospheric perspective, which gives distinction between the lower buildings and the more distant upper buildings.

The light source comes from the right, causing the left sides of the forms to appear shadowed.

Materials

Paper
19" × 24" (48cm × 61cm) medium-texture drawing paper; 10" × 8" (25cm × 20cm) medium-texture sketch paper

Pencils
.05 mechanical and 2B

Other
kneaded eraser; lightbox or transfer paper; ruler; triangle; T-square

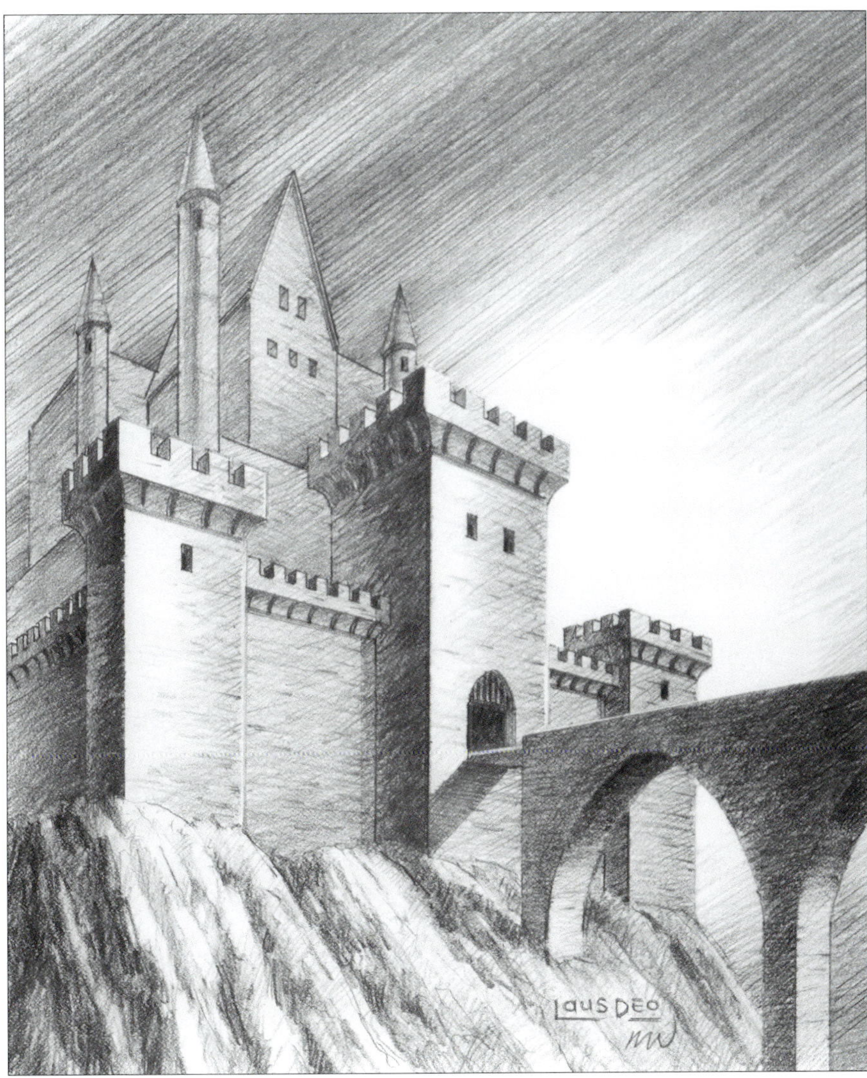

Medieval Castle
Graphite pencil on drawing paper
10" × 8" (25cm × 20cm)

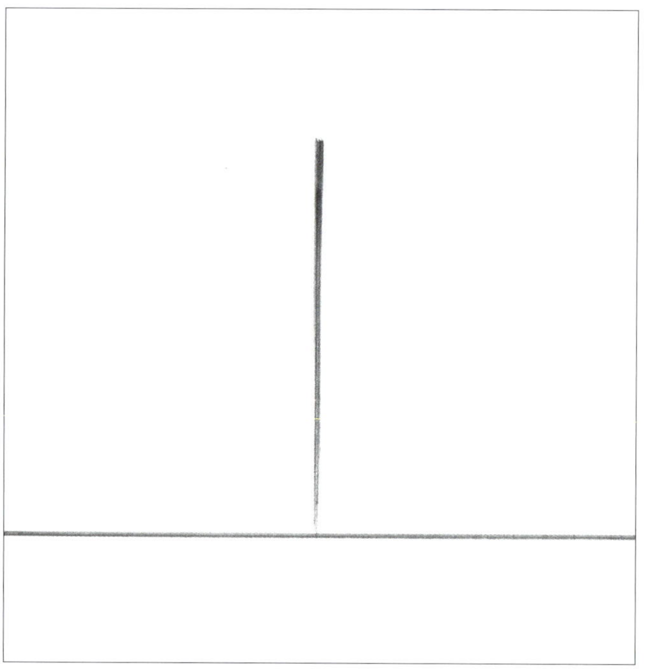

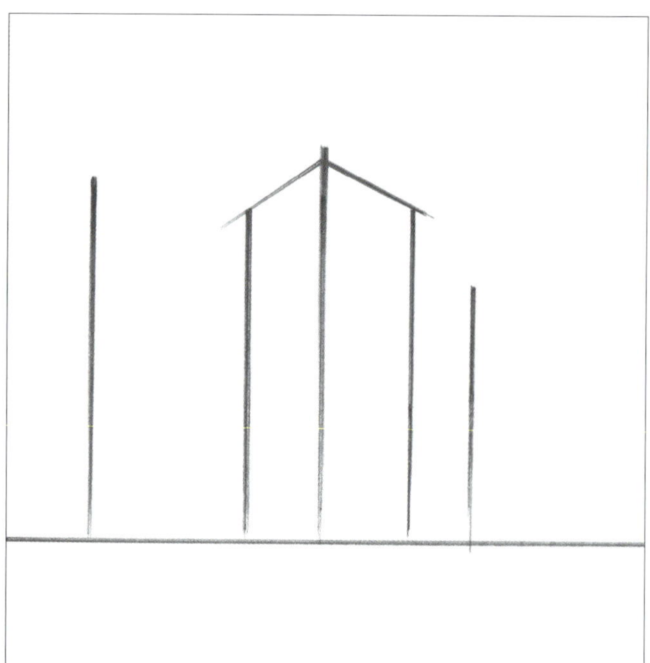

1 Sketch the Central Tower

Use a 2B pencil to sketch a line across a piece of sketch paper 4" (10cm) above the bottom edge as the horizon. Place the two vanishing points on the horizon 15½" (39cm) apart.

Add a vertical line 7" (18cm) from the left vanishing point as the front corner of the central tower. (These images do not show the vanishing points because they are cropped left and right of center, causing the front corner to appear at the center.)

2 Sketch the Central Tower and Side Towers

Sketch vertical lines for the front corners of the side towers. Make one line 2¾" (7cm) to the left of the central tower's front corner, the other 1⅞" (5cm) to the right. Sketch a box as the basis of the central tower. At a point 4¾" (12cm) above the horizon on the front corner line, add two orthogonal lines—one directed to the left vanishing point, the other directed to the right vanishing point. Add a vertical line as the left corner and another as the right corner. The base will later be defined by the rocky hillside, but for now the horizon can serve that purpose.

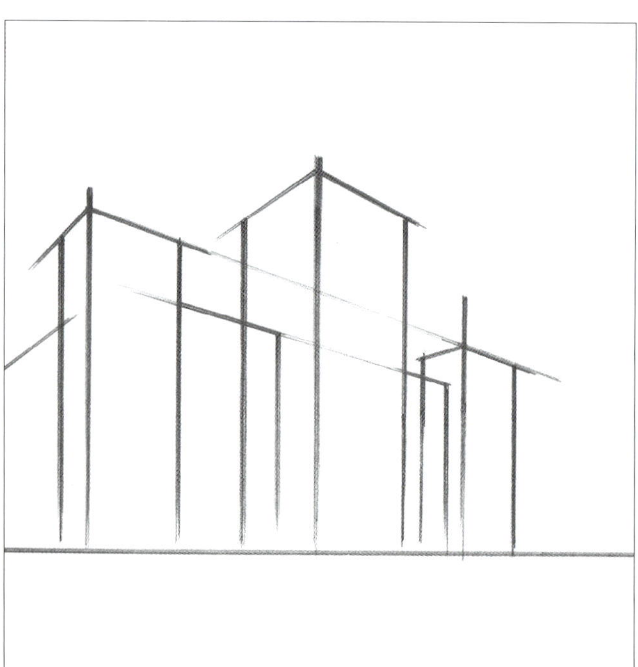

3 Sketch the Side Towers and Add Connecting Walls

Sketch the box forms of the side towers. At a point 4⅛" (10cm) above the horizon on the front corner line of the left tower, add orthogonal lines to both vanishing points. Because the side towers are the same height, the right orthogonal line will be used to construct both towers. Where the right orthogonal line intersects the front corner of the right tower, add a line directed to the left vanishing point. Add vertical lines as the side corners of the towers. Add vertical and orthogonal lines to form the walls that connect the towers.

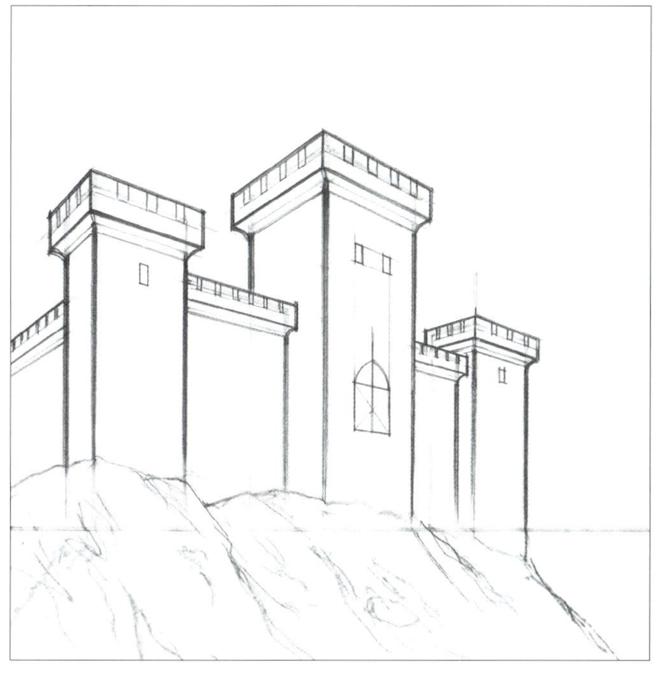

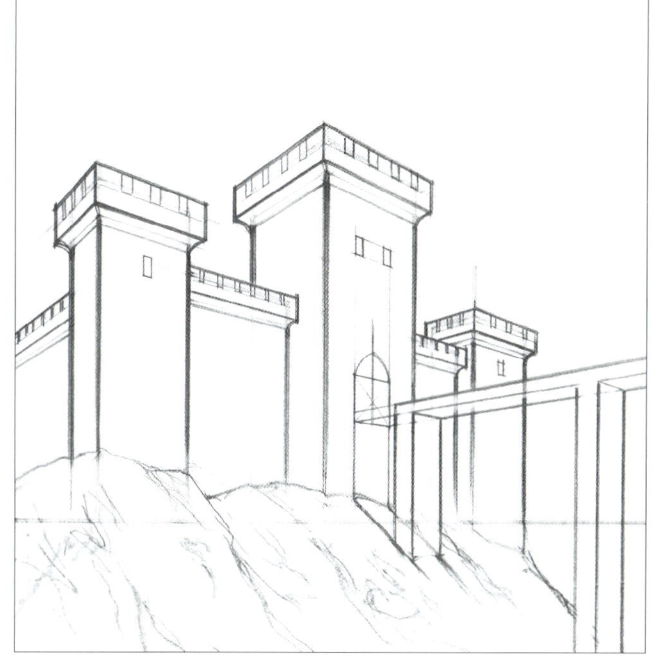

4

Develop the Towers, Walls and Hillside

Top the towers and walls with box forms. These are made by extending the top areas outward, then working down to form the sides and lastly closing off the lower sides. Erase any unwanted lines throughout the sketching process. Add an entrance, windows and merlons, along with lines to form the rocky hillside.

5

Begin the Bridge

Sketch the top of the bridge going out from the entrance along with the tall box forms of the supports. The placement of the base of the left support is determined by sketching lines down from the entrance, then down the hillside. These lines will intersect the vertical support lines at the base.

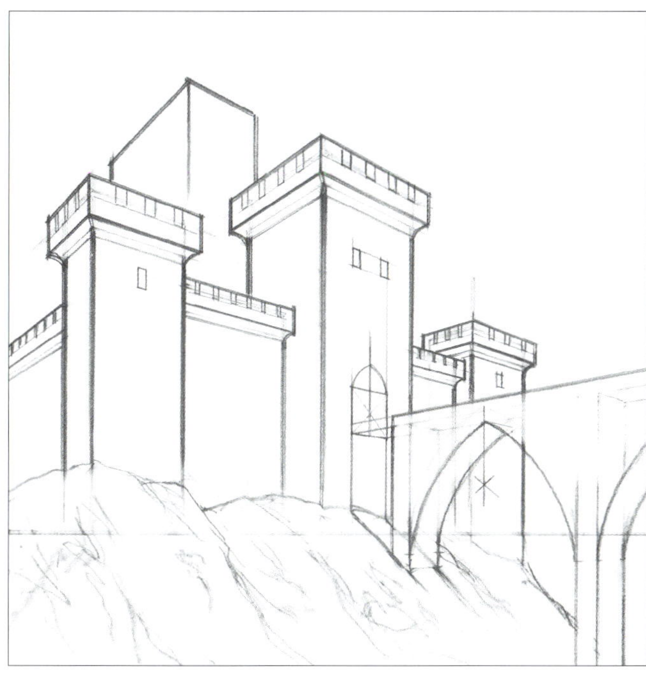

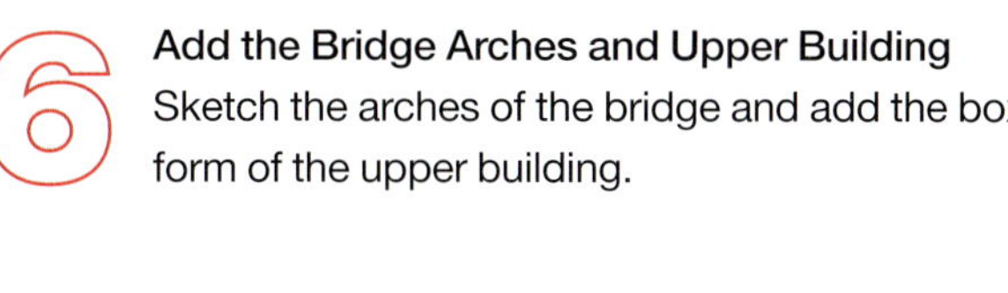

6

Add the Bridge Arches and Upper Building

Sketch the arches of the bridge and add the box form of the upper building.

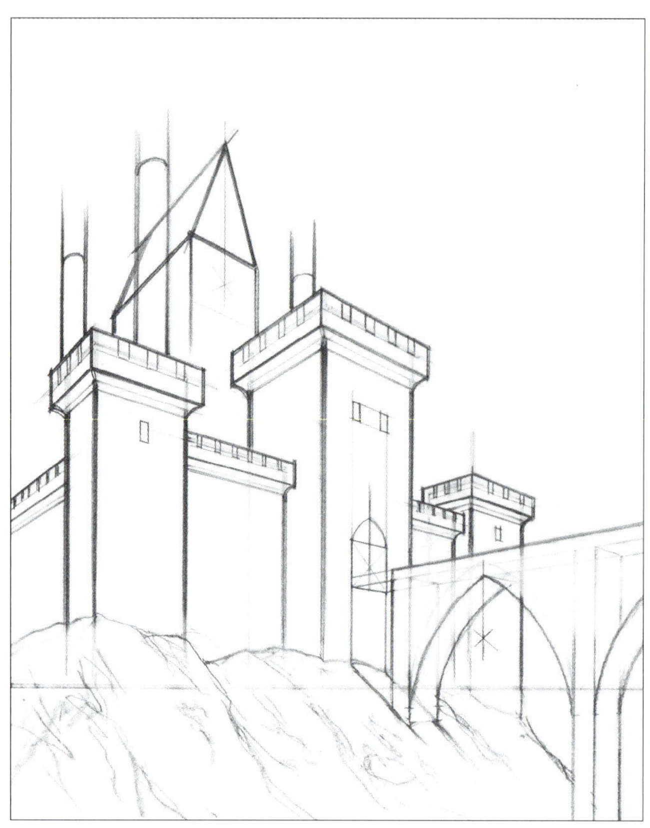

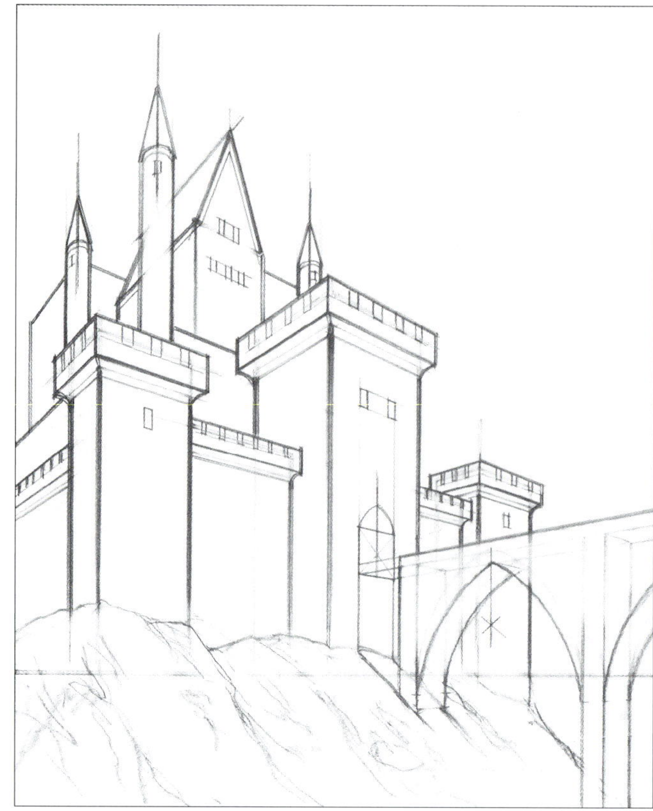

7 Add the Roof and Turrets

Add the roof to the upper building as well as the narrow cylindrical forms of the turrets.

8 Add Details to the Upper Buildings

Add details to the upper buildings, including the conical caps on the turrets, connecting walls and windows. The points for the caps on the turrets should be determined by first sketching a vertical line up from the centers of the cylindrical towers.

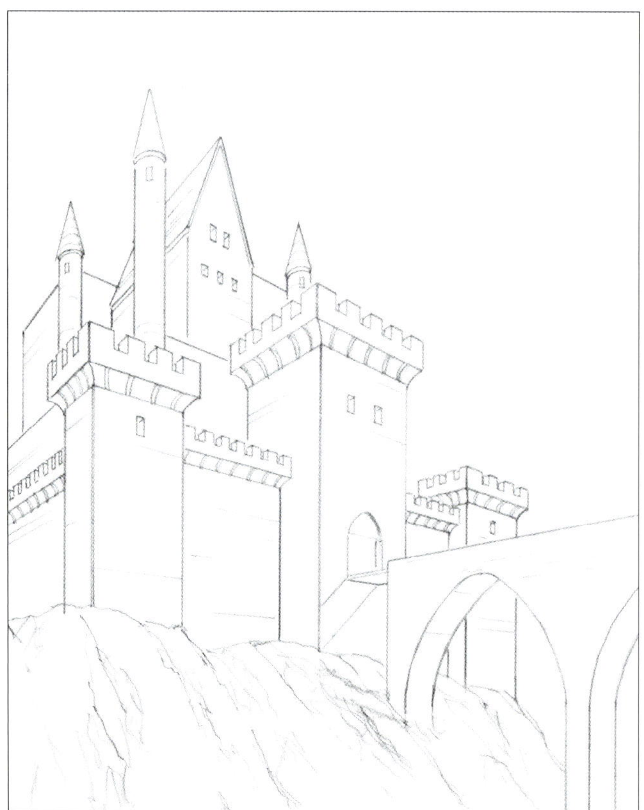

9 Trace or Transfer the Image and Add Details

Using a 2B pencil, trace or transfer the structural sketch onto drawing paper. Add details such as lines for the stonework and shadows. The merlons at the top of the tower and walls are three-dimensional and should be drawn as small box forms.

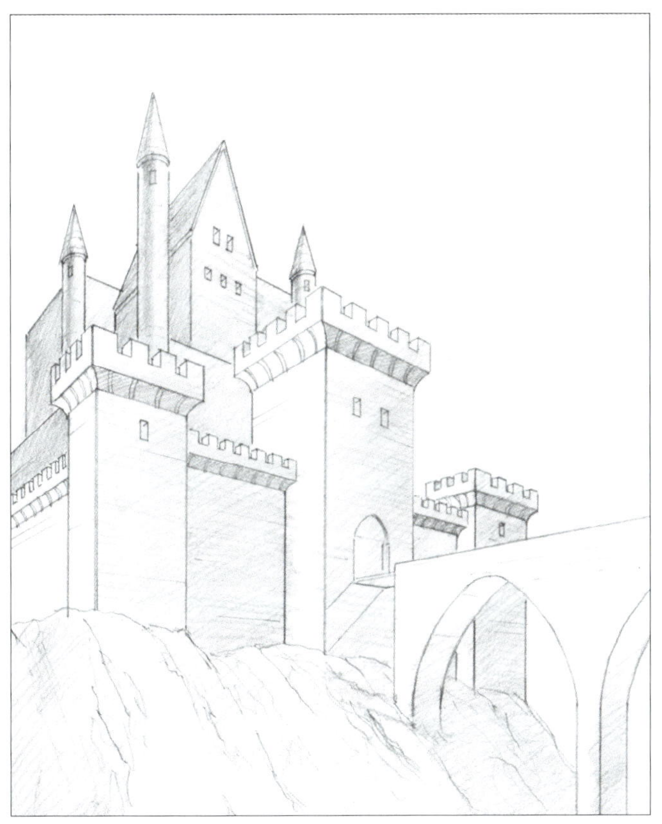

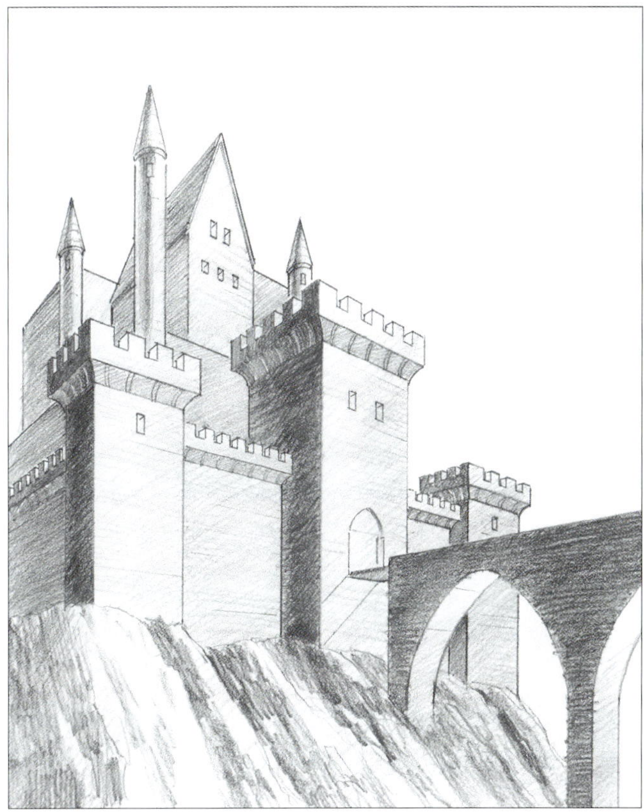

10 **Add the Light Values**

Add the light values with a 2B pencil.

11 **Add the Middle Values**

Add the middle values by building up pencil strokes. Use a mechanical pencil to add details and some dark regions.

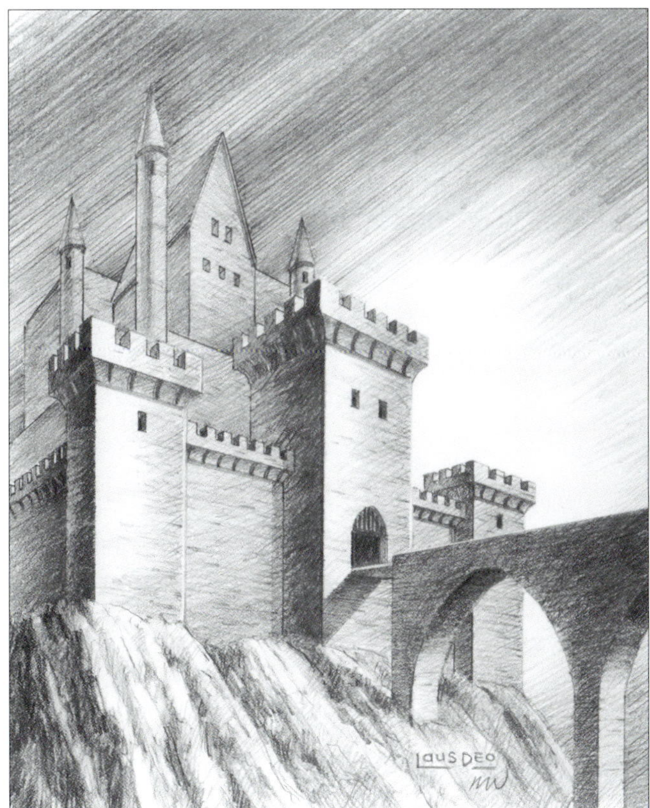

12 **Add Dark Values and Details**

Continue adding dark values and details to complete the drawing. Some areas may be lightened with a kneaded eraser.

The lower portion of the castle, being closer to the viewer, should have greater contrasts and be more detailed than the upper portion to emphasize atmospheric perspective.

Add values to the sky, contrasting with the lower buildings and almost blending in with the upper buildings. Sign the front and write the date on the back.

Roadster

The Shelby Cobra had a lightweight British body that was fitted with a powerful American V-8 engine, making it a legendary racer in its day.

This drawing involves transposing the angles of the orthogonal lines to sketch a box shape without plotting the vanishing points, then chiseling away to form the round body.

The upper contours reflect the sky, while the sides reflect the pavement and the distant landscape. Smooth value transitions along with sharp contrasts give a shiny appearance.

The light source comes from the left, causing the vehicle's shadow to spread into the right foreground. The light also bounces off the windshield causing a highlight.

A simplified version of this drawing can be made by leaving out the hood scoop, side pipes and roll hoop.

Materials

Paper
8" × 10" (20cm × 25cm) medium-texture drawing paper; 8" × 10" (20cm × 25cm) medium-texture sketch paper

Pencils
.05 mechanical, 2B and 6B

Other
kneaded eraser; lightbox or transfer paper; ruler; straightedge; triangle

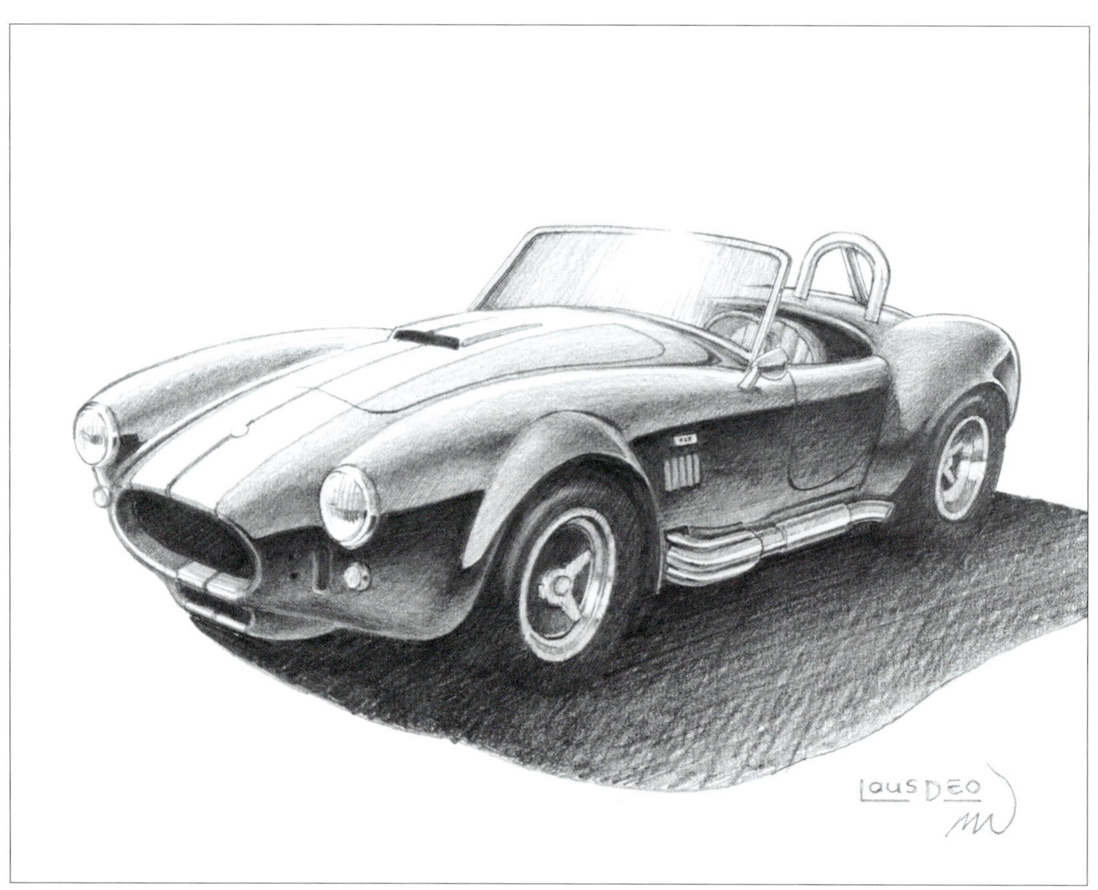

Roadster
Graphite pencil on drawing paper
8" × 10" (20cm × 25cm)

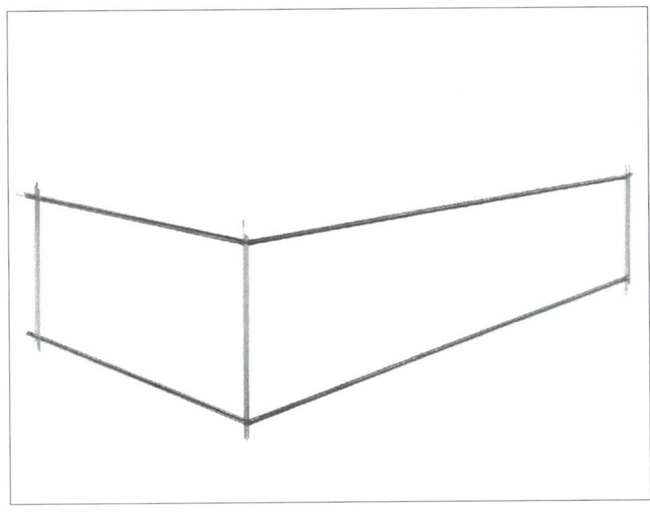

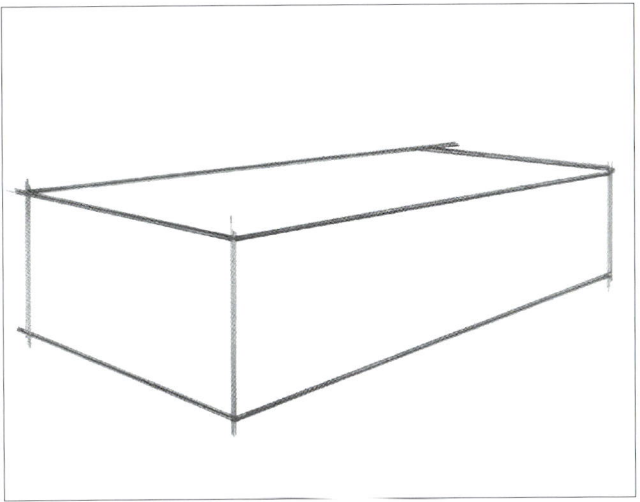

1 Sketch the Front and Side of the Box

Using an 8" × 10" (20cm × 25cm) piece of sketch paper and a 2B pencil, sketch a vertical line for the front corner and another line 5¾" (15cm) to the right for the back corner. Sketch the two orthogonal lines 2¾" (7cm) apart at the front corner to create the side of the box. Sketch a vertical line 3½" (9cm) to the left of the front corner as the left corner. Sketch the two orthogonal lines from the front corner to create the front of the box.

2 Complete the Box Form

Sketch an orthogonal line from the top left corner and another from the top back corner to complete the box form. This form represents the outermost dimensions of the body and will be chiseled away and rounded for the finished form.

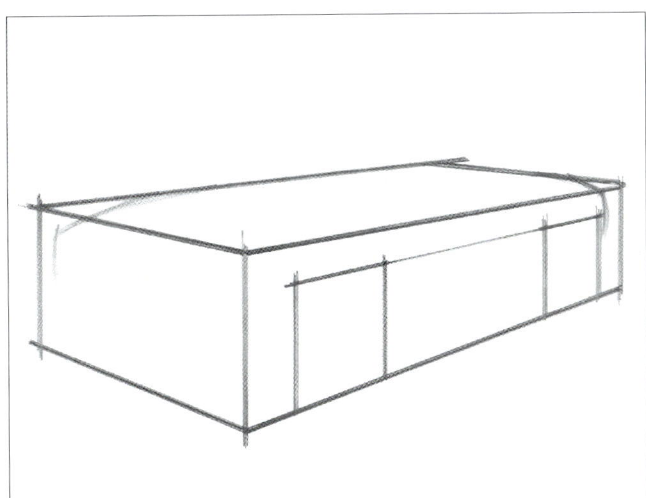

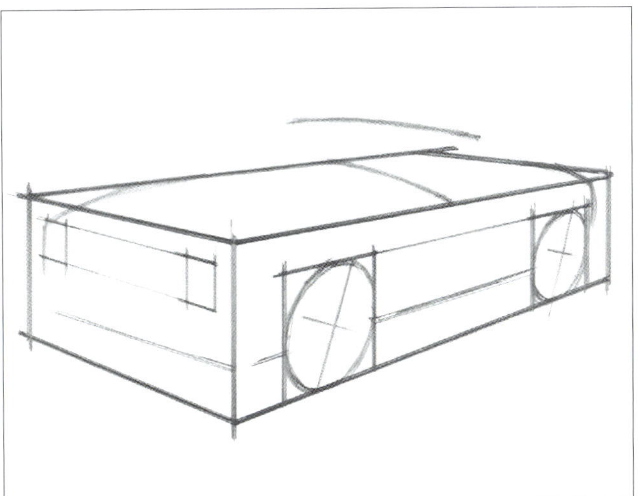

3 Block in the Tires and Begin Chiseling Away at the Form

Block in the outer form of the tires. Sketch the left corner, the back corner and a curved line for the top of the left front fender.

4 Continue Blocking in the Features

Continue to chisel away at the box form. Block in the headlights and sketch the top and bottom of the windscreen. Add the elliptical forms of the tires.

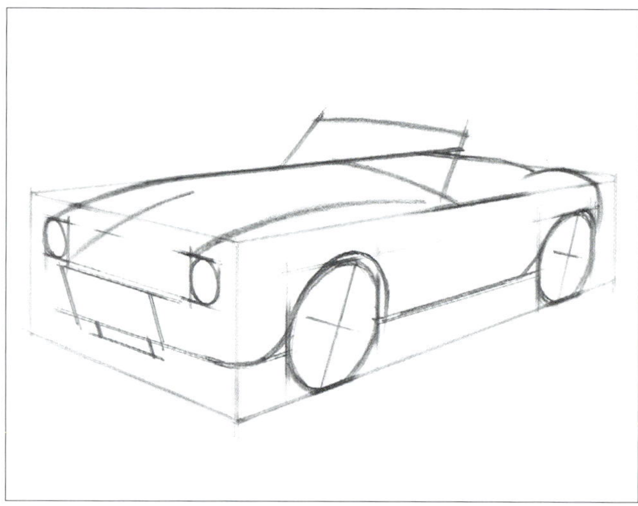

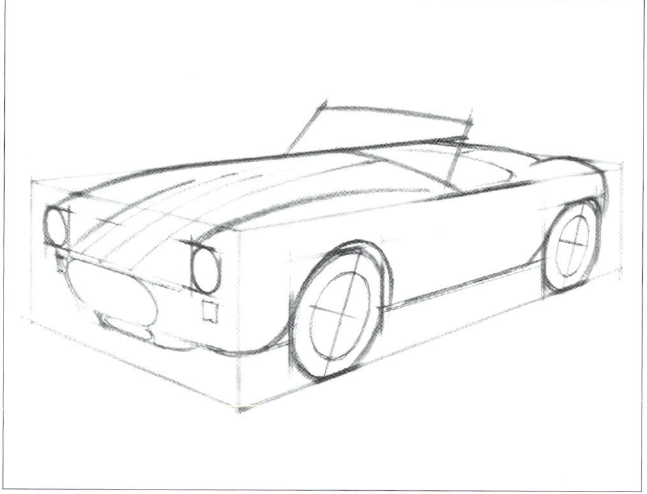

5 Continue Developing the Form

Chisel away at the top of the back of the box sketch. Round the fenders and wheel openings and block in the front openings to develop the form of the body. Also add the sides to the windscreen and round the headlights. Unwanted lines can be erased throughout the development of the structural sketch.

6 Form the Front and Begin Adding Details

Round the front openings and contour the lower front of the body. Begin adding details including the interior opening, the wheel rims and the stripes. Block in the turn signal lights.

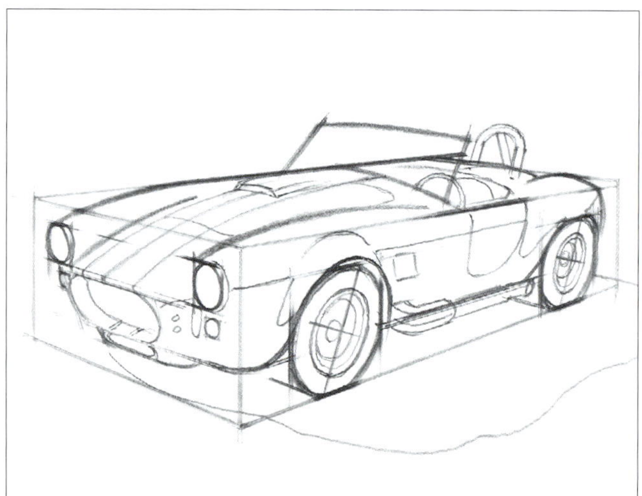

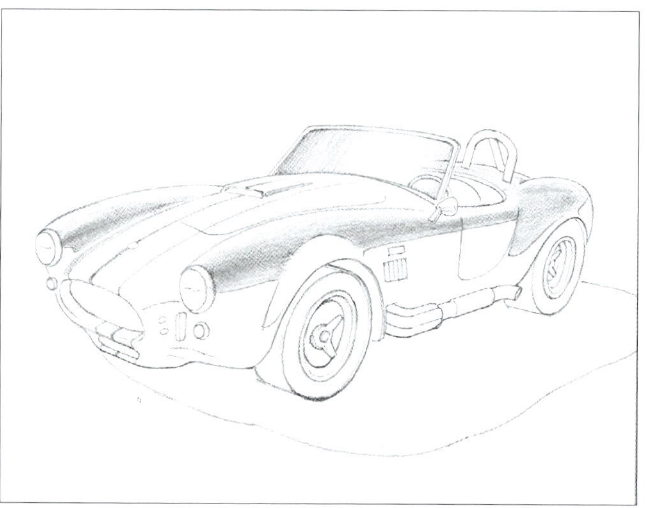

7 Add More Details, Shadows and Reflections

Add more details including the hood scoop, steering wheel, side pipes and roll hoop. Lines for the shadows and reflections should also be added during this step.

8 Trace or Transfer the Image and Add the Light Values

Using a 2B pencil, trace or transfer the sketch onto drawing paper. Leave out any unwanted lines.

Begin adding the light and middle values to the scene using a 2B pencil. Smooth pencil strokes should be used to shade in the contours of the bodywork of the automobile.

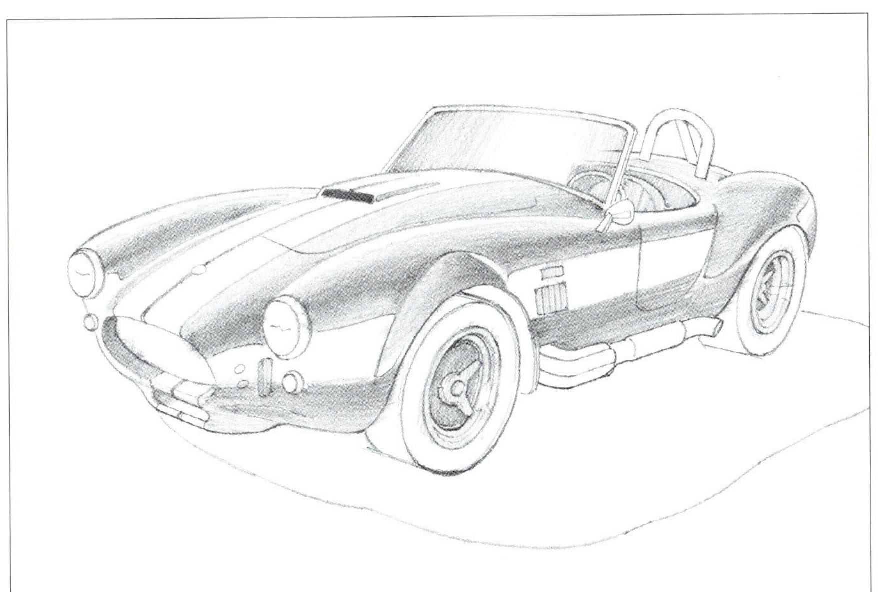

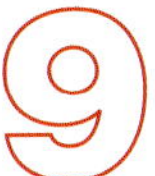

Add the Middle Values

Add the middle values by building up the pencil strokes.

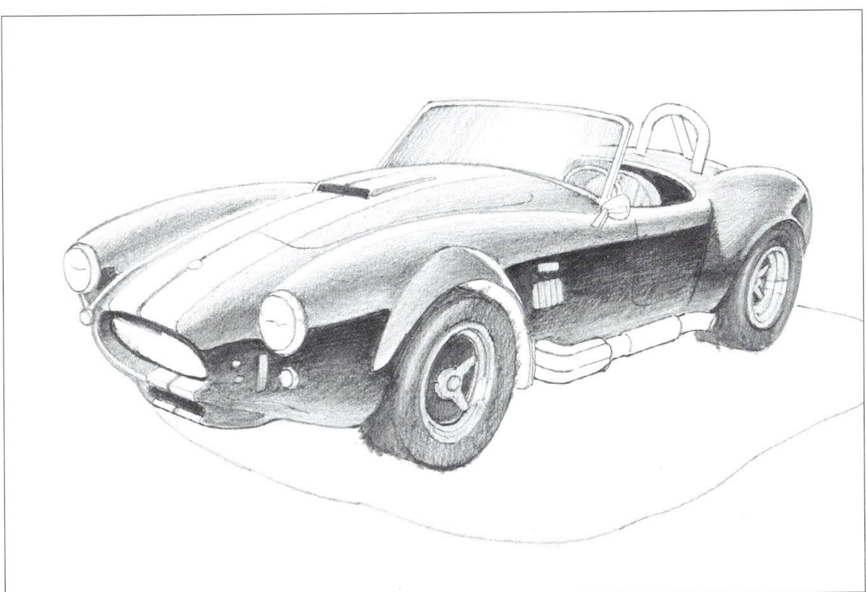

10 Add the Dark Values

Add dark values to the sides of the body, making the top edge a sharp contrast against the previous smooth shading. Darks should also be added to the wheels.

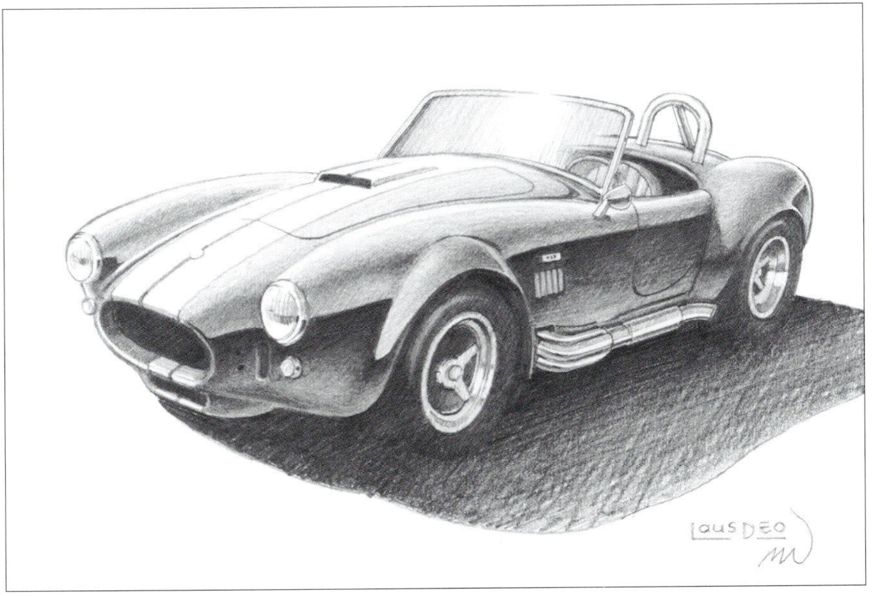

11 Continue Adding Darks and Details

Continue adding darks and details with 2B, 6B and mechanical pencils. Lighten areas as needed with a kneaded eraser. Sign the front and date the back of your completed drawing.

Battersea Power Station

With its stark, angular forms, the Battersea Power Station is an intriguing subject for observing and drawing two-point perspective. Rising alongside the River Thames in London, this iconic building has been seen in numerous movies and pop-culture venues. Most of the structural lines are vertical, or are directed to the right or left vanishing points. The exception to this is the chimneys, which narrow at the top and have ellipses.

This demonstration is done in three stages because of the many lines involved in completing the drawing. The first stage is a rough sketch. The second stage involves tracing the rough sketch onto tracing paper and adding more precise lines. The third stage involves tracing or transferring the sketch onto drawing paper and adding values to complete the drawing.

The light source comes from the upper left. Highly contrasting values emphasize the bold and imposing design of the architecture.

Materials

Paper
9" × 12" (23cm × 30cm) medium-texture drawing paper; 19" × 24" (48cm × 61cm) medium-texture sketch paper; 19" × 24" (48cm × 61cm) tracing paper

Pencils
2B and 6B

Other
kneaded eraser; lightbox or transfer paper; ruler; straightedge; triangle; T-square

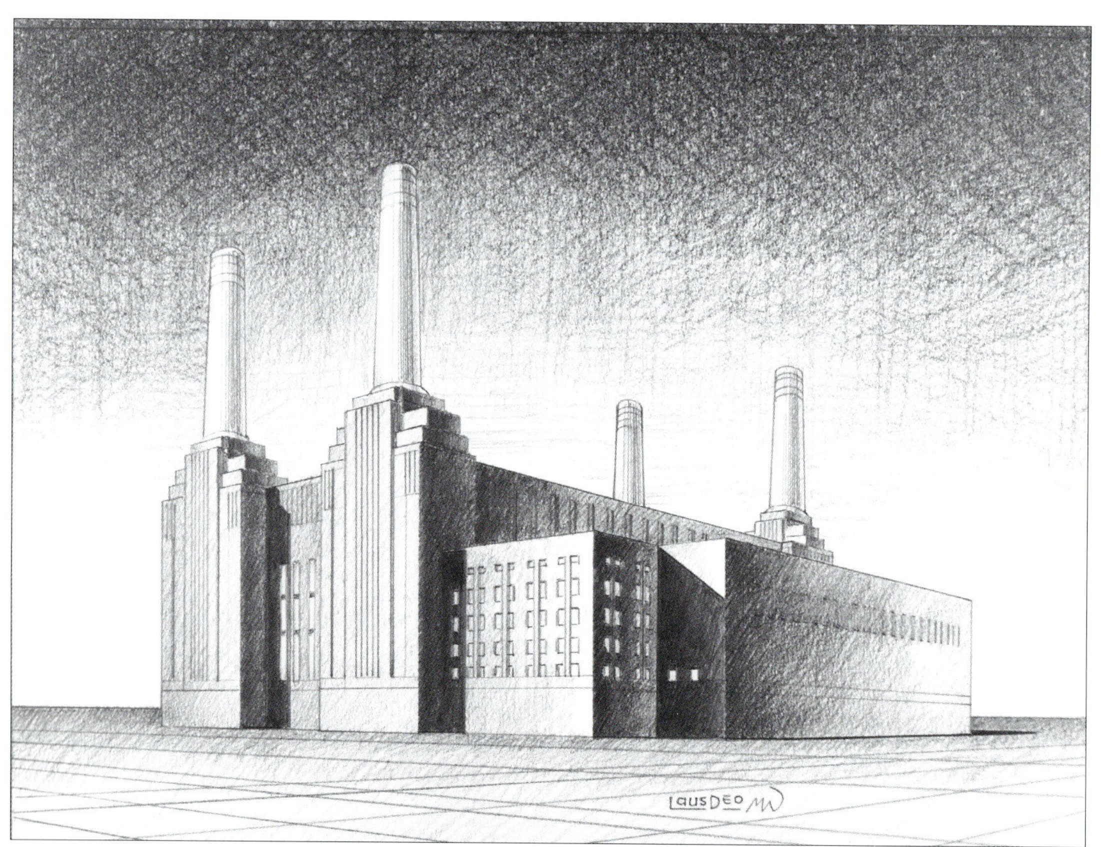

Battersea Power Station
Graphite pencil on drawing paper
9" × 12" (23cm × 30cm)

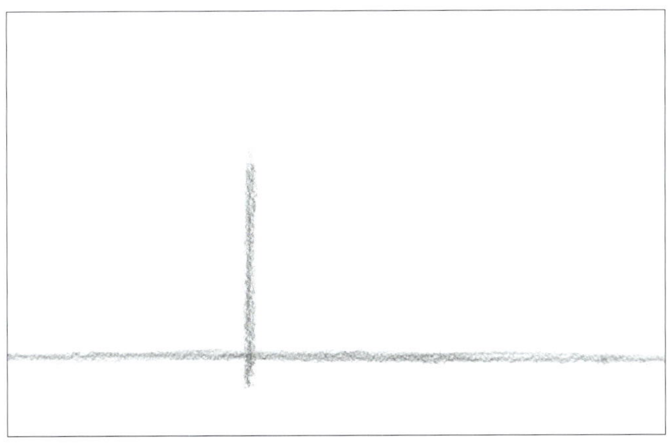

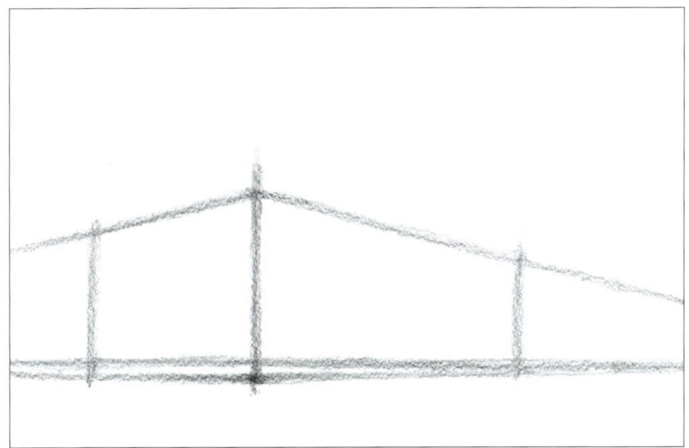

1 Start the Rough Structural Sketch

On a piece of sketch paper, start a rough sketch of the structure using a 2B pencil. To establish the vanishing points, the paper size is larger than what will be used for the finished drawing. Sketch a horizontal line about one third from the bottom edge of the paper for the horizon. Place the left vanishing point on the far left and the right vanishing point on the far right on the horizon with a distance of 23⅞" (61cm) between the two vanishing points. Sketch a vertical line 12¼" (31cm) from the left vanishing point as the nearest corner of the closest tower. (Although vanishing points were used to create the structural sketch, they were cropped out in order to show the images as large as possible.)

2 Sketch the Central Form

Sketch orthogonal lines that go from the previous vertical line at a point ¼" (6mm) below the horizon to the left vanishing point and the right vanishing point. Sketch orthogonal lines from the top of the vertical line at a point 3" (8cm) above the horizon to the left and right vanishing points. Add vertical lines, one 2⅞" (7cm) to the left of the first vertical line and one 4½" (11cm) to the right to form the sides of the towers.

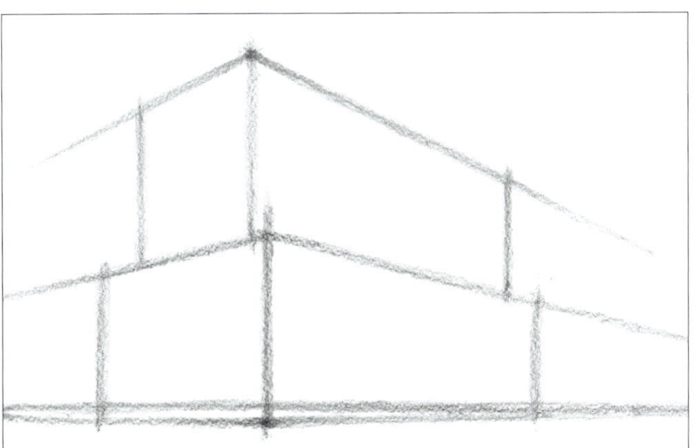

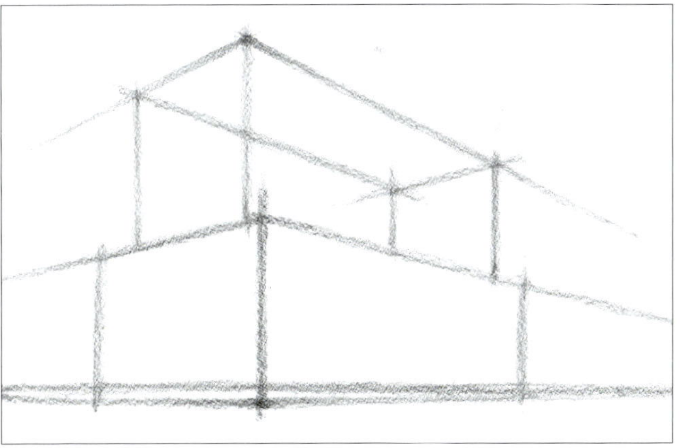

3 Place the Three Closest Chimneys

Sketch a vertical line ¼" (6mm) left of the previous central vertical line for the placement of the nearest chimney. From the new vertical line, at a point of 6⅛" (15.6cm) above the horizon, sketch an orthogonal line to the left vanishing point and an orthogonal line to the right vanishing point for the chimney's height. Add a vertical line on the left and another on the right for the approximate placement of the far left and far right chimneys.

4 Place the Distant Chimney

From the tops of the far left and right chimneys, sketch orthogonal lines to the left and right vanishing points. At their tangent, sketch a vertical line downward for the placement of the distant chimney.

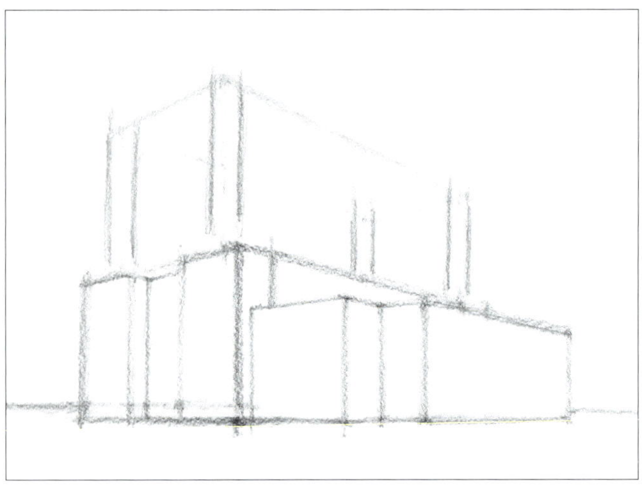

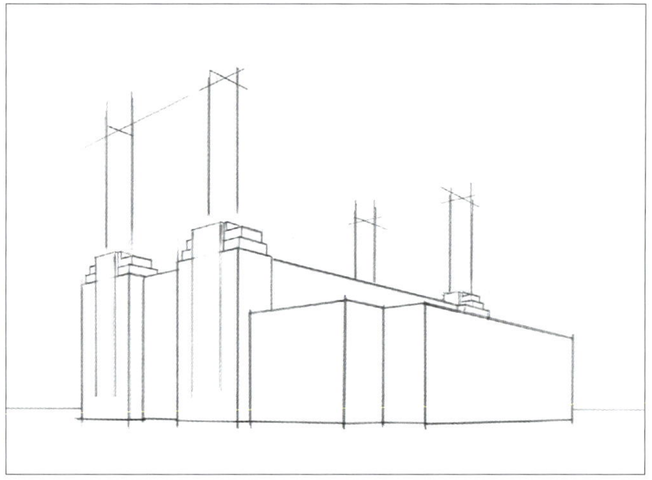

5 Continue Developing the Towers and Central Form and Sketch the Chimneys

Sketch lines to develop the box shapes of the towers and distinguish the central part of the building structure. Keep in mind that this building, with the exception of the chimneys, is just a cluster of box forms. Add box forms to the right side of the building by sketching the smaller box form connected to the central tower, then sketching the far right box form that is connected to the previous one. Erase any unwanted linework with a kneaded eraser. Sketch the basic forms of the chimneys extending up from the center of the towers with vertical lines.

6 Trace Onto Tracing Paper and Detail the Towers

Using a 2B pencil, lightly trace the structural sketch onto tracing paper, including the horizon and vanishing points. You'll get more precision by using a straightedge, T-square and triangle. Continue developing the form of the towers and begin adding details. The tops of the towers, along with the chimneys, are perhaps the most identifying features of this building.

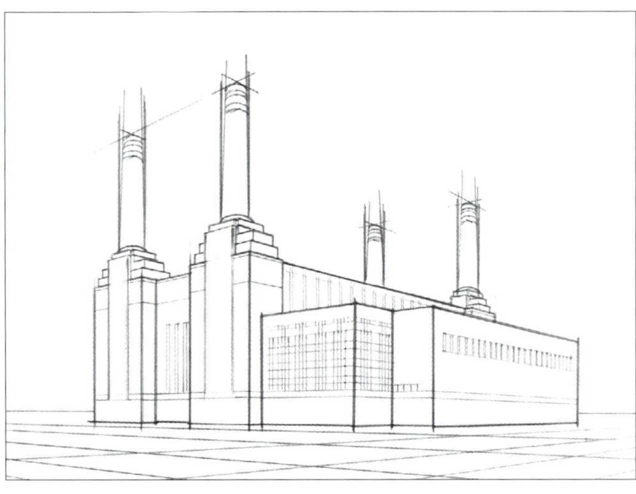

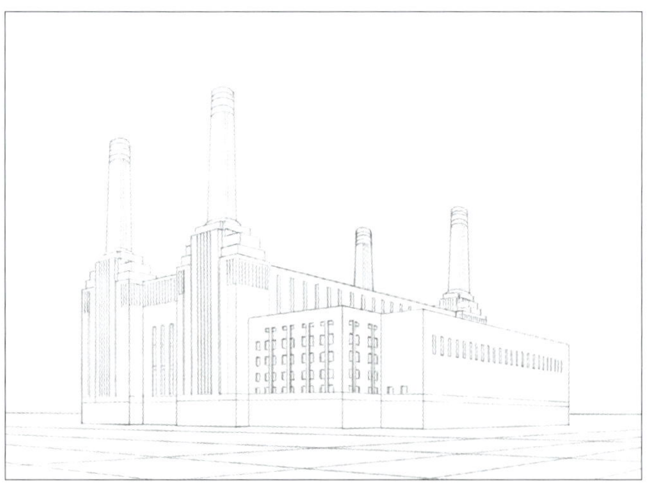

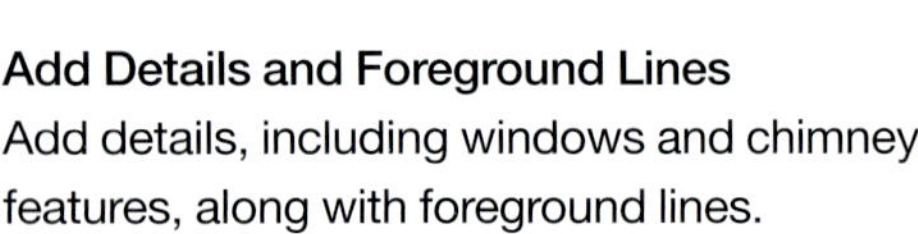

7 Add Details and Foreground Lines

Add details, including windows and chimney features, along with foreground lines.

8 Trace or Transfer the Image and Add Pattern Lines

Using a 2B pencil, trace or transfer the image onto drawing paper, omitting any unwanted lines. Add pattern lines for the bricks on the towers. (A smaller piece of paper is used for this stage of the drawing because the vanishing points are no longer necessary.)

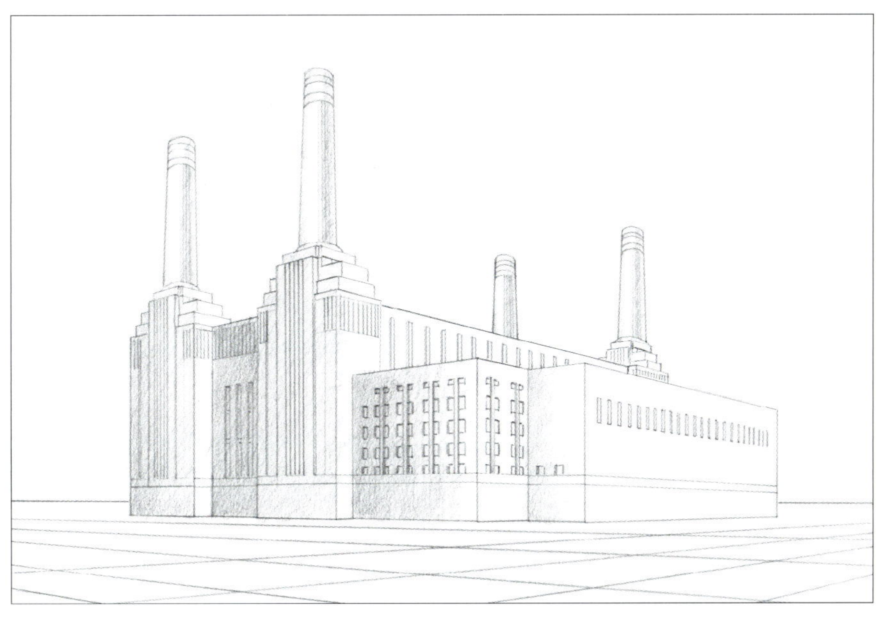

9 Add Light and Middle Values

Add the light and middle values of the building with a 2B pencil. Paper can be used as a frisket to create sharp edges.

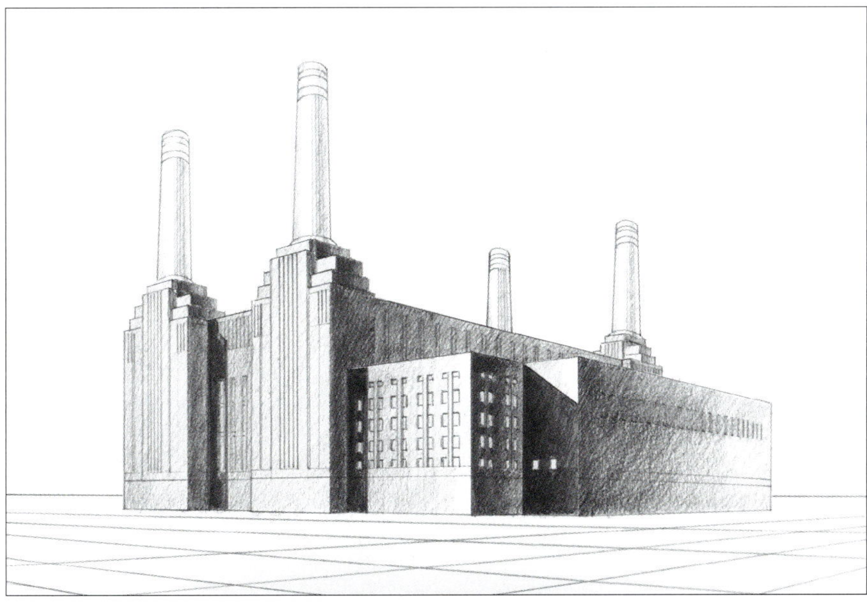

10 Add Dark Values

Add darker values to the building using 2B and 6B pencils.

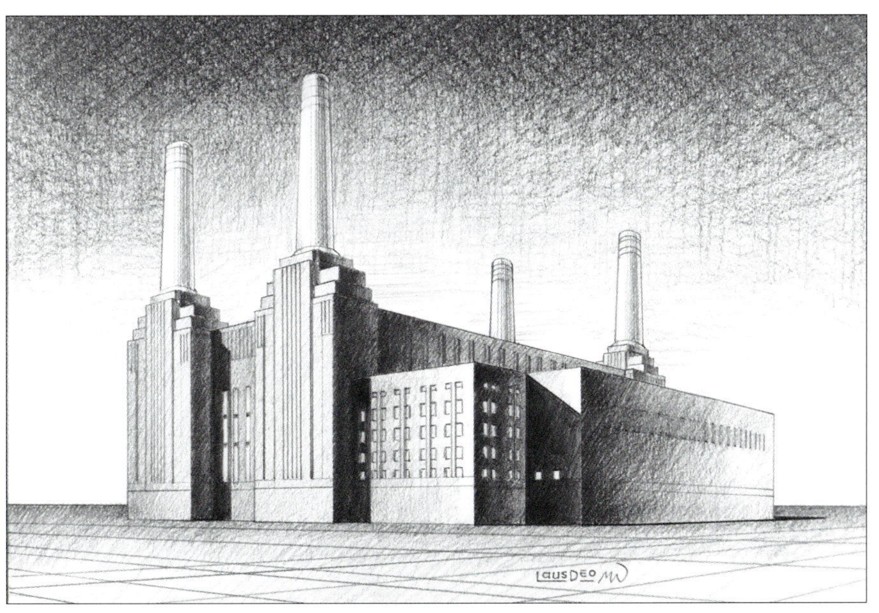

11 Add the Sky, Foreground and Details

Use a 2B pencil to add values to the sky, which darkens going up. Then darken the foreground, which lightens as it goes down. Add darks and details with 2B and 6B pencils. If needed, make adjustments by lightening some areas with a kneaded eraser. Sign the front of your drawing and write the date on the back.

Still Life with Books & Pottery

This still life is composed of books and pottery that, thought of in more basic forms, are boxes and cylinders. Two-point perspective is utilized, though there would be four vanishing points if the books were plotted out. The two lower books are aligned with each other, so they share the same two vanishing points. The top book is not aligned with the bottom books, so it has two vanishing points of its own. The light source is from the left, creating clearly defined shadows to the right of the objects.

Materials

Paper
8" × 10" (20cm × 25cm) medium-texture drawing paper; 8" × 10" (20cm × 25cm) medium-texture sketch paper

Pencils
2B and 6B

Other
kneaded eraser; lightbox or transfer paper; triangle

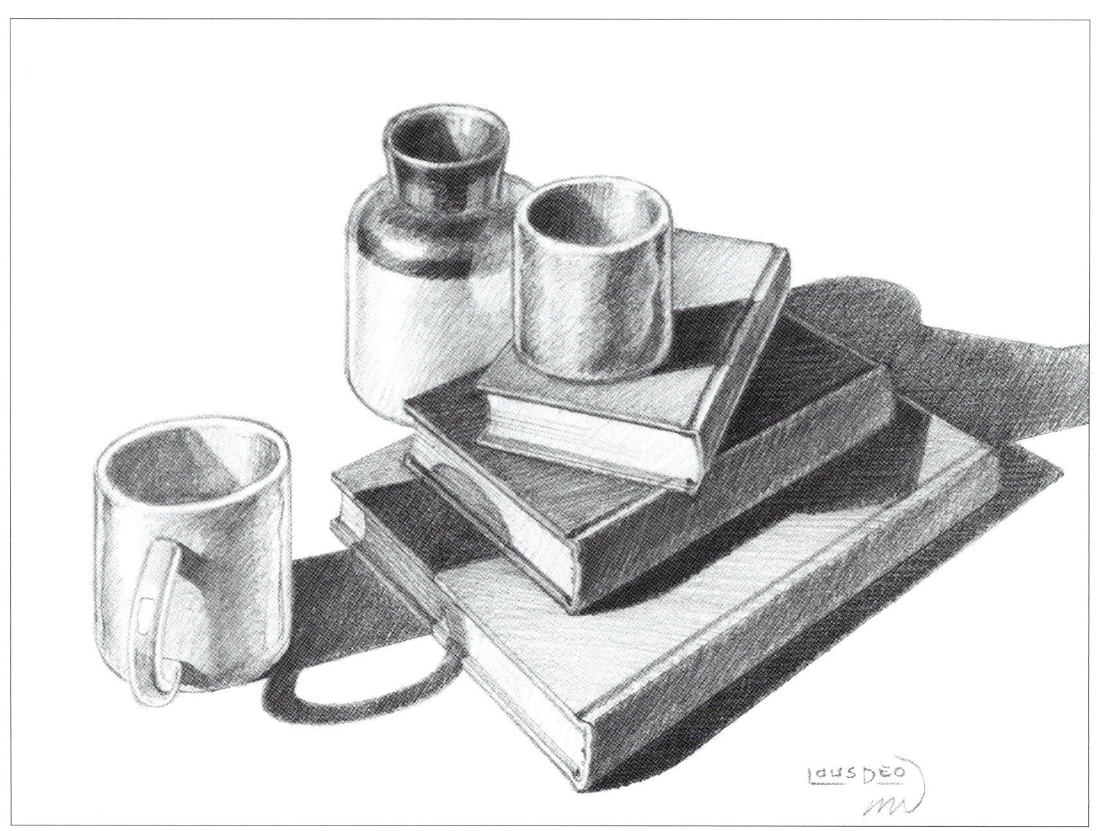

Still Life with Books and Pottery
Graphite pencil on drawing paper
8" × 10" (20cm × 25cm)

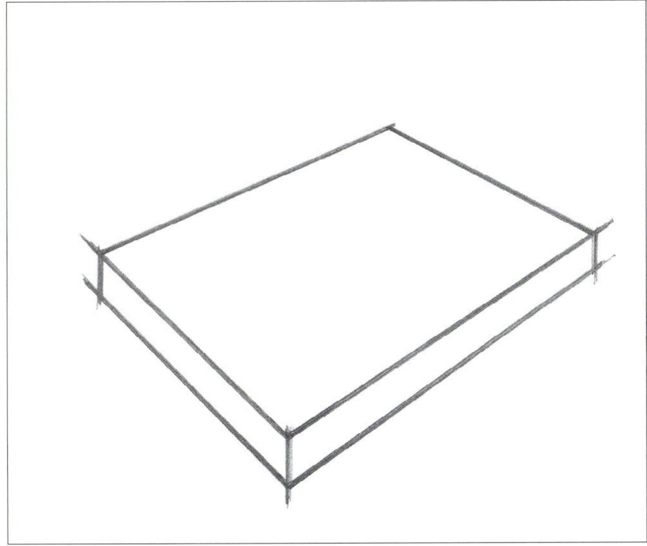

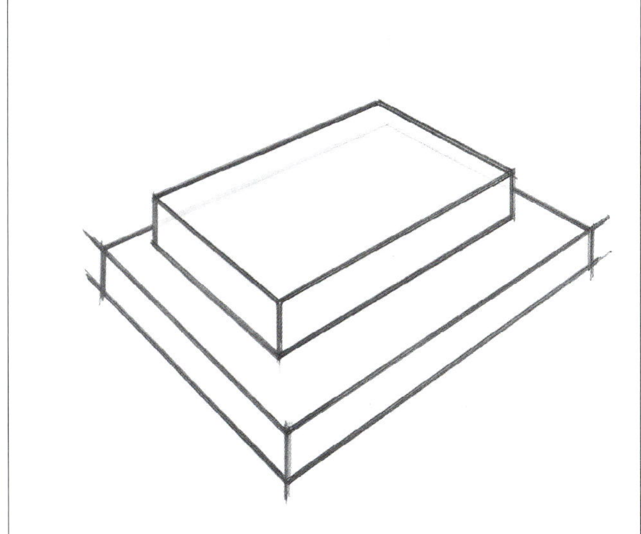

1 **Sketch the Lower Book**

Using a 2B pencil and a piece of sketch paper, begin the structural sketch by placing the front corner of the lower book with a vertical line. Add the left and right orthogonal lines from the front corner as the sides.

Sketch vertical lines for the left and right corners. From the point where the corner lines intersect the top orthogonal lines, sketch two more orthogonal lines to form the box shape of the lower book.

2 **Sketch the Middle Book**

Following the previous step, sketch the middle book, which rests on the lower book. Since the books align, they share the same vanishing points. Some lines can be erased during the sketching process so that the forms will be less confusing.

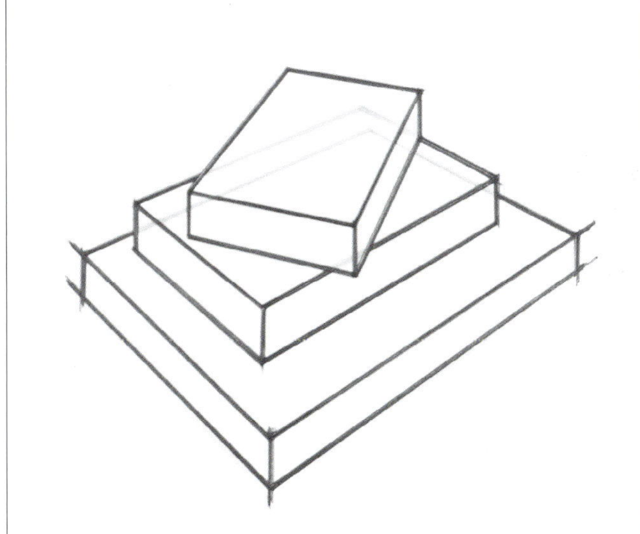

3 **Sketch the Top Book**

Sketch the top book following the same process as the lower and middle books. However, it does not align with the other two books, making the vanishing points and orthogonal lines different.

The Trouble with Tangents

Tangents occur when two or more elements line up or intersect each other. When composing art, tangents should generally be avoided because they can make a subject confusing for the viewer.

There are numerous tangents in this sketch. Can you spot them?

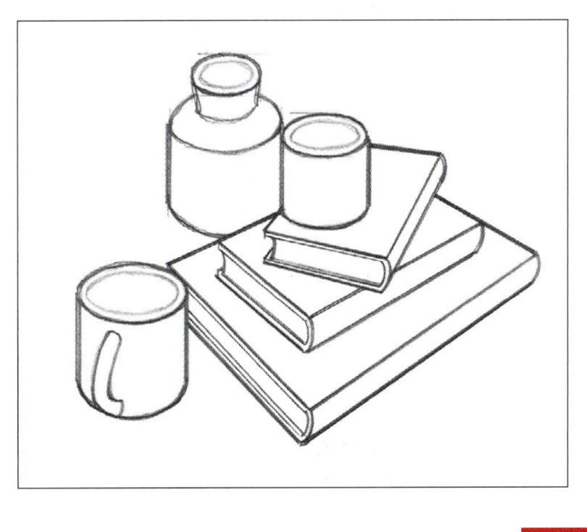

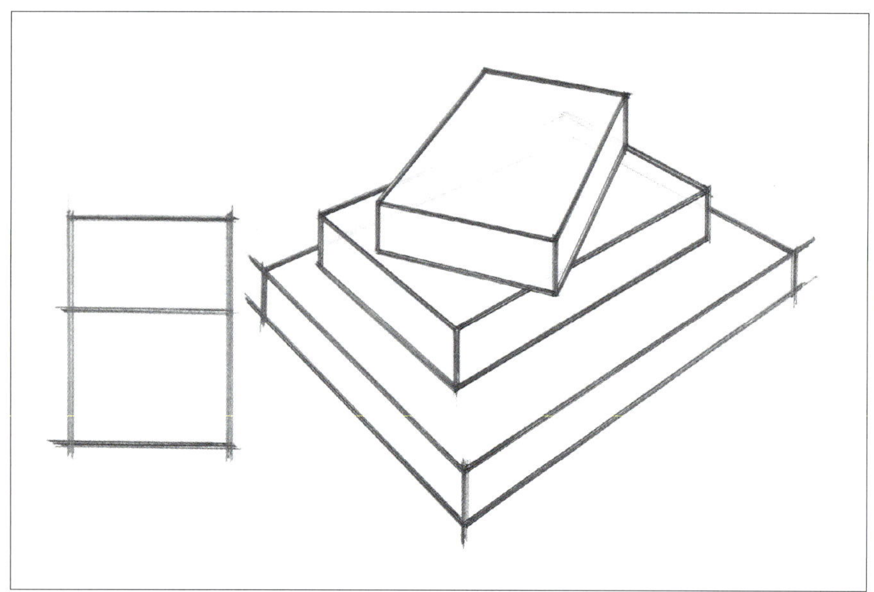

4 Block in the Left Mug

Proportion the width and height of the left mug, and block it in with vertical and horizontal lines. Add another horizontal line to proportion the top ellipse. Because of the relatively symmetrical form of these ellipses, a preliminary box form is not always needed to sketch them in.

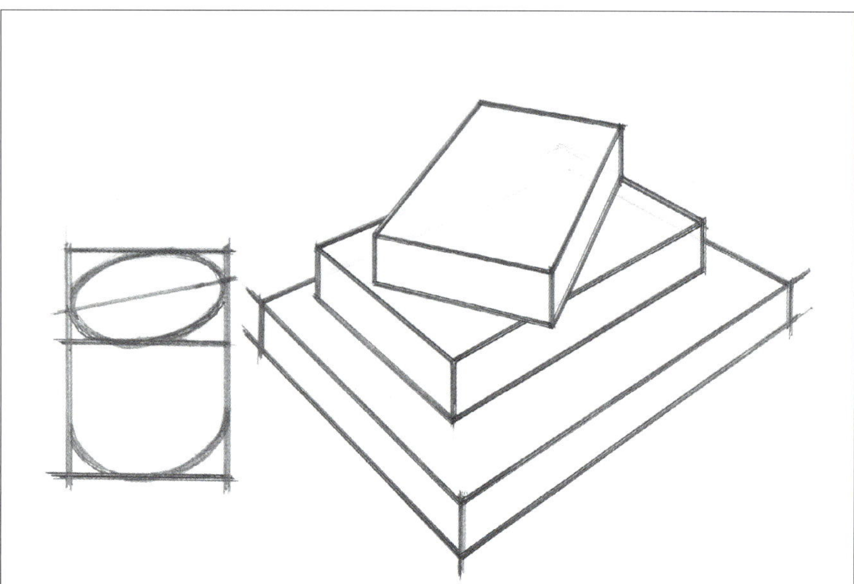

5 Build up the Mug

Sketch an angled line as the major axis of the top ellipse. Sketch the top ellipse. Next, sketch the lower portion of the bottom ellipse, which is shaped slightly rounder than the top ellipse. (The ellipses of this mug have a bit of peripheral distortion because they are placed off to the side.)

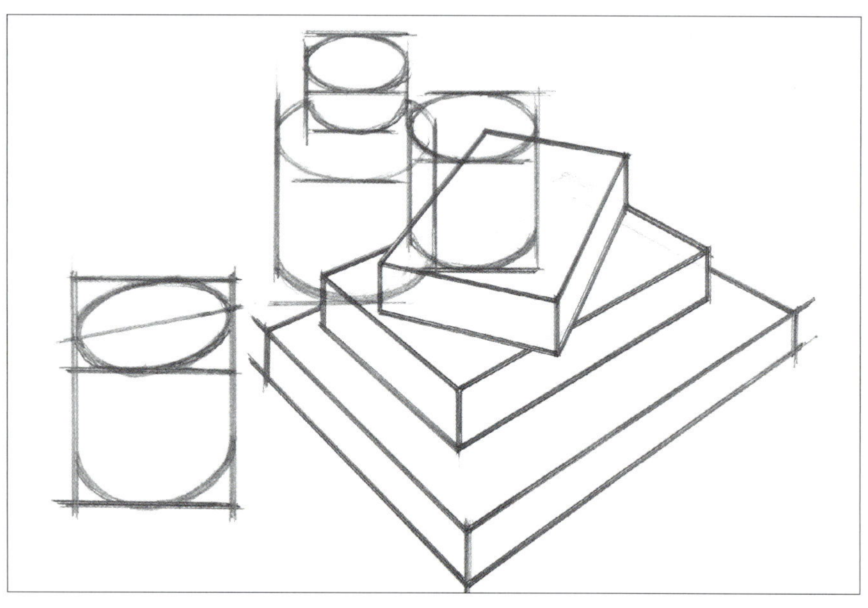

6 Sketch the Cup and Crock

Following the previous procedure, sketch the cup on the top of the books, then the crock behind the books. The crock can be sketched as a small cylinder on top of a larger cylinder. Both the cup and the crock have ellipses that are symmetrical.

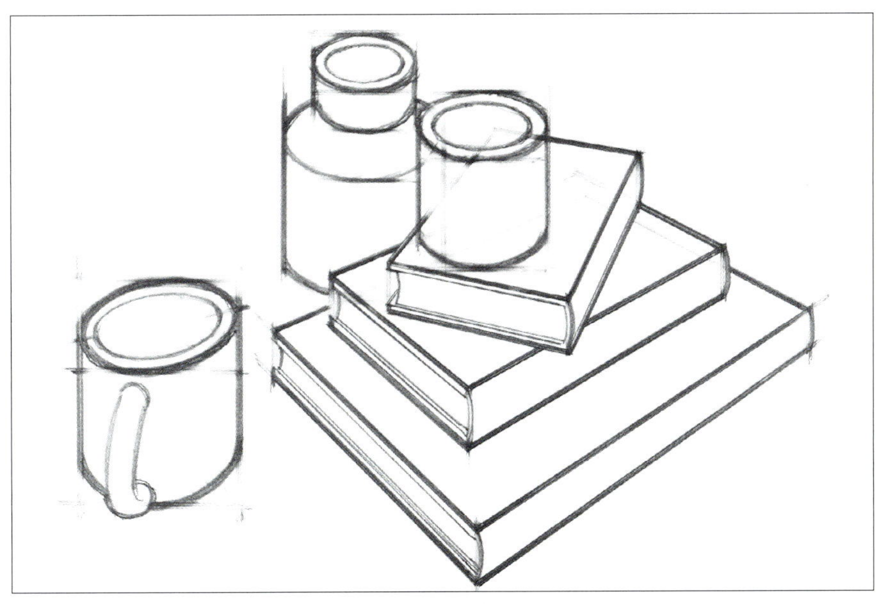

7 Develop the Forms

Develop the forms of the books and pottery including the handle to the mug. Erase any unnecessary lines to avoid confusion.

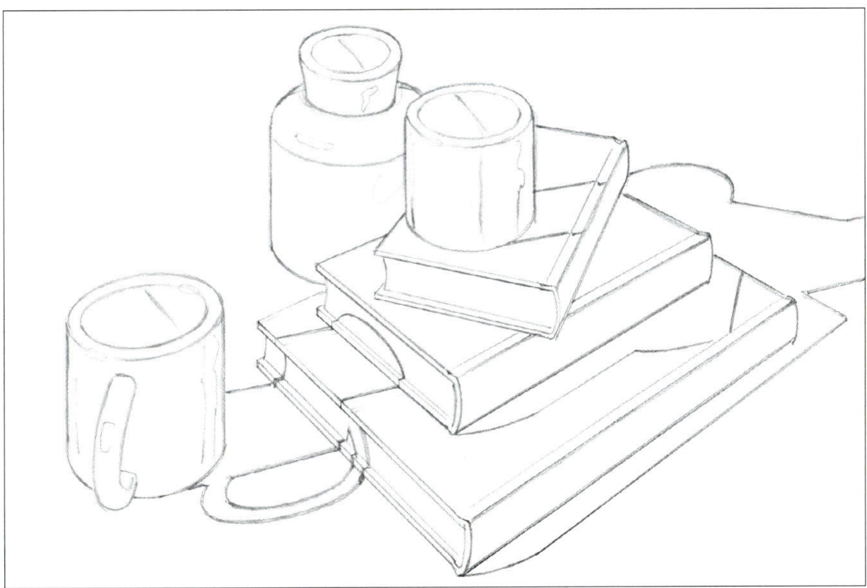

8 Trace or Transfer the Image

Using a 2B pencil, trace or transfer the structural sketch onto a sheet of drawing paper. Add more details such as shadows and highlights.

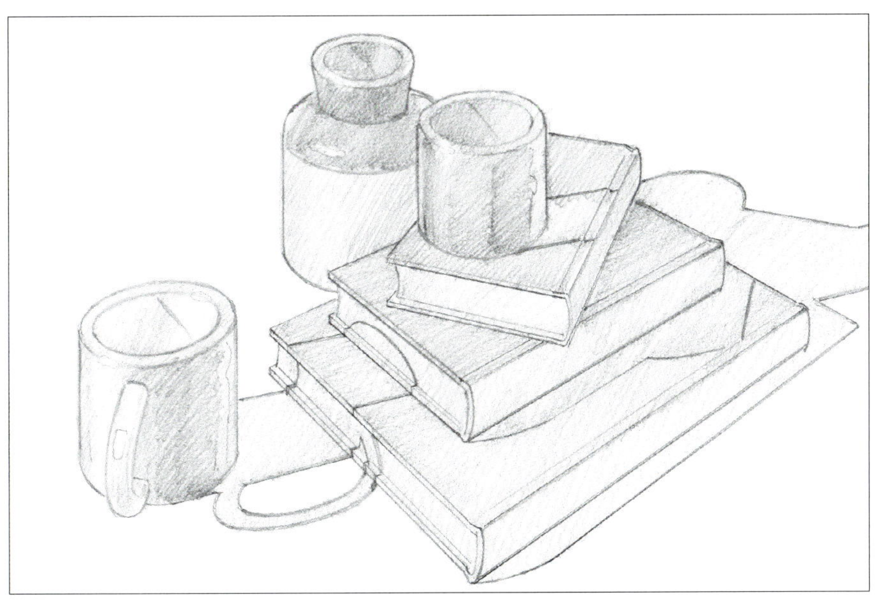

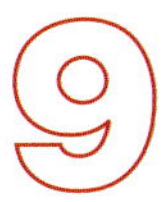

Add the Light Values

Add the lightest values to the scene using a 2B pencil.

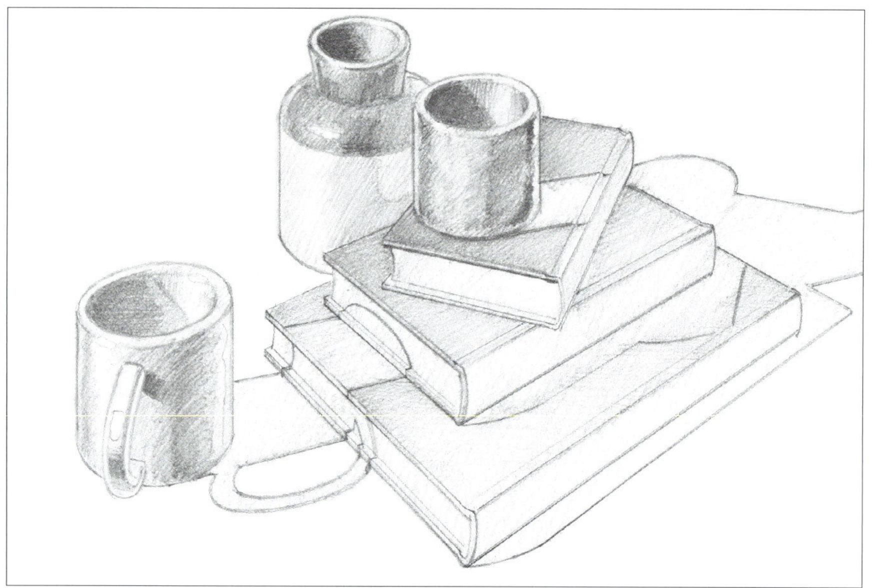

10 Add the Middle Values

Build up the pencil strokes to create the middle values.

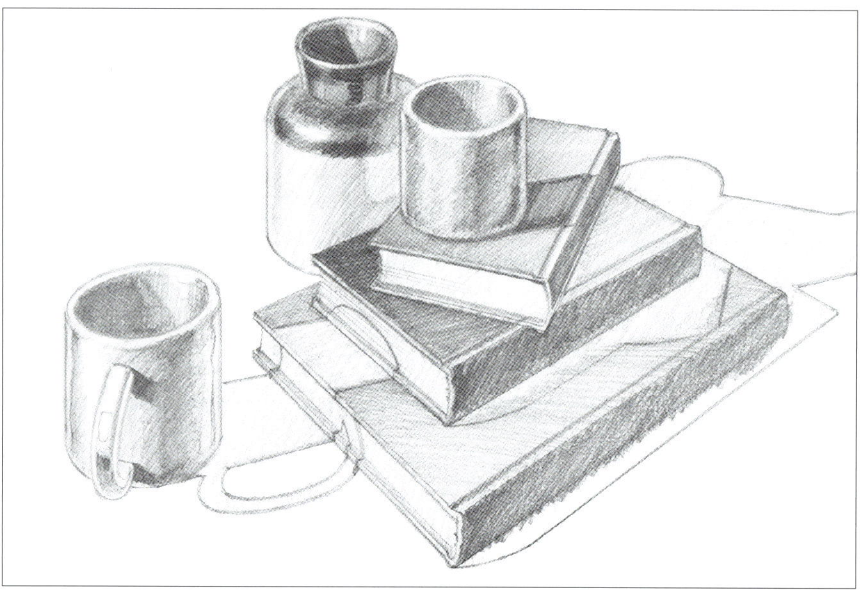

11 Add Dark Values and Details

Add dark values and details throughout the drawing with 2B and 6B pencils.

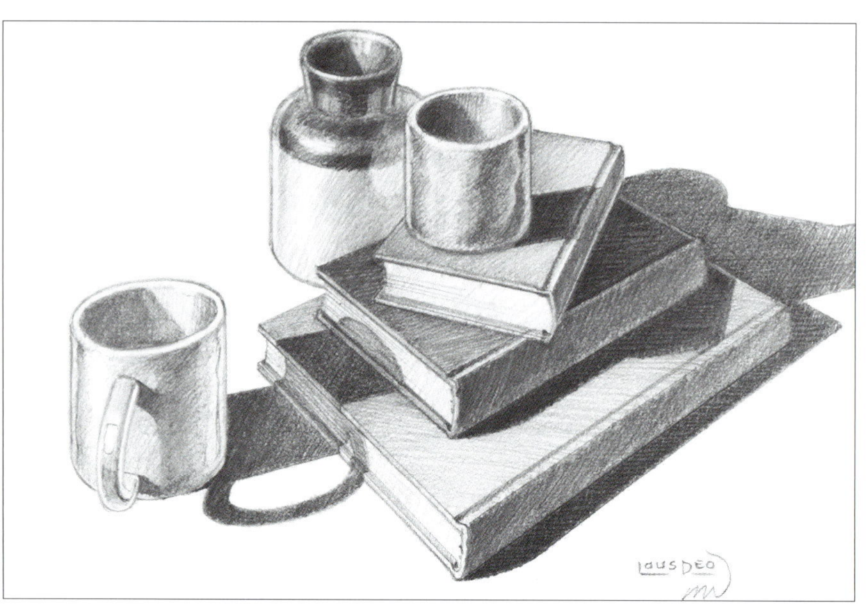

12 Continue Adding Details and Highlights

Continue adding details. Use a kneaded eraser to lighten some areas as needed. Sign the front of your drawing and write the date on the back.

City Scene with People

Two-point perspective and atmospheric perspective are used together to suggest depth in this city scene. The light source comes from the upper right, causing the right sides of the building to be lighter and the left sides to be darker.

This demonstration is very detailed and may take more time than the other demonstrations. However, the drawing can be simplified by changing the older style of the buildings, with their inset windows, to more modern architecture with fewer details and less ornamentation.

Materials

Paper
19" × 24" (48cm × 61cm) medium-texture drawing paper; 12" × 9" (30cm × 23cm) medium-texture sketch paper

Pencils
.05 mechanical and 2B

Other
kneaded eraser; lightbox or transfer paper; ruler; triangle; T-square

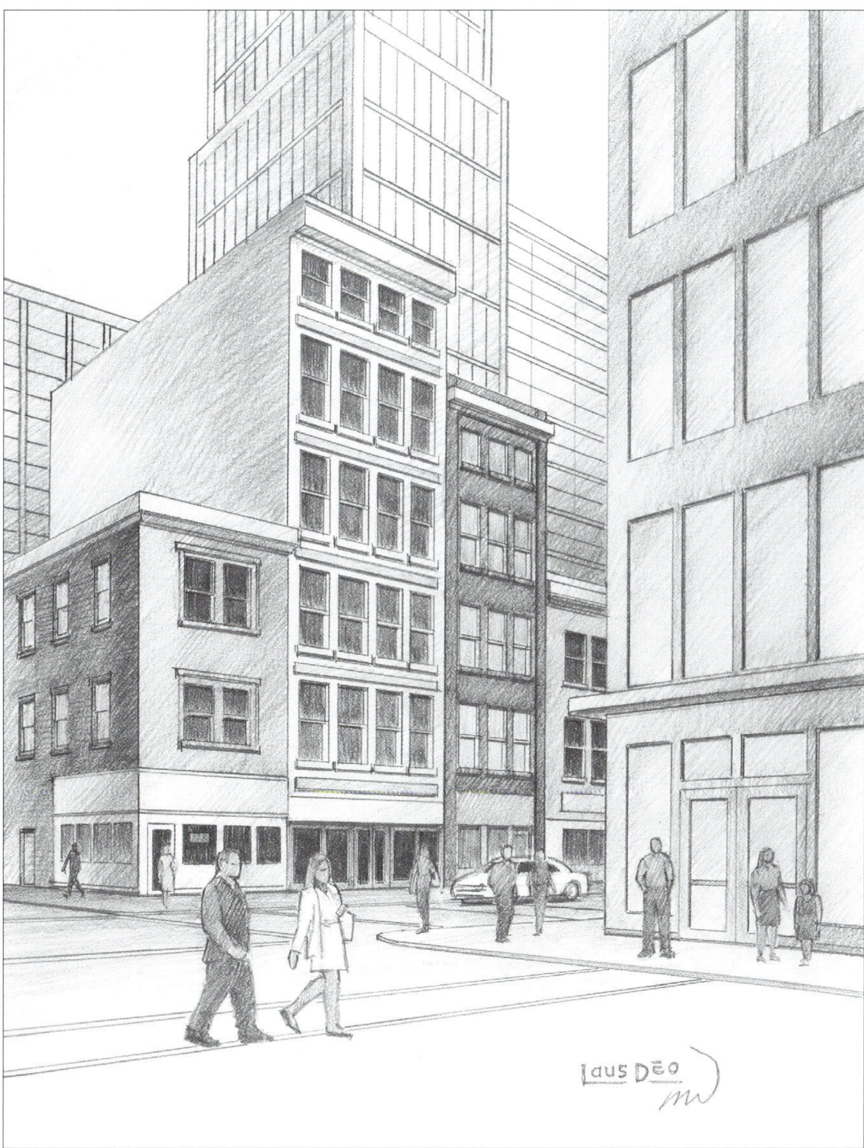

City Scene with People
Graphite pencil on drawing paper
12" × 9" (30cm × 23cm)

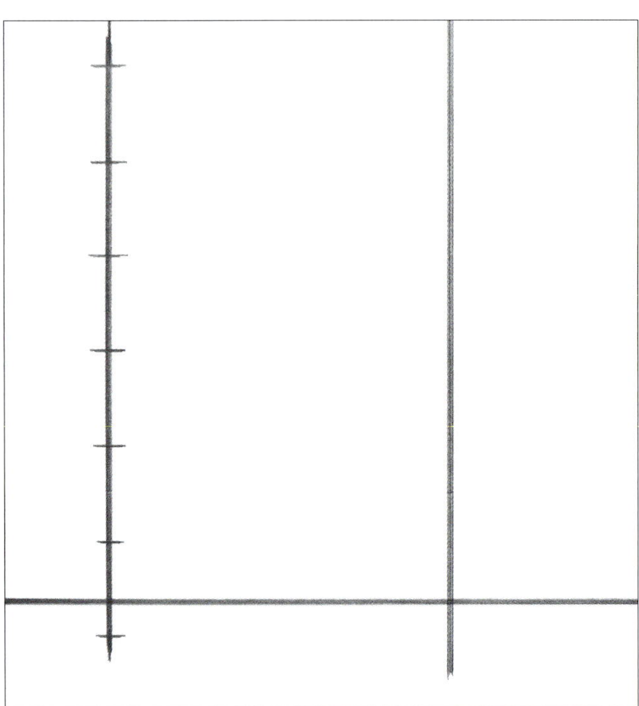

1 Sketch the Structural Foundation

Using sketch paper and a 2B pencil, sketch a line for the horizon 4" (10cm) above the bottom edge of the paper. Place two vanishing points on the horizon with a space of 22" (56cm) between them. Add a vertical line as the corner of the left building 6¾" (17cm) to the right of the left vanishing point. (To save space, the sides of the structural sketch, which include the vanishing points, have been cropped out and are not shown in this step or the following structural sketch steps.)

On the vertical corner line of the left building, mark the height of the floors of the buildings. The first mark is ½" (13mm) below the horizon, with additional upward marks being 1⅜" (3.5cm) apart from each another. Note that the first mark establishes where the ground plane is in relation to the horizon and at eye level. Sketch the right building corner by adding a vertical line 4¾" (12cm) to the right of the vertical corner line of the left building.

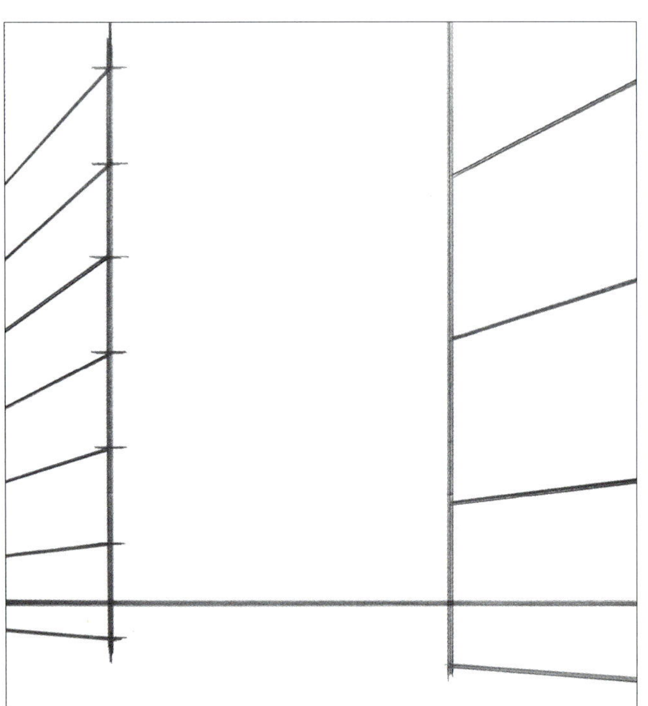

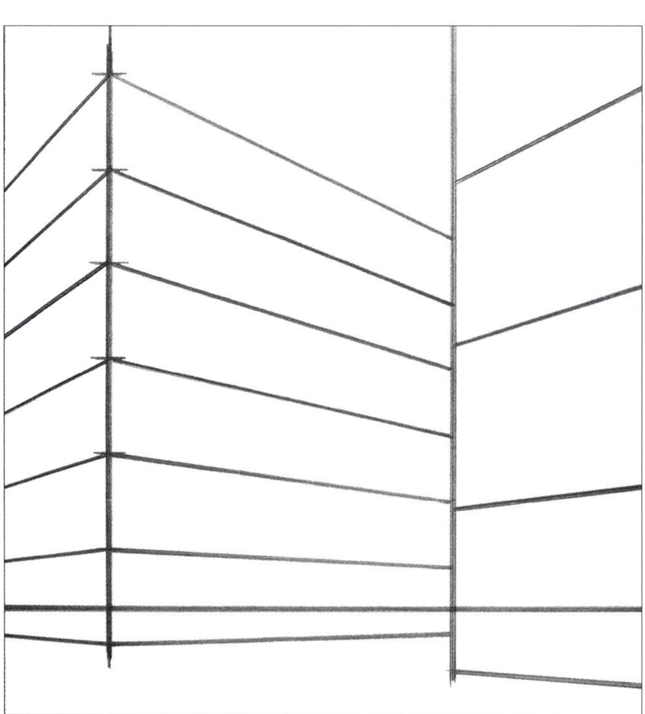

2 Add Orthogonal Floor Lines

Add orthogonal lines from the left vanishing point to the lines that mark off the floors of the left building. Continue the lines from the corner of the left building to the right building.

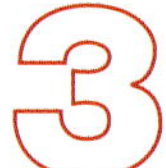

Add More Orthogonal Lines

Add orthogonal lines around the corner of the left building that are directed to the right vanishing point.

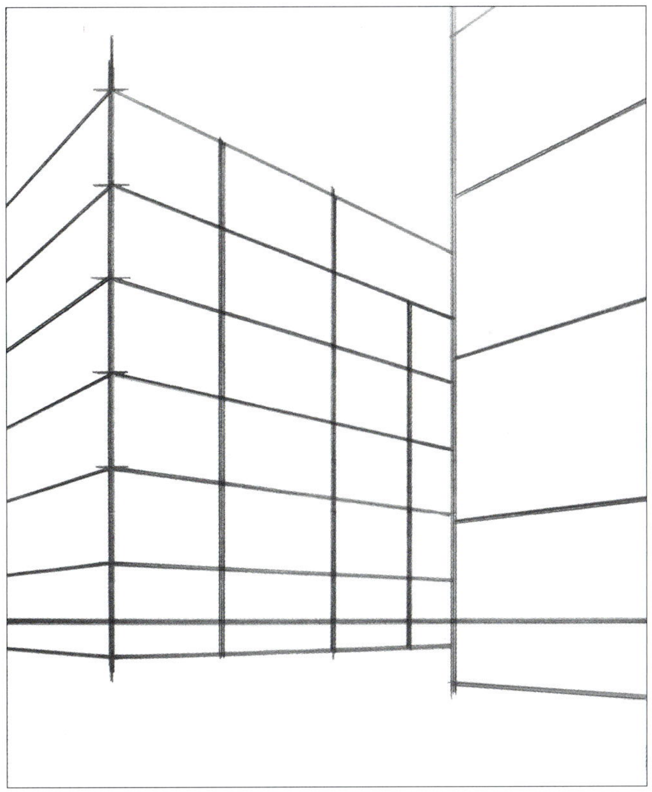

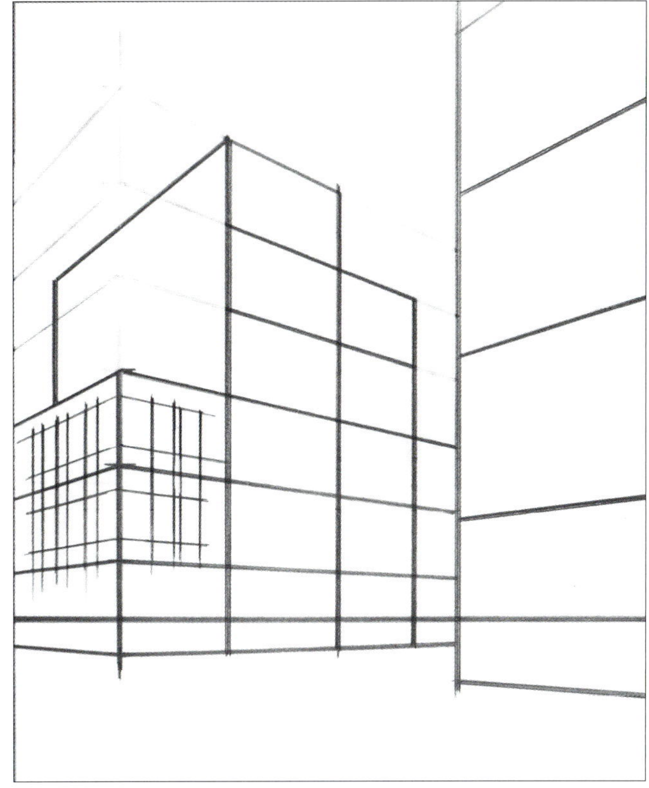

4

Add the Building Lines

Sketch vertical lines to distinguish the forms of the buildings.

5

Develop the Building Forms and Add Window Lines

Complete the box form of the buildings and add vertical and orthogonal lines for the windows of the far left building. Unwanted lines can be erased throughout the structural sketch process.

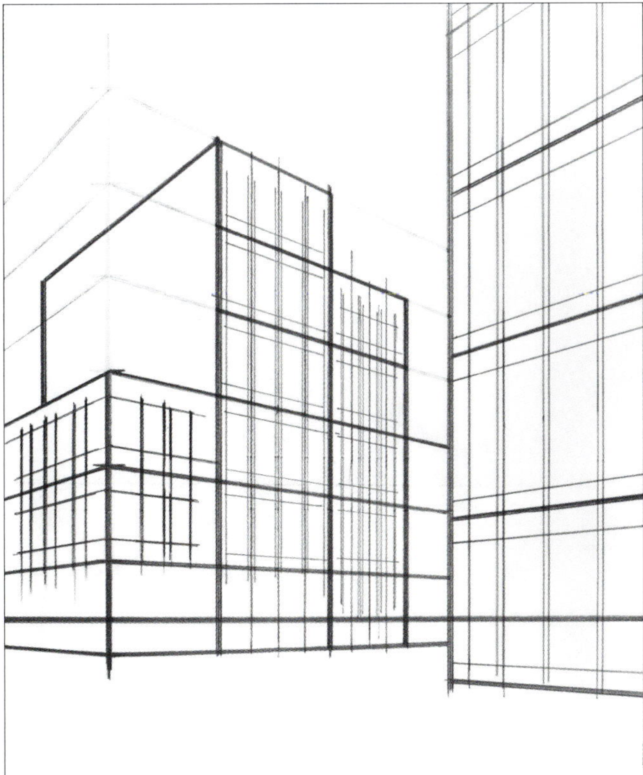

6

Add More Windows

Add windows to the other buildings by sketching vertical and orthogonal lines following the same process as the left building's windows. Areas can be subdivided for proper placement of lines.

Think Big, Then Small

It may be easier to sketch small, detailed forms, such as cars and people, bigger than the size needed for the finished drawing. The sketches can be reduced to the correct size using a copier, and the images can then be traced or transferred into place for the finished drawing.

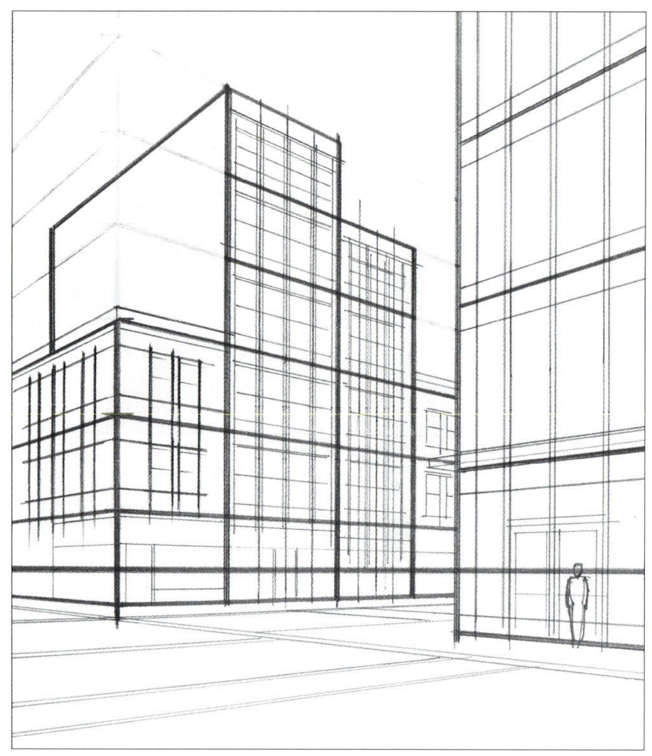

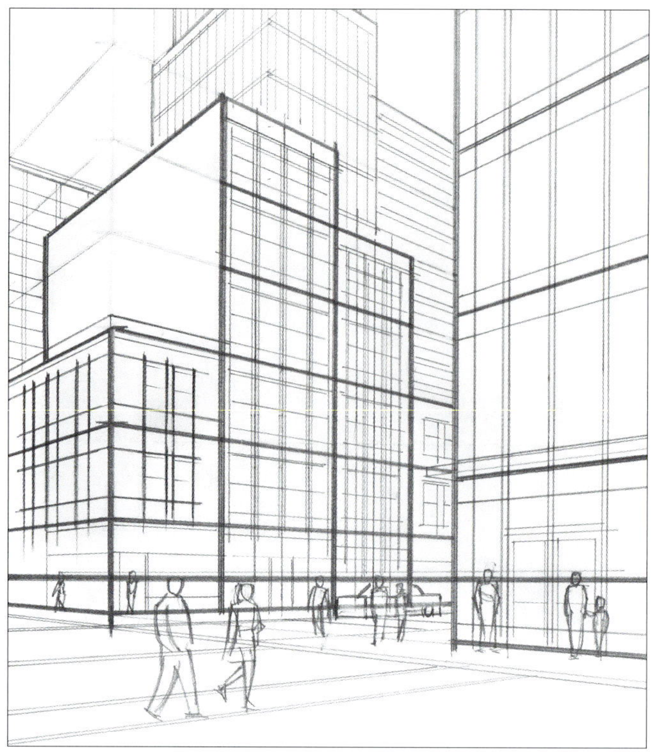

7 Add Details and a Person

Add details to the buildings, street lines and curbs. After sketching the doors of the right building, roughly sketch a person appropriate for the door height. The person's eyes should align with the horizon. This demonstration was drawn from the vantage point of an adult standing on a sidewalk. The eye level of any same-size adult standing on a sidewalk should align with the horizon in this scene.

8 Sketch More People, Distant Buildings and a Car

Add more people relative in size to the first person. People in the street will appear slightly lower than people on the sidewalk. Add distant buildings. Sketch the boxy form of a car on the street behind the people.

9 Trace or Transfer the Image

Trace or transfer the structural sketch onto drawing paper using a 2B pencil. Refine the forms of the people, buildings and car. The finer lines can be placed using a mechanical pencil.

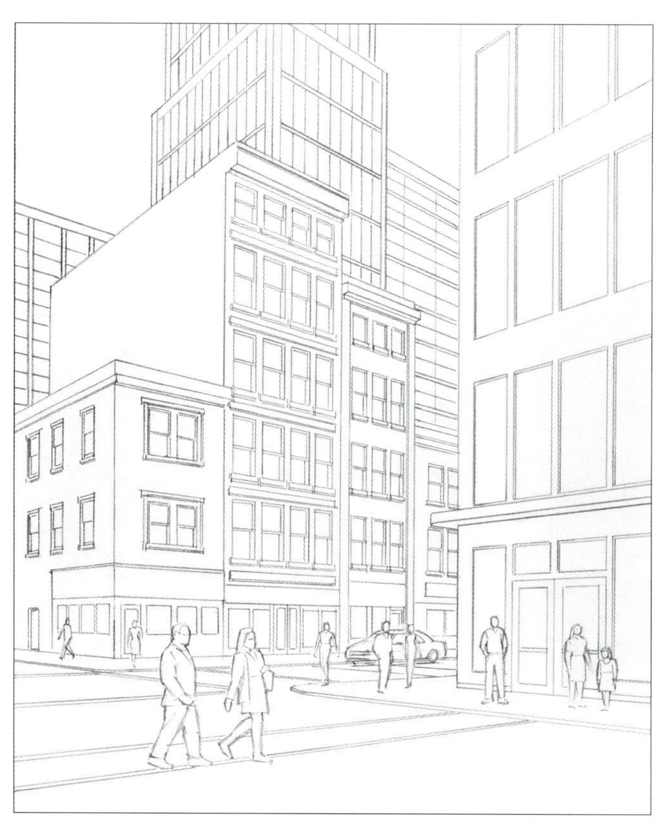

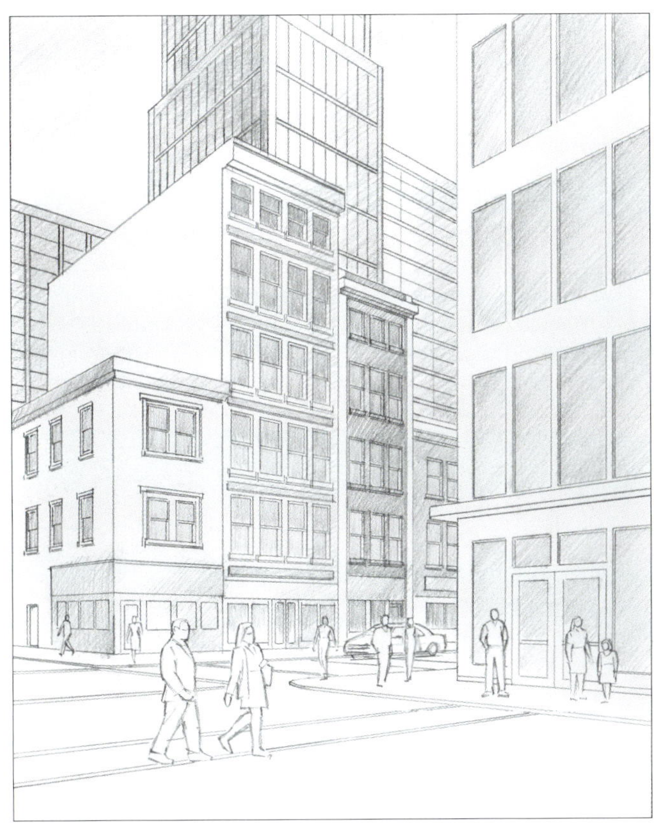

10 Add the Light and Middle Values

Add the light and middle values of the buildings with a 2B pencil. Paper can be used as a frisket to create the sharp edges.

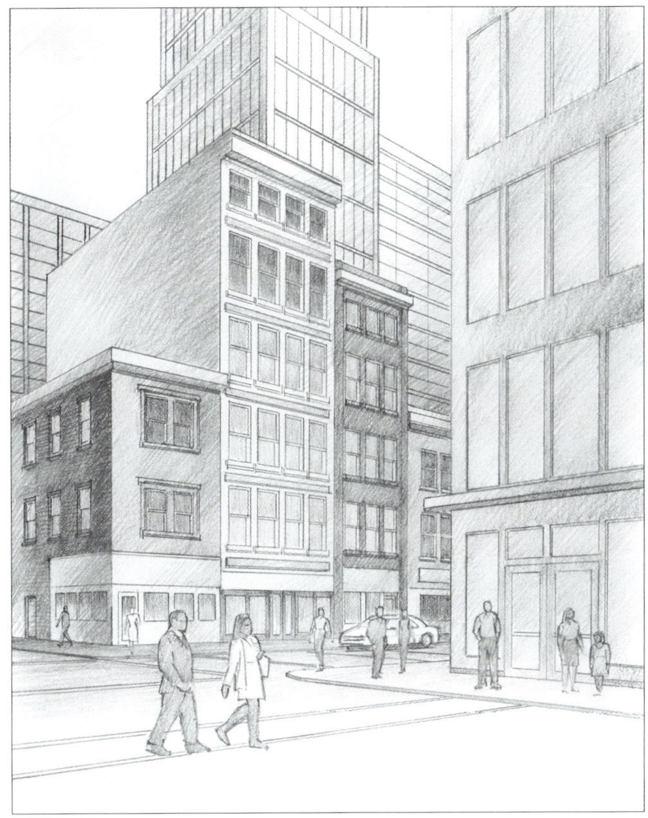

11 Continue Building up Values

Continue building up pencil strokes to add values. The distant buildings should have less detail and more muted values than the foreground buildings because of atmospheric perspective.

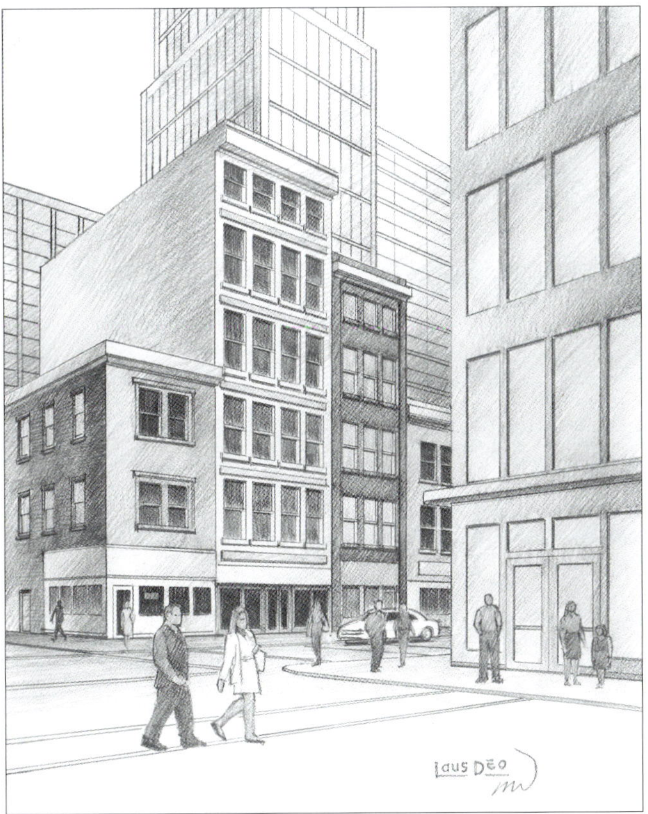

12 Add Darks and Details

Complete the drawing by adding dark values and details. Sign the front and write the date on the back.

Conclusion

You can apply what you have learned from this book to all of your artwork. The other books in our *Absolute Beginner* series are also great resources for learning different mediums and working with specific subjects as you continue on your artistic journey.

Have fun and keep up the good work!

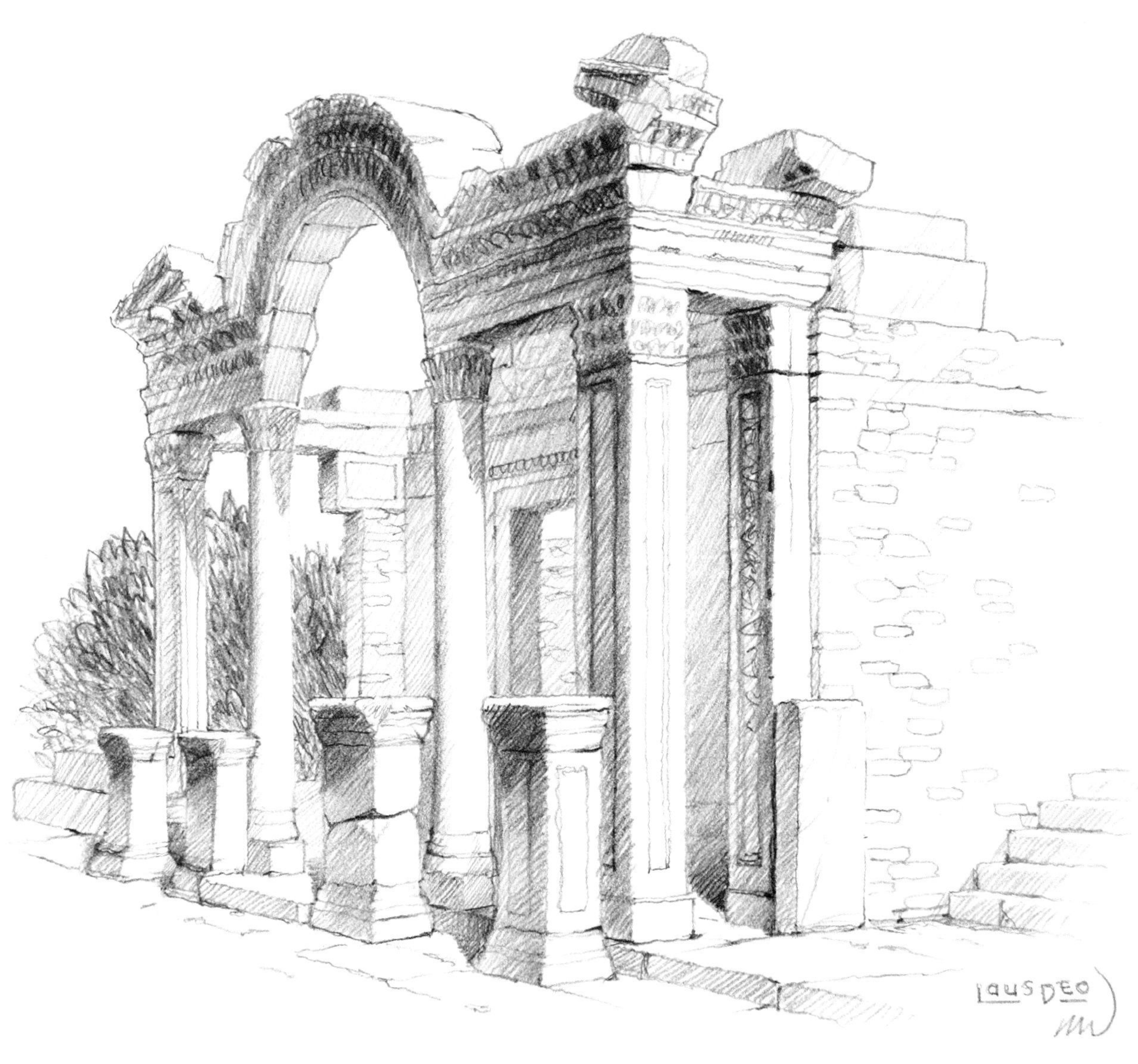

Ephesus Ruins
Graphite pencil on drawing paper
8" × 9" (20cm × 23cm)

Glossary

A

Accidental vanishing point. A vanishing point formed where lines of an inclined plane meet in the distance.
Aligning. Comparing the placement of elements and forms with the use of lines.
Angle ruler. A small, foldable ruler used to measure angles.
Atmospheric perspective. Also referred to as aerial perspective. Conveys depth through values, colors and the definition of elements.

B

Bisection. Half of a square or rectangle that is formed by drawing a centerline.
Blocking in. Sketching the most basic forms and proportions of a subject.

C

Centerline. A line drawn from the centerpoint of a square or rectangle.
Centerpoint. The point at the center of a square or rectangle determined by connecting opposite corners.
Central viewing area. The central portion of the field of vision.
Color wheel. A circular chart showing colors and their relationships to each other.
Complementary colors. Any two colors that are opposite to each other on the color wheel.
Concave. A form that curves inward.
Convex. A form that curves outward.
Cool colors. Colors that appear cool including greens, blues and violets.

D

Diagonal. That which is angled.
Drawing board. A smooth-surfaced, sturdy board used as a support for sketching and drawing.

E

Elevation. The height at which a scene is viewed from.
Ellipse. A circle in perspective that is symmetrical side to side and top to bottom.
Eraser shield. A thin metal shield used to protect areas of artwork while erasing.
Eye level. The height of the eyes of the viewer, which will also be level with the horizon.

F

Field of vision. This includes the central viewing area and peripheral area of a scene.
Foreshorten. The shortened appearance of an object because it is viewed straight on.
Frisket. A sheet of paper used to cover parts of a drawing to control the placement of pencil marks.

G

Graphite pencil. A pencil with graphite as the lead.
Ground plane. The surface below the horizon such as land or water.

H

Horizon. The line where the sky meets the land or water.
Horizontal. That which is sideways, parallel to the horizon.

I

Inclined plane. A slanted, flat area.
Isometric drawing. A three-dimensional drawing that lacks the use of vanishing points; similar to an oblique drawing.

K

Kneaded eraser. A putty-like gray eraser.

L

Lead. The general term for the core of a pencil.
Lead holder. Also called a clutch pencil. A mechanical pencil that uses graphite the width of a standard pencil lead.
Lightbox. A box with an interior light used for tracing sketches.
Light source. The origin of light in a scene or composition.
Linear perspective. Depth expressed with lines making use of a horizon and vanishing points.
Lines of diminishing distances. Lines that are placed increasingly closer to one another the more distant they are from the viewer.

M

Major axis. A line that represents the widest distance of a circle in perspective.
Mechanical pencil. A pencil that uses narrow, refillable graphite.
Minor axis. A line that represents the narrowest distance of a circle in perspective.
Multi-point perspective. Depth expressed with lines (linear perspective) making use of three or more vanishing points.

O

Oblique drawing. A three-dimensional drawing that lacks the use of vanishing points; similar to an isometric drawing.
One-point perspective. Linear perspective that uses just one vanishing point.
Orthogonal lines. Lines that are directed to a vanishing point, such as railroad tracks.

P

Parallel lines. Lines that are the same distance apart, such as railroad tracks. With linear perspective, parallel lines may appear to meet, forming a vanishing point.
Pencil extender. A wooden sleeve that lengthens a shortened pencil, making it easier to use.
Peripheral area. The area of the field of vision that is beyond the central viewing area.
Perpendicular. At a right angle or 90°.
Perspective. The representation of depth in art.
Plastic eraser. Also called a vinyl eraser. A soft, nonabrasive eraser.
Primary colors. The three most basic colors: red, yellow and blue.
Primary object. The object or form that casts a reflection.
Proportion wheel. A device for calculating the percentage for enlarging or reducing an image on a copier.
Proportioning. The process of comparing features of a subject to establish their correct sizes.

R

Reflecting surface. A surface that reflects an image, such as water or a mirror.
Reflection. An image cast on a surface.
Reflection base. The place at which a primary object reflects off the reflecting surface.

S

Secondary colors. Colors created by mixing two primary colors, including oranges, greens and violets.
Sketch. An unfinished study of a subject.
Slip sheet. A sheet of paper used under the hand to prevent smearing a drawing.
Straightedge. A piece of wooden or plastic material used for drawing straight lines.
Structural sketch. A sketch of a subject showing the structural form without values.
Subdividing. To form proportionally smaller units of a square or rectangle.
Symmetrical. Evenly balanced from side to side.

T

T-square. A T-shaped tool used with a drawing board to create horizontal lines.
Tangent. The meeting point of two or more elements.
Transfer paper. With graphite on one side, this paper is used for transferring sketches onto drawing paper.
Transposing angled lines. Duplicating the angled lines of a subject.
Triangle. A clear plastic triangular tool used with the T-square for making straight lines.
Two-point perspective. Depth expressed with lines (linear perspective) making use of two vanishing points.

V

Value scale. A strip of paper or cardboard used to gauge degrees of values from white to black.
Vanishing point. A point formed where parallel lines meet.
Vantage point. The place from which a scene is viewed.
Vertical. That which is straight up and down, perpendicular to the horizon.

W

Warm colors. Colors that appear warm, including reds, oranges and yellows.

Index

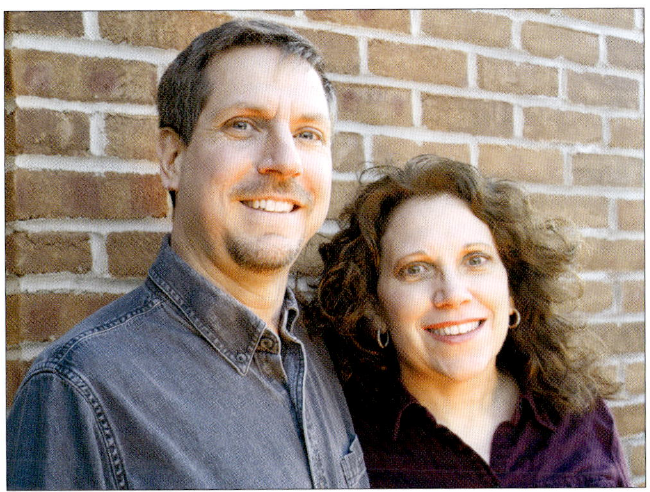

Photograph by Hannah Willenbrink.

About the Authors

Mark and Mary Willenbrink, the best-selling authors of the *Absolute Beginner* series, enjoy encouraging others to pursue their creative potential. Besides writing and illustrating books, Mark specializes in fine art and teaches art classes and workshops. Mark and Mary live with their family, border collie and two cats in southwestern Ohio. For more information on their latest books and workshops, visit shadowblaze.com and check out Mark's Facebook fan page at facebook.com/MarkWillenbrinkArtist.

Dedication

Laus Deo. Praise to God.

This book is dedicated to the Illustrators Lunch Group, a gathering of colleagues and friends that are so much more than artists who meet for lunch.

Acknowledgments

To Christina Richards, thank you for the time, energy, expertise and wisdom that you poured into our book; you have gone above and beyond with your support.

A special thank you to David Hartz and Thomas O. Miller for sharing your "virtual" expertise with us.

Thank you to all of the F+W Media team who worked behind the scenes to make this another outstanding *Absolute Beginner* book: designers Wendy Dunning and Jamie DeAnne, production coordinator Jennifer Bass and copyeditor Jeff Suess.

 Published by North Light Books, an imprint of F+W, A Content and eCommerce Company, 10151 Carver Road, Suite 200, Blue Ash, Ohio, 45242. (800) 289-0963. First Edition.

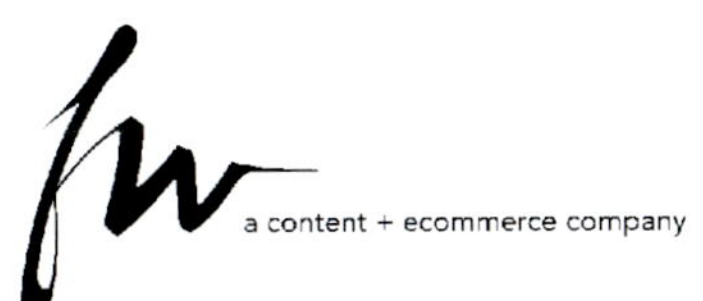

21 20 19 18 17 5 4 3 2 1

DISTRIBUTED IN CANADA BY FRASER DIRECT
100 Armstrong Avenue
Georgetown, ON, Canada L7G 5S4
Tel: (905) 877-4411

DISTRIBUTED IN THE U.K. AND EUROPE
BY F&W MEDIA INTERNATIONAL LTD
Pynes Hill Court, Pynes Hill, Rydon Lane, Exeter, EX2 5AZ, UK
Tel: (+44) 1392 797680
Email: enquiries@fwmedia.com

ISBN 13: 978-1-4403-4368-1

Edited by Christina Richards
Designed by Wendy Dunning and Jamie DeAnne
Production coordinated by Jennifer Bass

Metric Conversion Chart

To convert	to	multiply by
Inches	Centimeters	2.54
Centimeters	Inches	0.4
Feet	Centimeters	30.5
Centimeters	Feet	0.03
Yards	Meters	0.9
Meters	Yards	1.1

Ideas. Instruction. Inspiration.

Receive FREE downloadable bonus materials when you sign up for our free newsletter at artistsnetwork.com/Newsletter_Thanks.

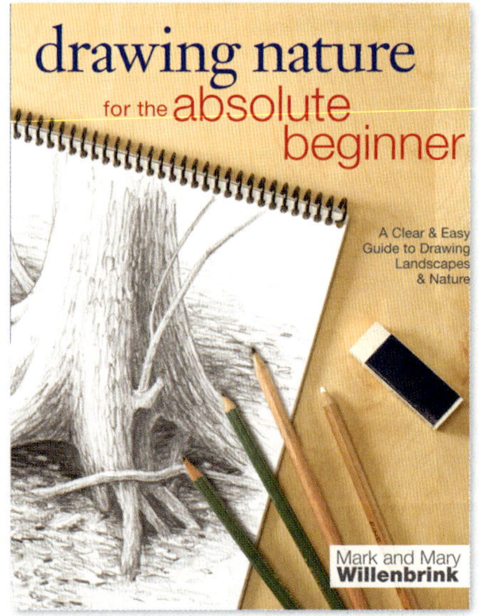

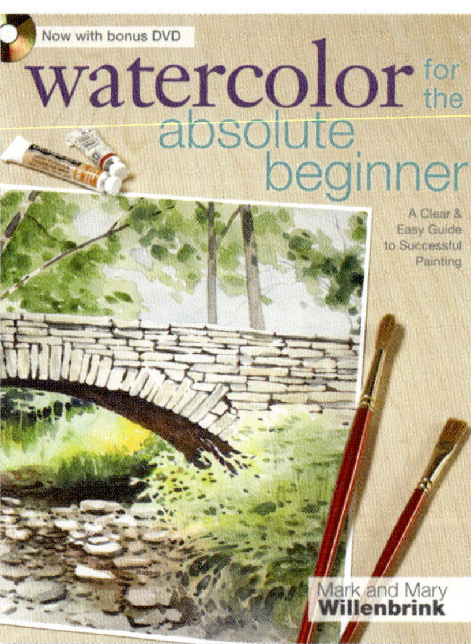

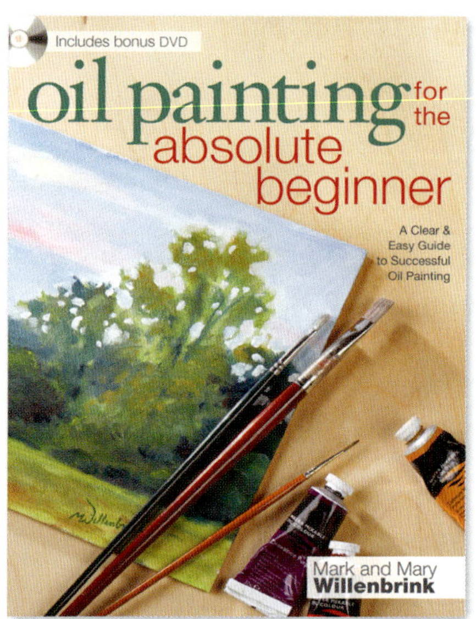

These and other fine North Light products are available at your favorite art & craft retailer, bookstore or online supplier. Visit our websites at artistsnetwork.com and artistsnetwork.tv.

Find the latest issues of The Artist's Magazine on newsstands, or visit artistsnetwork.com.

Follow North Light Books for the latest news, free wallpapers, free demos and chances to win FREE BOOKS!

Get your art in print!

Visit **artistsnetwork.com/splashwatercolor** for up-to-date information on *Splash* and other North Light competitions.

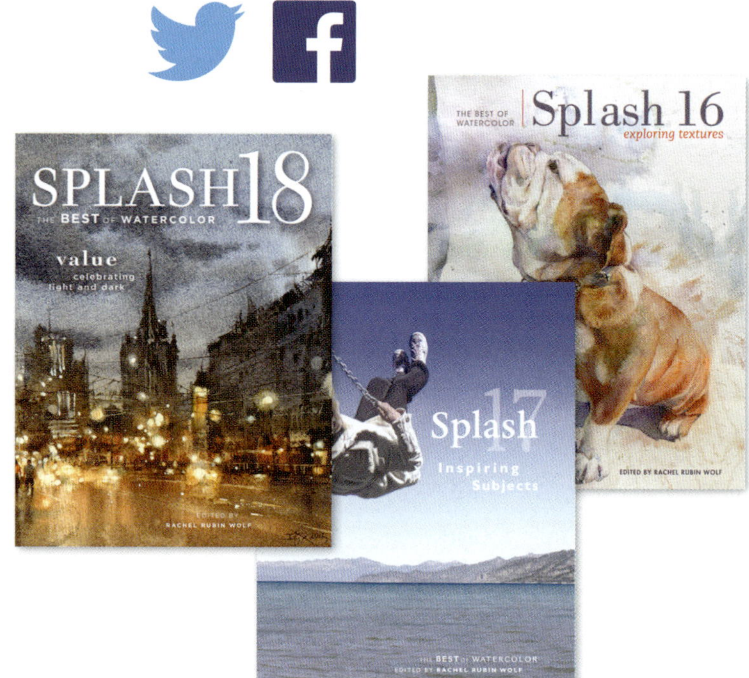